Tracing the Economic Transformation of Turkey from the 1920s to EU Accession

Tracing the Economic Transformation of Turkey from the 1920s to EU Accession

By

Tevfik Nas

LEIDEN • BOSTON
2008

This book is printed on acid-free paper.

Library of Congress Cataloging-in-Publication Data

Nas, Tevfik F.
Tracing the economic transformation of Turkey from the 1920s to EU accession / by Tevfik F. Nas.
p. cm.
Includes bibliographical references and index.
ISBN 978-90-04-16792-6 (hardback : alk. paper) 1. Turkey—Economic policy. 2. European Union—Turkey. 3. Turkey—Politics and government. I. Title.
HC492.N37 2008
330.9561'02—dc22

2008014030

ISBN 978 90 04 16792 6

PRINTED IN THE NETHERLANDS

To Paula

CONTENTS

ILLUSTRATIONS

Figures

Tables

ACKNOWLEDGMENTS

Without the dedicated and admirable work of Turkish scholars who have been contributing to the growth of an extensive literature on Turkey's economic and political transformation, from the early 1920s to the present, this manuscript would not have been complete. Above all, comments, insights, and suggestions from an anonymous reviewer skillfully directed me to the most relevant sources in this broad literature and significantly improved the analysis of this timely title that could have easily overlooked important issues and developments in the economic transformation of Modern Turkey. I also gratefully acknowledge the contributions that I received from Professor Aykut Kibritçioğlu of the Faculty of Political Sciences, Ankara University, and Professor Erinç Yeldan from Bilkent University and Amherst College. Valuable comments and contributions from Professor Mark Perry and Professor Paula Nas, both from the University of Michigan-Flint, greatly enhanced the content of the book. I am especially thankful to Mark for creating the figures and grateful to have beside me my devoted critic, and most valuable colleague, my wife Paula, and our two precious children, Megan and Jonathan, who patiently listened, debated, and enthusiastically provided their valuable insight on many important details, from start to finish, in completing this highly demanding project. Finally, special thanks go to the College of Arts and Sciences, University of Michigan-Flint, for its financial support, to Ms. Bonnie Granat for her expert editorial assistance, and Brill editors, Nienke Brienen-Moolenaar, Hylke Faber, and Marjolein Landowski for making this project possible.

CHAPTER ONE

INTRODUCTION

On October 3, 2005, the European Union foreign ministers reached a landmark agreement on an accession framework with Turkey and held their first ministerial meeting marking the official opening of full membership talks. British Foreign Secretary Jack Straw, whose country held the EU Presidency at the time, declared the occasion "a truly historic day for Europe and for the whole of the international community." He went on to say that this was an important milestone in the European enlargement, ushering in a new era that "will bring a strong secular state" into the EU.[1] Straw's Turkish counterpart, Foreign Minister Abdullah Gül, was equally enthusiastic. In his accession conference statement, Gül acknowledged that full membership had been a "mutual contractual goal since the start of relations as underlined in the Ankara Agreement" and that Turkey was "at the threshold of a new and challenging process."[2]

The decision to start accession talks was a challenge, not only for Turkey but for the majority of the EU member states as well. An associate member of the EU since the 1963 Ankara Agreement and an applicant for full membership since 1987, Turkey has faced ongoing opposition from the majority of EU governments and the European public. Some countries had reservations and seemed unprepared to admit Turkey as a full member, but given the likely adverse consequences of an outright rejection, they campaigned heavily in favor of the idea of "privileged partnership" status, a form of strategic alliance that would politically and economically anchor Turkey to the EU. Seeing its future in the EU, Turkey, on the other hand, made it known that it would not consider any outcome short of full admission. To fully comply with the terms of entry into the EU, Turkey had been implementing far-reaching restructuring programs and introducing a wide range of legislative and

---

[1] The Council of the European Union, press conference on Turkey's accession to the European Union, October 3, 2005, Luxembourg.

[2] See "Turkish Accession Conference Statement Delivered By Minister Abdullah Gül," *Turkish Daily News*, October 5, 2005.

political reforms. Consequently, after carefully monitoring Turkey's progress toward accession, the European Commission made an assessment in favor of starting the negotiations.[3] The Commission's recommendation was subsequently endorsed on December 17, 2004 at the Brussels Summit and the opening of accession talks was scheduled for October 3, 2005.[4] On that day, after intense negotiations and last-minute amendments to the accession framework, which reemphasized both the full accession objective and the open-ended nature of the negotiation process, an agreement to open full membership talks with Turkey was finally reached by all 25 EU member states.

Because of circumstances unique to Turkey, full membership talks are expected to last much longer than those held with the last twelve nations that have joined the union. As highlighted in the Commission's report, issues surrounding Turkey's membership prospects are complicated and fairly comprehensive. They range from the challenges of future EU foreign policies, in view of Turkey's existing economic and political ties, to matters relating to budgetary and institutional changes in the EU that will likely result from Turkish full membership. In particular, the Commission expects the budgetary impact to be substantial, stating that specific impact would depend on EU policies and any special arrangements with Turkey agreed upon during the financial negotiations. What might also prolong the negotiation period is the magnitude of the financial consequences of Turkey's membership, which cannot be assessed prior to the establishment of the EU's financial perspectives. As the Commission's report and the 2004 Presidency Conclusions of the European Council both concluded, those financial concerns would be incorporated into the budgetary framework of the EU applicable for the period beyond 2014.

Given the size of its population, Turkey's influence on the decision-making process in the European institutions could also be significant, since the EU voting system is dependent on the size of each member state's population. Some other issues that would possibly lead to prolonged negotiations include the fear of increased migration of workers from Turkey, the alignment of key sectors in areas such as agriculture,

[3] Commission of the European Communities, *Recommendation from the European Commission on Turkey's progress towards accession*, COM (2004) 656 final, October 6, 2004, Brussels.

[4] The Council of the European Union, *Presidency conclusions*, December 16–17, 2004, Brussels.

transportation, energy, and the environment, and the management of the EU's new external borders.

Recognizing that admission talks will likely be long and tedious, proponents of Turkish membership argue that the improving economic and political profile of Turkey is reassuring, and that it reveals a capable nation eager to join the club of elite European democracies. An integral part of the West both economically and militarily, Turkey has participated in the core European economic and political institutions since 1949, and as a NATO member, it has devoted its vital strategic assets to the defense of postwar Europe.[5] Naturally, as the notion of a united Europe began to surface during the late 1950s, it seemed highly unlikely at that time to preclude Turkey's membership, and over the years, as European enlargements followed, Turkish membership came to be viewed as inevitable. However, despite geopolitical realities justifying Turkey's future in the EU, economic, political, and cultural differences continue to be at the heart of European skepticism: Turkey is not geographically in Europe, and it is too large and culturally too different for the EU to absorb. The skeptics further argue that Turkey's full membership, if it does indeed materialize, is likely to destabilize the Union and alter its "European identity," leading to the end of the European integration project.[6]

Despite such strong opposition, both official and unofficial bodies of the Union seemed convinced that the full membership status of Turkey has unquestionable strategic value for the EU and the region in general.[7] As reported by the Independent Commission on Turkey,

[5] Turkey became a member of The Council of Europe in 1949, joined The North Atlantic Treaty Organization (NATO) in 1951, and became a participant and full member of major European institutions such as The Organization for European Economic Co-operation (OEEC), The Conference on Security and Cooperation in Europe (CSCE), to name a few.

[6] The main argument against Turkey's future in Europe seems to center on cultural differences. As Grabbe (2004, 2) noted, "[T]he prospect of Turkey joining raises tricky questions about European identity. Few [European] politicians want to address these since they have no ready answers. In part, Turkish accession is unpopular in the EU because it forces Europeans to confront fundamental uncertainties about who they are, which values they share, and how open their societies can and should be." For more on the debate on Turkey's future in Europe and a discussion of the proponents' and opponents' views of Turkish membership, see Benhabib and Işıksel (2006), Casanova (2006), Grigoriadis (2006), Göle (2006), Keyder (2006), Le Gloannec (2006), and Kastoryano (2006).

[7] With respect to Turkey's role in the region, the European Commission stated, "The prospect of accession should lead to improving bilateral relations between Turkey and

for example, "Turkey's accession would offer considerable benefits both to the European Union and to Turkey. For the Union, the unique geopolitical position of Turkey at the crossroads of the Balkans, the wider Middle East, South Caucasus, Central Asia and beyond, its importance for the security of Europe's energy supplies and its political, economic and military weight would be great assets. Moreover, as a large Muslim country firmly embedded in the European Union, Turkey could play a significant role in Europe's relations with the Islamic world" (p. 43).[8]

Because it has provided valuable lessons and challenges for other emerging economies in the region, Turkey's admission to the rank of modern democracies would indeed be well-deserved recognition of its significant progress. Turkey moved into a multiparty system in the 1950s, and despite the political turmoil of the next five decades, the country eventually managed to create a relatively stable economic and political system. With its ongoing economic transformation and maturing democracy, it has reached a state of stability and is able to accommodate institutional settings compatible with contemporary norms of advanced societies.

Elevating Turkey's membership status to its current level and keeping its economic progress on track has not come without hard choices, however. During the second half of the twentieth century, Turkey did enjoy impressive economic growth, and in response to global economic developments, it managed to continually restructure its economy and successfully realign its macroeconomic policies. But the adverse effects of both domestic and external shocks, especially during the late 1970s and since the 1990s, have been costly and highly destabilizing. Balance of payments complications and persistent inflationary pressures prevailed throughout the period, and because of delayed reforms and the emergence of fiscal and financial crises, valuable resources were

---

its neighbors in line with principle of reconciliation on which the European Union is founded. Expectations regarding EU policies towards these regions will grow as well, taking into account Turkey's existing political and economic links to its neighbors." See Commission of the European Communities, *Recommendation from the European Commission on Turkey's progress towards accession*, COM (2004) 656 final, October 6, 2004, Brussels.

[8] Chaired by Martti Ahtisaari, former president of Finland, the Independent Commission on Turkey was formed in March 2004 to examine "the major challenges and opportunities connected with Turkey's possible accession to the Union." See Independent Commission on Turkey. *Turkey in Europe: More than a Promise?* September 2004, British Council and the Open Society Institute, Brussels.

depleted and inefficiently reallocated. Insufficient national saving and the reluctance of foreigners to provide capital made matters worse, leading to policy outcomes with little or virtually no emphasis on long-term capital formation.

Nonetheless, in recent years, particularly the period after the 2002 parliamentary elections, Turkish economic growth gained new momentum, boosted by positive developments with respect to Turkey's full membership prospects in the EU. Its GDP has been growing robustly since then, and the inflation rate, after hitting several highs above 100 percent during the last two decades, is finally at a single-digit level and falling.[9] While challenges still remain in areas such as income distribution, unemployment, and the environment, there is, most importantly, a political atmosphere in Turkey that is ripe for new ideas to further accelerate the modernization process.

This book examines the transformation of an emerging economy, a nation that rose from bare subsistence in the early 1920s to a thriving market economy as it approaches its EU destination. To develop a better understanding of Turkey's economic transformation, Chapter 2 reviews the liberal period of the 1920s as background and then highlights the main features of Turkey's inward-looking economic and policy environments that prevailed for more than four decades. Throughout the 1920s, Turkey had a free-market-oriented economy with minimal state involvement and international trade that was largely conducted under free trade arrangements. The economic setting, which seemed to emulate the most common features of a small open economy, was to some extent the product of resource constraints and an infrastructure inherited from the Ottomans, with an added constraint imposed by a wartime treaty calling for the government to maintain tariff rates at their September 1916 level. It was within such a liberal economic and policy environment that Turkey made a concerted effort throughout the 1920s to rebuild its economy. But after that decade of limited success with liberal economic policies and the end of the worldwide depression of the 1930s, it switched course, adopting protectionist trade measures and implementing a state-led, inward-looking growth strategy.

[9] Unless otherwise stated, the statistical data and descriptive information provided in this book are taken from the Central Bank of the Republic of Turkey, *The Quarterly Economic Information Report* (various issues), *Annual Report* (various issues), and the Electronic Data Delivery System.

Turkey faced another major restructuring decision nearly fifty years later, when the inward-looking, state-led industrialization that had dominated its policy making came to an end. During the late 1970s, Turkey experienced an increasingly worsening balance of payments along with a severe foreign-exchange crisis that brought the nation's economy to a standstill. To reinstate macroeconomic balances and restore confidence in the economy, Turkey embarked on an ambitious restructuring plan in the 1980s aimed at pursuing free-market reforms and changing course from import substitution to export promotion. Chapter 3 focuses on this important stage in Turkey's economic transformation; it examines key developments that led to the economic imbalances of the 1970s and describes in detail the circumstances prior to the introduction of the 1980 economic stabilization and structural adjustment program. The chapter provides an in-depth look at the program, makes an assessment of the stabilization and restructuring efforts that dominated the 1980s, and highlights the program's performance, particularly with respect to its impact on inflation, investment, and economic growth.

The focus of the book then shifts to some of the major economic and financial events of the last two turbulent decades of the twentieth century. This is the period in which Turkey intensified its post-1980 restructuring, while opening its economy to the rest of the world and simultaneously trying to deal with its internal economic and political complexities. The main highlights of the period were the 1994 financial crisis, policies to combat inflation, and the economic events that led to the electoral defeat of Bülent Ecevit's coalition government in 2002.

The destabilizing effects of the 1994 financial crisis, which erupted after several failed stabilization attempts, were extensive and clear reminders of the need for credible macroeconomic policy making. The economy grew more vulnerable to future crises, and inflation continued unabated despite the stabilization measures that were consequently introduced. Chapter 4 examines the policy responses of the Turkish monetary authorities and the reactions of the financial markets to the 1994 financial crisis with a brief assessment of this period and the outcome of stabilization measures that were subsequently put into action. Chapter 5 reviews possible causes of Turkish inflation, provides a discussion of the anti-inflationary policies during the last three decades, and outlines possible reasons for the failure to control inflation, specifically during the 1990s.

Chapter 6 analyzes the economic events that led to and followed the 2001 financial crisis that was triggered by a dispute between Prime

Minister Bülent Ecevit and President Ahmet Necdet Sezer and the adoption of a floating exchange rate regime, which was a major departure from the 1999 Disinflation and Fiscal Adjustment Program. The objectives of the Ecevit government during that period were to restore confidence in financial markets through greater interest rate and exchange rate stability, improve the resiliency of the economy against future crises, and move forward with inflation targeting and policies to promote sustainable economic growth. The details of how to achieve these goals were repeatedly set forth in the International Monetary Fund (IMF) letters of intent, with a clear emphasis on structural reforms, which included the completion of banking and public-sector restructuring and privatization, and the enhancement of fiscal transparency. However, as highlighted in chapter 7, the economic environment continued to deteriorate, leading to a new election and the defeat of Ecevit's coalition parties in 2002. Chapter 8 focuses on the restructuring efforts for the modernization of the Turkish economy and examines macroeconomic policies and outcomes during the post-election period.

The remainder of the book focuses on Turkish-EU relations and recent economic developments. Chapter 9 provides a brief history of the European enlargement and discusses developments since Turkey's application for full membership in 1987. Chapter 10 highlights the main economic developments and restructuring during the period prior to and after the 2004 Brussels Summit, a period that will go on record as the time when inflation finally dropped to single-digit levels, a seemingly impossible outcome given the long history of inflation in Turkey. And finally, Chapter 11 provides a concluding commentary on Turkey's full membership prospects in the EU.

Turkey's economic transformation has been unique in many respects, especially considering the obstacles that the country faced during the last century in one of the most politically unstable regions of the world. As noted in the concluding commentary, Turkey's close relations with the West, and in particular with the EU, has been an important factor, a stimulant for its accomplishments that should not be overlooked. Assuredly, however, the motivations behind Turkey's efforts have always been its desire to establish a modern economy, its appreciation of contemporary values and Western civilization, and its instinct for building bridges between East and West. Turkey, a nation that lacked key developmental resources and faced numerous financial constraints, has certainly proven its commitment to establishing a functioning market economy. And it is this lesson that we will begin to appreciate as we chronologically retrace Turkey's experience from the time of its emergence as a new republic in the 1920s to the present, as it approaches its EU destination.

We now begin our review and discussion by revisiting the post-World War I years and beyond.

CHAPTER TWO

AN OVERVIEW OF THE TURKISH ECONOMY: 1920–80

During the 1920s, Turkey's commerce and trade were severely disrupted by the wartime flight of human capital, and both the agricultural and manufacturing sectors were handicapped due to the loss of financial capital and the heavy war debt that had been inherited from the Ottoman government.[1] Most of the active industries in that period were small-scale food and textile establishments, and even those, which were fairly undeveloped by European standards of the time, were limited to accommodating the basic needs and priorities of a war-torn society.[2] Yet, despite such constraints, Turkey did not wait long to mobilize its limited resources. Inspired by the declarations of the 1923 Economic Congress, which reflected the views and expectations of various segments of Turkey's economically active population, the new republic targeted its development efforts at building infrastructure and increasing the production of essential goods and services for both domestic consumption and investment.[3] One notable outcome of the Congress was the clear affirmation of the sense of urgency in attracting foreign capital to aid in the revitalization of the economy, specifically for infrastructure investment and partnerships with domestic producers. Measures were also proposed to encourage the private sector to take an active role in industry. The private sector's presence in those years

[1] By the end of 1914, the total outstanding debt was approximately 28.2 percent of the total state revenue, and in 1924, in compliance with the Lausanne Treaty, 62.25 percent of the outstanding debt was turned over to the newly formed Republic of Turkey. See Kuyucuklu (1983, 190) and Ülken (1981, 81). There was also a dramatic decline in population from 16.3 million in 1914 to 13.6 million in 1927. See Tezel (2005, 137).

[2] Before World War I, there were about 282 industrial establishments, 22 of which were state owned, and approximately 85 percent of labor and capital belonged to foreigners and minorities. See Ülken (1981, 79).

[3] On February 17, 1923, more than 1,100 representatives from various sectors and socioeconomic groups assembled in the Western Anatolian city of Izmir. The purpose of this first economic congress of the new republic, which lasted until March 5 of the same year, was to produce a balance sheet identifying the existing assets and the size of the production capacity, and to set goals and priorities for economic growth and development. For the highlights of the congress proceedings, see Kuyucuklu (1983, 172–189) and Ülken (1981, 83–94).

was mostly in international trade and banking and was limited in the food and textile categories.[4] This lack of interest in industry was due in part to the inadequacy of the existing capital base. There were other reasons, though, such as the attractiveness of a trade sector that was free from protectionism, and the high risk of investing in industries that were open to foreign competition.[5]

The state's role in the economy during that period was minimal. Throughout the 1920s, state intervention was limited to legislation and decrees aimed at stimulating private capital accumulation, establishing an effective banking system, and allocating foreign capital to priority infrastructure development, such as highway and railroad construction.[6] As was universally the case at the time, fiscal policy did not yet exist as a stabilization tool. For the most part, Turkey had a balanced budget and reported fairly small surpluses, with the exception of a deficit in 1925.[7] State revenues, generated in part from customs duties, sales taxes on agriculture, and income from state monopolies, were fully used to match the budgetary expenditures. From 1926 to 1929, total budgetary expenditures as a percentage of GNP ranged between 12 and 15 percent. Only about 17 percent of that amount was allocated to investment expenditures and transfers to state enterprises, a fairly low percentage for a nation in the midst of postwar reconstruction.[8]

On the monetary front, there was no central bank and essentially no monetary policy. The amount of coins in circulation and the paper money issued by the Ottoman Bank, which had been performing the function of a central bank, remained almost constant. The money supply, however, which included demand deposits created by the banking sector in addition to coins and paper money, did increase in response to growing transactions demand for money.[9]

---

[4] Banking, in particular, was profitable and fairly attractive for the Turkish private sector, and it was encouraged and supported by the government. See Keyder (1981, 104–108).

[5] For more on this period, see Kazgan (1985, 281–90), Keyder (1981), Kuyucuklu (1983, 155–199), Sönmez (1982, 14–25), and Ülken (1981, 77–100).

[6] See Kazgan (1985, 287–90) and Sönmez (1982, 14–25).

[7] The deficit in 1925 was caused by the abolition of the agricultural tithe, which was replaced with other direct taxes on agriculture and was largely financed by borrowing. See Tezel (1982, 401).

[8] For a detailed analysis of government revenues and expenditures, see Tezel (1982, 387–414).

[9] In 1923, paper money (amounting to 130 to 140 million TL) and coins (amounting to 8 to 10 million TL) accounted for about one-third of the money supply. See Keyder (1981, 99).

Table 2.1 Output growth, 1924–1979

Year	GDP Growth rate	Industry		Agriculture		Service	
		Growth rate	% of total	Growth rate	% of total	Growth rate	% of total
1924	14.6	–7.1	8.5	27.2	47.8	8.4	43.7
1925	12.5	17.9	8.9	5.6	44.7	19.7	46.4
1926	18.2	14.8	8.7	31.8	49.9	5.7	41.5
1927	–12.7	19.4	11.9	–30.9	39.5	2.2	48.6
1928	10.8	–0.6	10.6	19.2	42.4	7.3	46.9
1929	21.5	3.8	9.1	42.6	49.8	6.6	41.2
1930	2.4	12.7	10.0	–3.9	46.8	7.2	43.2
1931	8.2	14.2	10.5	14.3	49.2	1.4	40.3
1932	–10.6	17.8	13.9	–28.8	39.3	3.9	46.9
1933	15.5	19.0	14.2	22.1	41.4	9.6	44.4
1934	6.3	13.8	15.3	2.7	40.1	6.6	44.6
1935	–3.0	–0.1	15.7	–6.1	38.8	–1.3	45.4
1936	23.1	–3.4	12.3	54.1	48.6	6.0	39.1
1937	1.5	10.3	13.4	–3.5	46.2	5.1	40.4
1938	9.5	15.7	14.2	5.4	44.4	12.1	41.4
1939	6.8	16.7	15.5	3.8	43.2	6.9	41.4
1924–29	10.8	8.0	9.6	15.9	45.7	8.3	44.8
1930–39	6.0	11.7	13.5	6.0	43.8	5.7	42.7
1940–49	0.7	–0.3	14.9	1.7	43.0	1.0	42.1
1950–59	7.1	9.2	14.2	6.6	39.6	6.8	46.2
1960–69	5.4	9.5	18.0	1.9	33.0	6.7	49.0
1970–79	4.7	6.1	19.8	1.9	25.6	6.0	54.6

Sources: TÜRKSTAT, *Statistical Indicators 1923-2005*; Central Bank of the Republic of Turkey, Electronic Data Delivery System.

This relatively free-market-oriented economic and policy-making environment prevailed until 1929. From 1924 to 1929, the GDP growth rate averaged 10.8 percent annually, largely due to impressive growth in agriculture, which, even with the drought year of 1927, was about 16 percent annually (see table 2.1). Growth in industry was less robust, averaging 8 percent annually despite some apparent increases in direct foreign investment and various measures that were introduced by the government.

The positive performance of agriculture during that period was to some extent the result of effective utilization of existing capacity that had been idle during the war. The government's efforts to provide more access to agricultural inputs were also considerable. As Keyder (1981) explained, "The agricultural policy of the state during the 1920s was designed to aid in the reconstruction of pre-war output levels. To this end the government sought to increase the amount of land under cultivation, supported tractor purchases, and legislated firmer rights of ownership on land. A parallel effect was produced by the transportation policy, which was designed to facilitate the marketisation of surplus, and commercialisation of agriculture" (p. 36).

Domestic industry was stimulated by various measures as well. In 1924, *İş Bankası* (Business Bank) was established to meet the financial requirements of the emerging domestic private industries. The 1913 Law for the Encouragement of Industry was modified and reintroduced in 1927, granting tax exemptions, reduced tariff rates, and subsidies to the private sector.[10] Yet, despite these measures, the growth of domestic industry was moderate, partly because domestic manufacturers were largely unprotected from competition by foreign manufacturers. The main reason Turkey was unable to protect its infant industries from foreign competition was that the government had to maintain tariff rates at their September 1916 level as had been mandated by the Lausanne Treaty.[11]

The economic and policy environment during the period 1924–29 was typical of a fairly small, open, and agriculture-based economy.[12] For the most part, Turkey's exports consisted of primary products for which it held a comparative advantage, and its imports included a wide range of consumption and capital goods under free trade arrangements.[13] Both interest rates and exchange rates were determined through undeveloped but free-market forces, and the inflows of foreign capital and short-term credit provided the only sources of domestic infrastructure and capital investments. Foreign capital inflows were mostly in large-scale manufacturing and mining, accounting for nearly two-thirds of the direct investment during the 1924 to 1930 period. The largest investment was in electricity, gas works, and other municipal services, and was followed by mining, cement, and food processing.[14]

With the onset of the Great Depression in 1929, this relatively liberal period in Turkey came to an end. In line with the rest of the world, the government adopted protectionist measures to counteract the external

[10] See Keyder (1981, 57–58).

[11] However, citing Kurmuş's 1978 study, Sönmez (1982, 17) claimed that overcoming the constraints of the treaty was possible, but the Turkish government deliberately chose not to do so.

[12] It is interesting to note that according to Kazgan (1985, 287–88), the free-market, outward-looking orientation of the economy in those years was somewhat comparable to the ideal economic and policy environments envisaged in the 1980 program.

[13] About 70 percent of total imports included a variety of consumption goods and services. The remaining 30 percent were investment goods. See Kazgan (1985, 283) and Ülken (1981, 100).

[14] See Keyder (1981, 60).

and domestic imbalances exacerbated by the worldwide depression that followed. The deterioration in external accounts was due in part to a sharp decrease in exports in 1929 that was precipitated by weaknesses in the agricultural sector that stemmed from a worldwide fall in the prices of primary products. It was also the result of a speculative rise in imports that peaked in October 1929, when Turkey was allowed to begin raising tariffs in accordance with the Lausanne Treaty. Moreover, the first installment of foreign debt that Turkey inherited from the Ottoman Empire became due in 1929, adding to the demand for foreign currency. These factors, combined with a declining inflow of foreign capital and the foreign-exchange crisis that followed, brought about the adoption of various protectionist measures in the forms of tariffs and quotas, foreign-exchange controls, and tax exemptions for a few basic imported goods.[15]

The Protectionist Period of the 1930s

In the wake of the worldwide depression of 1929–33, the world economy was suffering tremendously, and the intellectual tradition of classical economics, which had neither an apparent explanation nor a remedy for an economic downturn of such magnitude, was far from producing a cure. Interventionist Keynesianism thus followed, as did the new intellectual tradition of an increased role for the state as a stabilizing influence.

During the same period in Turkey, *etatism* emerged as a form of state interventionism different from the Keynesian approach in that its focus was on the allocation, regulation, and distribution functions of the state rather than the state's role as an economic stabilization force. As Öniş (1996) wrote, "From a liberal or pragmatic perspective, etatism was interpreted as a development strategy in which the state is forced to undertake an active entrepreneurial role out of necessity rather than for any ideological reasons. The corollary of this reasoning is a progressive reduction in the weight of state involvement in the economy as private capital matures and assumes the leadership role in economic affairs. A qualification is called for in the sense that there were also intellectuals who interpreted etatism in a different light, namely as an alternative,

[15] For the details, see Kazgan (1985, 291–95).

non-capitalist path of economic development, inspired to a certain degree by the relatively successful Soviet experience at a time when the major industrialized countries of the West were experiencing the deepest crisis of their history" (pp. 157–58).

At the time, there were several competing perspectives, all charging the state with the important task of overseeing and leading the industrialization process. Advocating "economic liberalism," one group of intellectuals who subscribed to the liberal perspective, based their argument on the premise that in an inherently self-regulating economy, the private sector would still need encouragement until it becomes self-sustaining and should not be replaced by the state. Another group advocated "economic etatism," which allowed for state planning and gradual, but eventual, removal of the state's role in the economy. But the group of intellectuals who conceptualized a non-capitalist path, those who belonged to the *Kadro* (Cadre) movement (attributed to the views of a group of intellectuals writing for a monthly journal called *Kadro* between 1932 and 1934), had a much more radical view of state involvement in the economy. They advocated a centralized state with ownership of economic enterprises and state planning that would facilitate resource allocation rather than leaving it to the private sector.[16] As Türkeş (2001) wrote, for these three views, "[T]he desired economic development meant a self-sustaining, industrialized national economy. All three advocated the state's intervention in the economy, although each differed on the question of the extent of the state's intervention, as well as in their objectives. All three advocated 'etatism,' but each put the emphasis on different aspects" (p. 107). The case for those who advocated economic liberalism, according to Türkeş, "was difficult to argue in Turkey, where the private sector remained anxious for protection and assistance by the state" (p. 96). There was also no universal support for the *Kadro* movement (Hale 1980). Clearly, the liberal or pragmatic perspective, which evolved considerably along the lines of the proposals of economic etatism, dominated the etatist era and left its mark on the interventionist economic policies and development planning that were subsequently implemented.

[16] In a comprehensive study of the intellectual origins of etatism and the Kadro movement, Türkeş (2001) revealed further divisions among various interpretations on the subject of economic development and the role of the state. For more on the Kadro movement and other interpretations of etatism, also see Okyar (1965), Hale (1980), and Türkeş (1998).

During the 1930s, interventionist policies certainly made sense, and they had far-reaching effects. Despite the efforts of the government to boost domestic private industry throughout the 1920s, none of the existing private entities had the resources needed to assume a leadership role in promoting industrialization. Private industries were in their infancy, they needed state support, and above all, they lacked necessary financial strength and maturity. Interventionist policies did not just improve the trade balance and accelerate the formation of private capital—they paved the way for a more systematic and direct involvement of the state in economic policy making as well.[17] After the 1930s, the Turkish state reaffirmed itself as the driving force of industrialization, producing goods and services in key sectors and at the same time encouraging and supporting the formation of private capital.

Turkey was not alone in implementing inward-looking industrialization policies, however. During the three decades after the end of World War II, a large number of newly independent nations embraced inward-looking development policies and relied heavily on protectionism and import-substitution industrialization. As outlined in Krueger (1992), "Several interrelated strands of thought contributed to policy formulation in pursuit of industrialization. First, there was the widespread belief in the 'weakness' of domestic economic activities and their inability to compete with established industries abroad. Second, there was a strong suspicion of the market mechanism, and a belief that the government would have to assume responsibility for development. Third, there was a strong tendency to discount the value of the traditional economic activities" (p. 7).

Policy responses in the developing world varied broadly, but overall many of the measures introduced during that period became the defining characteristics of an evolving inward-looking development strategy. In a lengthy analysis of the industrialization policies of seven developing countries, Little, Scitovsky, and Scott (1970) found that the nations' ability to import manufactured goods was drastically reduced not only because of the fall in the value of their primary goods exports but also

[17] The role of the state in the economy should not be underestimated, even during the pre-1930 liberal period. As Kongar (1998, 349–56) argued, the role of the state from the very early years of the republic was to create Western-style liberalism, and for that it was essential to encourage and support private initiatives. Kongar also argued that the vision and the role of the state after the 1930s became more systematic but remained pretty much the same.

because industrialized countries were unable to supply manufactured goods. After the Great Depression, there was a widespread shortage of manufactured goods, and commodity prices were rapidly falling. There were several other factors that led to a strong desire for self sufficiency, economic independence, and import substituting industrialization, including the following: (a) duties on trade were a relatively easy form of taxation, (b) import restrictions provided investment opportunities for local and foreign businessman to invest in import-substituting industries, (c) import substitution provided high profits and thus a direct source of savings for expansion, and (d) there were already established markets for these industries.

Because of these and other country-specific factors, most nations thus increasingly turned to import-substitution industrialization and protectionism. By fostering infant industries under heavy protectionism and redeploying society's scarce resources away from agriculture to industry, they hoped to be able to check the growing gap between themselves and the industrial countries.[18] At the time, with shrinking export markets and a decrease in developing countries' share of total world exports, such an economic transformation seemed almost inevitable. Of course, the role of government in this process was not limited to securing domestic markets for the emerging infant industries. In some countries, the role of state in the development process was extended beyond import substitution and protectionism to include the functions of coordination and planning as well. Even though planning took different forms in different countries, it was implemented more formally in the Asian countries and less so in most Latin American countries (Little, Scitovsky, and Scott, 1970, 35–41). Overall, though, as Chenery (1975) wrote, planning techniques, which were viewed as experimental during the early 1960s, gained wide acceptance in the 1970s; they were useful forms of "systematic economic analysis as a basis for government policy," and for most state plans, growth was not the only objective. He also observed that the "modification of social objectives and the introduction of new constraints, particularly in the areas of improved income distribution and employment possibilities" ranked high as priorities with planners (Chenery, 1975, xi–xii).

---

[18] For a review and analysis of the development policies during the postwar years, see Little, Scitovsky, and Scott (1970), Healey (1972), and Edwards (1993).

During the 1970s, planners in most developing countries assumed a central role in coordinating the inward-looking policies. And, as examined next, to some extent this was also the case in Turkey. Having already established the roots of its state-led, inward-looking development strategy during the late 1920s, and having experimented with industrial plans since the early 1930s, Turkey certainly was equipped with an economic and policy environment conducive to furthering and deepening its industrialization process with its unique state planning organization.

The World War II Years and Beyond

At the beginning of the 1940s, most macroeconomic indicators in Turkey were on a downward trend, with the exception of the trade balance, which looked favorable due to declining imports. GDP growth was weak, inflation was on the rise, and the state budget was under considerable pressure because of wartime defense spending. However, there were some improvements in the growth rate of real output in both agriculture and industry. GDP, which had decreased by an annual average of 6.6 percent during the first half of the 1940s, resumed its growth after 1946 with an impressive performance, averaging a 10.9 percent annual increase during the second half of the decade. After recording negative growth rates for most of the 1940s, both agricultural and industrial sectors also managed to recover from their economic slump. However, on the budgetary front the situation was not as impressive. To finance the growing public expenditures that had resulted from excessive defense spending, the government introduced new taxes and raised the existing ones. Nevertheless, significant amounts of public expenditures still had to be financed by increasing the money supply.[19]

The only bright spot was the trade balance. Due to increased protectionist measures and the high premium importers had to pay for foreign currency, the volume of imports dropped, especially during the war years. The nonavailability of imports, partly due to disruption of trade routes, was also a reason for their slow growth. The decline in exports was mild during the early years of World War II. But because

[19] Consequently, the expanding money supply, combined with import constraints and widespread shortages of consumer and producer goods, finally led to an upsurge in inflation. See Sönmez (1982, 39).

of the high foreign demand for agricultural and other primary products, exports increased considerably throughout the remainder of the decade. A surplus in the trade account resulted between 1940 and 1946 that later turned into a deficit after the 1946 currency devaluation when imports began to rise partly because importers no longer had to pay a high premium for foreign currency.[20]

This was a decade of stalling industrialization and continually searching for more effective planning. In 1933, in the midst of the emerging protectionism, the government had introduced its first industrialization plan for the expansion and diversification of industrial output. Several state enterprises were created to produce both consumption and investment goods and to provide production prospects for the private sector's growth in key industries.[21] The majority of the manufacturing plants built were in industries such as textiles, paper, ceramics, chemical products, and iron and steel. These plants were expected to generate demand for domestic raw materials and to produce a variety of basic finished products, thereby decreasing dependency on imported goods.[22] Financial intermediaries were also established to finance and manage these new enterprises: *Sümerbank* (Sumerian Bank), founded in 1933, was in charge of manufacturing broadly, and *Etibank* (Hittite Bank), created in 1935, was to be active in the areas of mining and power supply.[23]

As a result of the 1933 industrial plan, the growth rate of industrial output accelerated. After declining in two consecutive years, the growth rate of total industrial output increased by 10.3 percent in 1937 and 15.7 percent the next year (see table 2.1). However, growth in the agricultural sector was relatively slow. In the second half of the 1930s (excluding the year 1936, when output rose by 54 percent, and the down years of 1935 and 1937, when growth was negative), this sector managed to grow by only single digits, in part because of the change in the internal terms of trade in favor of industry and the implementation of selec-

---

[20] The devaluation was introduced in 1946 to align the nominal value of the Turkish lira with its trade value. Before then, importers paid a slightly higher premium for foreign currency than the exporters. See Hale (1981, 73).

[21] By the end of the 1930s, state enterprises accounted for nearly 10 percent of the total number of industrial establishments that were active, an increase from 2.1 percent in 1932, and captured approximately 50 percent of the total industrial output. See Kongar (1998, 354–56).

[22] About 16 plants were established in these sectors, where previously imports comprised approximately 50 percent of total imports. See Ülken (1981, 105–7).

[23] For a detailed account of the period, see Sönmez (1982, 30–36), Hale (1980, 100–117; 1981, 53–85), and Kongar (1998, 353–56).

tive price controls in the agricultural sector. Also during this period, the volume of imports as a percentage of GNP declined, as expected, and the trade balance, which was in deficit during the 1924–29 period, turned positive.[24]

A second five-year follow-up plan was introduced in 1938 to deepen and vertically expand the import-substitution process that had been put into motion with the first industrial plan in 1933. Unfortunately, nearly all of the projects that were proposed under this highly ambitious plan, which was revised within a year of its preparation, had to be abandoned because of World War II (Tezel 1982, 275–83). During the rest of the 1940s, further planning activities followed, with some implementation, but none of the proposed designs offered anything new. The prepared documents were mostly revisions worked out as part of an ongoing planning preparation process. In essence, all of the plans seemed to comport with the idea of state-led industrialization evolving along the same principles that had formed the basis of the 1933 industrial plan.[25] Clearly, the 1933 industrial plan provided the impetus for Turkey's industrialization. With it, import substitution became the official priority, marking the beginning of a period of state-led industrialization with a unique state-private sector partnership that would endure for more than four decades.

There was a brief return to liberalization during the early 1950s as a result of the increased foreign-exchange availability that stemmed from the Marshall Plan and easy credit markets. Export growth due to the Korean War and the rapid increase in imports that it led to also coincided with attempts at liberalization involving the removal of most restrictions on foreign trade, including automatically granting import licenses for most goods (Şenses 1983, 288). However, these attempts were short-lived; rising inflation, an overvalued Turkish lira (TL), and a widening trade deficit soon led to renewed protectionist measures and a return to more intense state interventionism.[26] During

[24] See Kazgan (1985, 289–95) and Sönmez (1982, 33–35).

[25] Most projects that were introduced during the 1945–46 plan were completed during the last part of the 1940s and the beginning of the 1950s. For a detailed analysis of the planning initiatives during the 1940s, see Tezel (1982, 262–302).

[26] During 1950–53, growth performance was impressive, averaging 11.5 percent, but the trade deficit increased significantly. Exports rose by 50 percent, and imports rose by about 86 percent. That led to the implementation of the protectionist measures beginning in the last quarter of 1952. For a detailed analysis of the period, see Kazgan (1985, 296–314) and Sönmez (1982, 40–58).

the second half of the 1950s, inflation accelerated, GDP growth slowed, and foreign debt continued to accumulate. Deteriorating terms of trade in agriculture and the decrease in exports were adversely affecting the trade balance and growth. Imports decreased, as did the size of the trade deficit. But widespread shortages of imported goods and the lack of foreign currency continued, which led to the introduction of the 1958 austerity program and the devaluation of the overvalued Turkish lira. The main goals of the program, which was also supported by a standby agreement with the IMF, were to lower inflation, balance the budget, and increase exports. The results, though, fell short of expectations: Both exports and imports rose during the next two years, causing the trade deficit to increase to its pre-crisis levels. The GDP growth rate remained below its 1958 level, and both the budget deficit and foreign debt continued to rise.[27]

The Turkish government, however, could not fully carry out the 1958 austerity program because it was overthrown by the military in 1960. Using powers granted by the 1961 constitution, the new government formed after the coup and those that followed intensified import substitution under heavy protectionism and a series of five-year development plans.[28] The main objectives of the first five-year plan (1963–67) were high growth, self-sufficiency in development finance, and achieving the needed capital accumulation to further import-substitution industrialization.[29] The economy, stimulated mostly by domestic sources, managed an impressive 6.5 percent annual average rate of GDP growth in this first five-year period (see table 2.2). That was followed by a 5.4 percent annual average growth rate, driven by workers' remittances and foreign savings, during the second development plan period (1968–72). Also during that period, the annual average growth rate of agriculture was 1.8 percent, and its relative share in GDP decreased to 30.6 percent from its earlier level of 31.7 percent in the period 1963–67.

The third development plan (1973–77) followed a strategy that included deepening import substitution into intermediate and capital goods and allowing for the prospect of Turkey joining the European

[27] For more on this period, see Kazgan (1985, 317–18), Sönmez (1982, 57–58), and Kongar (1998, 357–61).

[28] For a detailed analysis of the five-year development plans, see Aktan and Baysan (1985, 60–73) and Kongar (1998, 361–411).

[29] For the details see Kopits (1987).

Table 2.2 Output growth during the five-year plan periods

Five-year Plan Period	GNP	GDP	Industry		Agriculture		Service	
	Growth rate		Growth rate	% of total	Growth rate	% of total	Growth rate	% of total
1963–1967	6.6	6.5	11.2	19.0	3.2	31.7	7.2	49.3
1968–1972	6.3	5.4	8.4	17.8	1.8	30.6	8.3	51.6
1973–1977	5.3	6.0	8.7	20.3	1.2	24.2	6.0	55.5

Sources: TÜRKSTAT, *Statistical Indicators 1923–2005*; Central Bank of the Republic of Turkey, Electronic Data Delivery System.

Customs Union. This highly ambitious document aimed at establishing an economic structure similar to those of the member nations of the Union, which at the time was called the European Economic Community. To achieve this long-term objective, the third plan projected increased production capacity of intermediate and capital goods in the hope of energizing industries in which Turkey had a comparative advantage.[30]

The external shocks of the early 1970s, particularly the energy crisis of 1973–74, did not weaken the industrialization drive. Turkey remained on a high-growth path and performed exceptionally well, especially when compared to the growth performance of other countries facing similar resource constraints.[31] However, toward the end of the 1970s, increased dependence on imported inputs created foreign-exchange shortages; that, combined with serious imbalances resulting from the external shocks, led to a significant decline in the growth rate of output, an increase in inflation, and the debt crisis of the late 1970s.

Import-Substitution Policies

Import-substitution policies were instrumental in the development of Turkey's resource base. A unique state interventionism that was developed during the 1960s radically changed the resource base by producing intermediate inputs at subsidized values and keeping the domestic prices of the imported goods below their world-price equivalence. These and

[30] By the end of 1977, the share of industry in the GNP reached 21.3 percent, which was a significant increase (from 17.1 percent in 1963).

[31] During the period 1965–80, the average GDP growth in the lower middle income countries was 5.5 percent, and globally the growth rate was about 4 percent, about 2.2 percentage points below Turkey's. See World Development Report (New York: Oxford Press, 1992).

other measures, such as maintaining an overvalued domestic currency and redistributing income in accordance with state-oriented industrialization policies, kept the cost of production at low levels, thus helping the profit margin to rise in the industrial sector.[32] By accelerating private and public investment in key industries, import substitution was aimed at establishing a self-sufficient economy, changing the agricultural character of the economy, and generating new sources of export earnings.

Backed by a high level of protection, the strategy proved to be useful in several industries, essentially intermediate and consumer goods. Industries in which these policies were heavily concentrated included iron and steel, chemicals, metals, and transportation equipment. In some industries, such as food, textiles, clothing, cement, and petrochemicals, not only were imports eliminated but exports were also realized.

In spite of import-substitution policies, however, the import of some goods, such as machinery, electronic equipment, iron, and steel, steadily increased over the years. Imports of these goods had increased partly because of the capital input requirements of the import substitution industries and partly because of the size of these industries, which had not grown enough to fulfill domestic requirements.[33] As industrialization progressed, the need for imports increased, and as a result the import program became more restrictive and increasingly dependent on foreign currency.

During the period 1963–70, import-substitution policies were implemented without serious foreign-currency and imported-input constraints. Despite occasional shortages of imported inputs and moderate foreign-exchange availability, Turkey was able to progress from the production of consumption goods to the production of intermediate goods. After 1970, however, benefiting from the 1970 devaluation of the Turkish lira that had led to increased export earnings and workers' remittances from abroad, import substitution intensified at the consumer goods level. The domestic market became more attractive for consumption goods, and demand for imported inputs began to rise.

With the onset of the oil crisis of 1973–74, energy became more expensive, and the prices of imported inputs rose. Reluctant to give up

---

[32] For more on the state-oriented industrialization strategy, see Keyder (1984) and Pamuk (1984).

[33] Imports may increase in other related home industries as well. As noted in Healey (1972), even though the idea was to reduce imports in the designated industries, more imports were induced in newly stimulated home industries.

Table 2.3 Selected macroeconomic indicators, 1975–1979

Year	GNP	GDP	Inflation	Export	Imports	Trade balance	Current account	Budget deficit
	Growth rate			In million $		% of GNP		
1975	6.1	7.2	19.9	1,401	4,739	−7.0	−3.5	−0.8
1976	9.0	10.5	16.9	1,960	5,129	−5.9	−3.8	−1.2
1977	3.0	3.4	44.6	1,753	5,796	−6.6	−5.1	−4.3
1978	1.2	1.5	36.5	2,288	4,599	−3.5	−1.9	−1.5
1979	−0.5	−0.6	81.2	2,261	5,069	−3.4	−1.7	−3.1

Sources: TÜRKSTAT, *Statistical Indicators 1923–2005*; Central Bank of the Republic of Turkey, Electronic Data Delivery System; State Planning Organization, *Economic and Social Indicators 1950–2006*.

its industrialization drive, the Turkish government deliberately delayed the necessary cost adjustments that should have reflected the rising energy prices and continued its price support policies. By deferring the necessary internal adjustments to the external shocks, policy makers created an economic environment with "largely unnoticed build-up of price and incentive distortions in 1973–77, which caused not only a stagnation in exports, but also a rapid rise in the intensity of imported inputs in current production" (Celasun 1990, 39). Among other factors, Turkish intervention in Cyprus and the 1975 U.S. embargo on military shipments to Turkey also added further strains on the current account and public finances. The current account that had been in surplus in 1972 and 1973 turned into deficit during the remaining years of the 1970s. To meet the public sector's rising borrowing requirement and to finance the growing deficits, the government followed easy monetary policy and resorted to short-term borrowing.

After 1976, an overvalued Turkish lira further raised the demand for imported goods; that widened the trade deficit, which in turn raised the demand for more foreign currency (see table 2.3). Thus, an increasingly worsening balance of payments, accompanied by the external shocks of the mid-1970s, led to severe shortages of essential goods and production bottlenecks and resulted in high inflation and the debt crisis of 1977.

The Debt Crisis of the Late 1970s

The public sector, which was the driving force behind the growth strategy, initially relied on both domestic savings and foreign-exchange receipts to meet borrowing requirements. However, as the public-sector borrowing requirement (PSBR) reached unmanageable levels, due to excessive spending after the 1973–74 oil crisis, external borrowing intensified.[34] The growth strategy that required the needed capital accumulation, in order to deepen the import-substitution industrialization, "amplified the impact of oil price increases," and as a force underlying the crisis it also required uninterrupted inflows of short-term capital (Öniş 1986, 9). As a result of the accommodating response of the monetary authority, short-term external borrowing practices, in particular, increased, which planted the seeds for the 1977–79 debt crisis. That crisis led to the implementation of several austerity programs by the end of the 1970s.

The short-term borrowing scheme that was used contributed to the crisis. Even though foreign borrowing was being secured largely for public-sector investment, it was the private sector that was engaged in short-term borrowing (Rodrik 1988, 64). Under the exchange-rate guarantees extended by the Central Bank, the private sector was borrowing heavily and turning the funds over to the public sector. There was no currency risk for short-term debt, and that made this form of borrowing quite lucrative.[35] But this form of borrowing, even though it was secured by exchange-rate guarantees, soon led to an increased expectation of domestic currency depreciation. However, such a financing scheme was not sustainable, and by 1977 Turkey was unable to service its short-term debt.

Rising monetary aggregates and the supply limitations from widespread shortages of imported inputs caused inflation to accelerate. During the period 1973–77, the Central Bank relied heavily on sterilization to lessen the expansionary effects of public-sector credits. This allowed for a moderate monetary expansion and kept inflation relatively low. However, as foreign-exchange receipts began to decline, due mainly to the 1973–74 oil crisis, declining export earnings, and the lack of external borrowing, the Central Bank had to stop the sterilization practice and heavily monetize the growing budget deficit (Celasun 1990, 41). In March 1978, to relieve the economy from escalating inflationary pressures, Demirel's government devalued the Turkish lira

[34] See Kopits (1987, 2).

[35] One form of borrowing, which was called "Convertible Turkish Lira Deposit" (CTLD), accounted for 48.9 percent of all short-term debt and 21.7 percent of all debt by the end of 1977 (Rodrik 1988, 164). For more on CTLD, also see Celasun and Rodrik (1989, 194–98).

and raised interest rates. The government also lowered its expenditures and significantly raised prices for the products produced by the state economic enterprises (SEEs). As a result, the current account deficit narrowed, but credits to the public sector and the money supply both continued to increase.

In March 1979, the Ecevit government introduced a similar austerity program that placed more emphasis on utilizing domestic resources and lowering dependency on foreign inputs. The Turkish lira was further devalued, and interest rates were raised. Consequently, there were some improvements to the balance of payments account, but despite the contractionary policies that were being implemented, public-sector credits and monetary aggregates continued to rise, which led to higher inflation. The situation worsened in 1979 as the second wave of rising oil prices continued to shock the Turkish economy. Despite a stagnant economy and high unemployment, inflation rose by 81.2 percent in 1979, and the annual percentage change in real GDP turned negative (–0.6 percent) for the first time in more than two decades (see table 2.3). The inability of demand-management policies to restrain domestic demand and the failure of the 1978 and 1979 devaluations to improve current account balances finally led to the introduction of the 1980 stabilization and structural adjustment program. As Celasun and Rodrik (1989) concluded, "Until January 1980, the various adjustment measures undertaken by the authorities can be described as 'too little, too late.' The reduction in government spending was only half-hearted, and exchange rate policy, albeit more active, lagged behind rising inflation. The policymakers were too conscious of political support to administer radical shock treatment, and too divided to implement any feasible alternative" (p. 198).

By the end of the 1970s, it was clear that further expansion of import substitution would have been inefficient and costly. While the rest of the industrializing world was rapidly moving into a high-tech era, deepening the import-substitution industries in Turkey would have required substantial amounts of physical capital and human resources. It was also infeasible to continue with inward-looking policies as the developing world, particularly the newly industrializing countries, became increasingly involved in export promotion policies.

During that period, academic interest in export promotion as an alternative development strategy, which dated back to the 1960s, was on the rise. Covering different sub-periods from the early 1960s to the late 1970s, several researchers found strong evidence of a positive association between export promotion and economic growth. They reported better growth performance in countries implementing a policy of export promotion than in those nations that had adopted an inward-looking industrialization strategy.[36] However, performing causality tests between exports and growth for 37 developing countries, Jung and Marshall (1985) questioned the validity of export-promotion policies and found supportive evidence for export promotion only in a few instances. Reviewing some of the multicountry studies on trade policy, Edwards (1993) also concluded that "[a]lthough these cross-country investigations have unearthed significant information on trade practices in a score of countries, they have been subject to two limitations. First, invariably the authors have found it extremely difficult to compute satisfactory indices of protection and trade orientation, and second, these studies have not been able to provide a fully convincing theoretical framework that links commercial policy, trade orientation, and growth" (p. 1361).

Despite these limitations, it was well documented in the literature that the growth performance of East Asian economies that had been implementing export-oriented trade policies since the mid-1960s was far superior to the performance of Latin American countries experimenting with protectionism and import-substitution policies. Beginning in the 1970s, a growing number of nations started to rethink their decades-old protectionist policies, and as supply shocks of the 1970s, inflation, and the debt crises continued to destabilize their economies, the new economic liberalism, which was based on free-market-oriented allocation and an outward-looking trade regime, became the dominant development strategy.

We conclude our overview of the Turkish economy for the period 1920–80 with the following observations.

1. In retrospect, despite the limited supply of productive resources, particularly during the early years of the Republic, and despite the shock waves of the worldwide depression that followed, the outcome of both the relatively liberal period of the 1920s and the protectionist years of the 1930s was impressive and should not be overlooked. The value of the GDP nearly tripled in two decades, labor productivity increased significantly, and the structure of the economy changed

[36] See, for example, Balassa (1978), Tyler (1981), Feder (1982), Nishimizu and Robinson (1984), and Bell, Ross-Larson, and Westphal (1984).

slightly in favor of industry.[37] The share of industry in total output increased from 8.5 percent in 1924 to 15.5 percent in 1939, a respectable transformation considering the resource constraints that had to be overcome at the time.

2. The improvements in key economic indicators were the product of the forceful drive that Turkish society had as a postwar nation. They were also the result of the government's determination and ability to turn the nation around despite limited finances and an almost nonexistent resource base. Certainly the development of the new republic was empowered by its victory in the War of Independence in 1922 and the Treaty of Lausanne that followed. With this landmark treaty, Turkey was able to free itself from some of the economic restrictions that it had inherited from the Ottoman Empire and move forward as an independent nation enjoying the freedom of designing its own development strategy and macroeconomic policies.
3. The adoption of protectionist measures, induced by the worldwide depression of 1929–33, and the state-led inward-looking strategy that followed were well timed. The strategy not only provided the needed capital accumulation to further the import-substitution industrialization, which was the driving force behind the growth strategy, but also promoted a unique state-private sector partnership that lasted more than four decades.
4. By the end of the 1970s, Turkey's state-led industrialization was halted, largely due to the supply-side shocks of the 1973 oil crisis. Even though the government tried not to hamper the industrialization drive, and attempted to adapt to the shocks by changing the sources of its financing requirements, it had to finally give in because of the deteriorating economic conditions and heavy foreign debt. Higher costs for both energy and imported inputs drastically increased the public sector's borrowing requirement, which was initially being met by an easy monetary policy and short-term external borrowing. That eventually led to high inflation, acute shortages of foreign currency, and high budget and trade deficits.

[37] As reported in a recent study by Altuğ and Filiztekin (2006, 17), during the period from 1928 to 1939 there were significant increases of both aggregate labor productivity (the ratio of GDP to total employment) and relative sectoral productivity (the productivity of each sector divided by the aggregate productivity) in sectors such as manufacturing, services, and utilities.

5. The performance of most nations experimenting with inward-looking industrialization and protectionism during the post-World War II years up until the 1970s varied. As country studies began to emerge pointing out the relatively more favorable performance of East Asian countries that followed outward-oriented growth policies over the majority of developing nations that followed inward-looking policies—and moreover, as a result of concerns over accumulation of third world debt and the debt crisis that it led to—a new policy of economic liberalization and market-oriented development began to emerge.
6. By the end of the 1970s, in view of changing economic and financial conditions both at home and abroad, Turkey's forty-year-old, state-led industrialization was no longer sustainable. Therefore, major revisions in Turkey's development and growth strategy had to be made, and that led to the dramatic change in macroeconomic policy making as well as the critical stabilization and economic restructuring of the 1980s, which we turn to next.

CHAPTER THREE

STABILIZATION AND RESTRUCTURING DURING THE 1980s

Throughout the 1970s, excessive public- and private-sector spending in Turkey contributed to high inflation, greater dependency on imported inputs, and severe foreign-exchange shortages that ultimately led to the introduction of the 1980 stabilization and structural adjustment program. Prior to the program's implementation, exchange rates were fixed, and even with occasional devaluations, the Turkish lira was continually overvalued. In addition to the chronic imbalances of the external accounts and huge fiscal deficits that were behind the public sector's unsustainable borrowing requirement, economic inefficiency was also an issue. Widespread price controls and selective subsidies were common, interest rates were administered, and unique to Turkey, the public sector was becoming increasingly more active in the traditional areas of the private market—producing private goods and services, an economic function rarely seen in any other contemporary free-market economy. Monetary and fiscal instruments also needed refocusing. For decades, both monetary and fiscal policies, instead of being used for macroeconomic management purposes, were applied as a means of financing Turkey's giant state economic enterprises (SEEs). The money supply changed in direct relation to total credit expansion, and monetary policy was aimed at controlling private and public spending by setting borrowing limits within Turkey's not-yet-mature banking system.

It was presumed that the 1980 stabilization and structural adjustment would improve the situation. In addition to the drastic measures intended to stabilize the economy, major structural reforms were also included in the program. These were designed to encourage export promotion and gradually remove trade barriers and foreign-exchange restrictions. The expected outcomes were lower inflation, an improved balance of payments, and a smooth transformation of Turkey's inward-looking growth strategy into an outward-looking, export-driven industrialization through further restructuring.

This chapter provides an in-depth look at Turkey's 1980 program and the key events that gradually led to it. A brief overview of stabilization and restructuring experiences of other countries during the 1980s is followed by chronological details of political and economic developments in Turkey before the program's introduction. The chapter concludes with an assessment of Turkey's stabilization and restructuring efforts that dominated the 1980s, and highlights of the program's performance, particularly with respect to its impact on inflation, investment, and economic growth, are discussed.

Restructuring Experiments in the 1980s

Stabilization and structural adjustment programs were fairly popular in the 1980s, offering a variety of measures to restore macroeconomic balances and revitalize an economy by strengthening its free-market dynamics. Common components of such programs were anti-inflationary monetary and fiscal policies, exchange-rate adjustments, and measures to liberalize international trade and finance. In most countries' experiments, these components worked as follows: domestic demand was restrained by means of anti-inflationary monetary and fiscal policies; competitiveness in external markets was restored by way of exchange-rate adjustments; and aggregate supply was stimulated through trade liberalization and improved market conditions. The stabilization components emphasized demand-management measures. A combination of tight fiscal and monetary policies slows down an economy, thus reducing real income and the price level. Consequently, when price expectations begin to change, the economy regenerates itself with improved productivity and efficiency.

These neoliberal programs, largely introduced in reaction to the insufficiency of and dissatisfaction with Keynesian demand management policies of the 1970s, gained considerable ground during the late 1970s and the 1980s, mostly in advanced market economies where stagflation stubbornly remained a major macroeconomic challenge. They also gained acceptance in less developed countries, where they were referred to as the "Washington Consensus."[1] These programs were especially prevalent in those countries that had relied on both protectionist and inward-oriented policies to industrialize their economies for the previous three decades. As Summers and Pritchett (1993) wrote:

[1] The term "Washington Consensus" was first used by John Williamson in 1989 to refer to the stabilization and structural adjustment package proposed by Washington-based institutions such as the IMF, the World Bank, and the U.S. Treasury Department. We will return to this issue in chapter 10.

"Developing nations from Mexico to Malaysia have made changes in their economies that dwarf anything achieved by Ronald Reagan. The design of structural adjustment programs directed at the four '... ations'—stabilization, liberalization, deregulation, privatization—has become a cottage industry" (p. 383).

Both politicians and development economists hoped that these neoliberal programs would lower inflation, and through restructuring, generate long-term growth in real output and exports. Yet after a decade of experimentation with these programs, the overall outcome was not quite what was expected. The evidence from the late 1980s substantiated only some of the neoliberal claims, mainly showing reduced inflation and increases in real GNP growth spurred by the supply-side tax incentives, particularly in the developed countries (Feldstein 1986, 26–30) but not necessarily in the developing world. In the United States, an economic recovery began in 1983, and most other advanced OECD member nations followed with rather low GDP growth rates and high unemployment (Bruno and Sachs 1985, 10). In Britain, inflation declined, industrial growth accelerated, and exports increased; however, unemployment performance was poor, and income equality was not improving.[2] In France, *theorie de l'offre*, the French version of supply-side economics, raised hopes for an economy of "well-tempered" freedom.[3] In Portugal, one of the least-advanced members of the OECD at the time, liberalism transformed a nation that was on the brink of economic disaster in 1983 into a booming economy where the indicators were all moving in a favorable direction.

Most of the developing world, however, remained unsure of the stabilization, growth, and development value of this new liberal strategy.[4] In the majority of these stabilization experiments, the failure to adopt

---

[2] Layard and Nickell (1989, 219) noted, "Compared with a Callaghan/Healey government for the last ten years, Mrs. Thatcher has raised unemployment and inequality, and reduced inflation. Though she has raised productivity, the verdict on output is uncertain."

[3] The *theorie de l'offre* consisted of across-the-board tax reductions to stimulate capital growth and investment. In addition, it included measures to restore price-setting freedom, privatize national companies and banks, and achieve a transition from a regulated economy to a free-market economy through the judicial system. See Edouard Balladur's commentary, "What France's Economic Policy Means," *Wall Street Journal*, April 10, 1987.

[4] For a comprehensive review of the theoretical models investigating the relationship between trade orientation and growth, with accompanying country specific analyses, see Edwards (1993).

appropriate fiscal, monetary, and exchange-rate policies caused high inflation and output losses, considerably exacerbating the adverse effects of the external shocks of the 1970s and early 1980s.[5] In the Southern Cone, the inability to coordinate the current and capital accounts, and the use of the exchange rate as an anti-inflationary tool, caused a failure to achieve the highly acclaimed liberal targets of the *Talbita* (the pre-announced rate of devaluation) policy.[6] In Brazil, despite the *Crusado* plan, monthly inflation reached 40 percent by the end of 1989, with large sums of external and domestic debt outstanding. In Argentina, the initial success of the *Austral* plan was followed by accelerated inflation and a cycle of failed stabilization attempts.[7]

But there were a small number of success stories. By the mid-1980s, Korea, which had experienced a sharp decline in output in 1980, was quickly recovering—with high investment growth and a substantial trade surplus. It was meeting its debt service obligations and paying off its external debt.[8] Mexican adjustment and restructuring policies, after several failed stabilization programs that were introduced after 1981, led to remarkable outcomes toward the end of the decade. Its heterodox stabilization program was successful in reducing inflation, achieving macroeconomic stability, and increasing economic efficiency (Ortiz 1991). Chile's stabilization program and its trade reform were also successful. Rising productivity in the tradable sector, diversified exports,

[5] The 1973–78 and 1978–83 external shocks included increases in oil prices, a slowdown of world trade, and increases in the interest rates in global financial markets (Balassa 1986). For more specific factors associated with external shocks and policy responses, see Tanzi (1986), and for the analysis of the exchange rate policy response, specifically, see Khan (1986).

[6] Summarizing the results of a World Bank research project, Corbo, de Melo, and Tybout (1986) reported that policy reforms in Uruguay, Chile, and Argentina had started during the second half of the 1970s. During the early phase of the stabilization and liberalization programs, all three countries did well, but as they became increasingly open to foreign capital inflows the programs failed to generate the expected outcomes. For a summary of the other country experiences, see Edwards and Teitel (1986) and Bruno et al. (1991).

[7] For detailed analyses of both the *Crusado* and *Austral* plans, see Cardoso (1991), Heymann (1991), and Kiguel and Liviatan (1991).

[8] According to Collins (1990), Korea's adjustment differed from the experiences of other countries. High rates of investment in export industries, a stable policy environment, and capital inflow were the main factors that helped Korea's quick recovery after 1980. "Korea's experience should not be construed as an example that a country in the midst of a prolonged economic crisis, with a depleted capital stock and a history of political reversals and mistakes, can simultaneously undertake structural adjustments together with restrictive macroeconomic policies, transfer resources abroad and revive stagnant growth rates" (p. 107).

and periodic adjustments in the exchange rate led to the highest rate of growth in Latin America during the second half of the 1980s (Edwards 1993, 1373–75). Finally, as detailed in the next section, Turkey was hailed as an exemplary country that had made considerable progress toward a free-market economy by means of its orthodox stabilization and adjustment program.

Turkey's 1980 Stabilization and Structural Adjustment Program

Between March 1975 and November 1979, Süleyman Demirel and Bülent Ecevit, two of the most prominent figures in Turkey's political landscape, switched back and forth as prime minister three times, and each time they were handed the job they claimed that they had inherited an economy in ruins (see table 3.1). In December 1979, when Demirel became prime minister, the economic fundamentals were not very different from those that had existed 18 months earlier, when Ecevit had taken over. The economic environment was fragile, not only because of mismanagement during the previous administration, as alleged by the opposition, but also because of a severe payments crisis that had stalled the economy. Widespread shortages of basic goods, rising inflation and unemployment, and a lack of liquidity to carry on the day-to-day operations of the state were some of the critical problems that needed immediate attention.

As mentioned in the previous chapter, Turkey had already experimented with stabilization packages twice since 1978. Nevertheless, the economy was not improving. A new vision to move Turkey beyond repeated stabilization attempts was needed. Turkish bureaucrats from the Treasury, the Central Bank, and the State Planning Organization, each of which had been mastering the art of crisis management during Turkey's most difficult times and had seen no improvement in economic fundamentals, agreed that some form of restructuring was an absolute necessity. Experts from the IMF, the World Bank, and the OECD were also aware of the gravity of the macroeconomic situation. Despite the failure of previous stabilization attempts, these experts still had no better alternative than offering similar programs based on neoliberal policies in order to stabilize the economy and operationalize restructuring in the Turkish context. So as not to repeat the same policy mistakes that led to previous foreign-exchange crises, the experts agreed that it was

Table 3.1 Governing parties, coalitions, and prime ministers in Turkey, 1950–2007

Term	Prime Minister	Governing Party/Coalition	Term	Prime Minister	Governing Party/Coalition
05/22/1950–03/09/1951	Menderes	DP	06/21/1977–07/21/1977	Ecevit	CHP
03/09/1951–05/17/1954	Menderes	DP	07/21/1977–01/05/1978	Demirel	AP-MSP-MHP
05/17/1954–12/09/1955	Menderes	DP	01/05/1978–11/12/1979	Ecevit	CHP
12/09/1955–11/25/1957	Menderes	DP	11/12/1979–09/12/1980	Demirel	AP
11/25/1957–05/27/1960	Menderes	DP	09/20/1980–12/13/1983	Ulusu	Non-civilian
05/30/1960–01/05/1961	Gürsel	Non-civilian	12/13/1983–12/21/1987	Özal	ANAP
01/05/1961–11/20/1961	Gürsel	Non-civilian	12/21/1987–11/09/1989	Özal	ANAP
11/20/1961–06/25/1962	İnönü	CHP-AP	11/09/1989–06/23/1991	Akbulut	ANAP
06/25/1962–12/25/1963	İnönü	CHP-CKMP-YTP	06/23/1991–11/20/1991	Yılmaz	ANAP
12/25/1963–02/20/1965	İnönü	CHP	11/21/1991–06/25/1993	Demirel	DYP-SHP
02/20/1965–10/27/1965	Ürgüplü	AP	06/25/1993–10/05/1995	Çiller	DYP-SHP
10/27/1965–11/03/1969	Demirel	AP	10/05/1995–10/30/1995	Çiller	DYP
11/03/1969–03/06/1970	Demirel	AP	10/30/1995–03/06/1996	Çiller	DYP-CHP
03/06/1970–03/26/1971	Demirel	AP	03/06/1996–06/28/1996	Yılmaz	ANAP-DYP
03/26/1971–12/11/1971	Erim	National unity coalition	06/28/1996–06/30/1997	Erbakan	RP-DYP
12/11/1971–05/22/1972	Erim	National unity coalition	06/30/1997–01/11/1999	Yılmaz	ANAP-DSP-DTP
05/22/1972–04/15/1973	Melen	caretaker	01/11/1999–05/28/1999	Ecevit	caretaker
04/15/1973–01/26/1974	Talu	AP-CGP	05/28/1999–11/18/2002	Ecevit	DSP-ANAP-MHP
01/26/1974–11/17/1974	Ecevit	CHP-MSP	11/18/2002–03/14/2003	Gül	AKP
11/17/1974–03/31/1975	Irmak	caretaker	03/14/2003–08/29/2007	Erdoğan	AKP
03/31/1975–06/21/1977	Demirel	AP-MSP-MHP-CGP	08/29/2007–present	Erdoğan	AKP

Sources: The Grand National Assembly of Turkey and The Republic of Turkey Ministry of Foreign Affairs.

Note: Democratic Party (*Demokrat Parti*, DP), Republican People's Party (*Cumhuriyet Halk Partisi*, CHP), Justice Party (*Adalet Partisi*, AP), Republican Peasant People Party (*Cumhuriyetçi Köylü Millet Partisi*, CKMP), New Turkey Party (*Yeni Türkiye Partisi*, YTP), Republican Reliance Party (*Cumhuriyetçi Güven Partisi*, CGP), National Salvation Party (*Milli Selamet Partisi*, MSP), National Movement Party (*Milli Hareket Partisi*, MHP), Motherland Party (*Anavatan Partisi*, ANAP), True Path Party (*Doğru Yol Partisi*, DYP), Welfare Party (*Refah Partisi*, RP), Democratic Left Party (*Demokratik Sol Parti*, DSP), Democratic Turkey Party (*Demokratik Turkiye Partisi*, DTP), Justice and Development Party (*Adalet ve Kalkınma Partisi*, AKP).

essential for Turkey to abandon its state-led industrialization, its restrictive trade regime, and its financial repression. They also believed that to achieve those ends, the country had to employ adjustment measures that were in accordance with an outward-looking free-market-oriented structural adjustment and stabilization program. From the perspective of the IMF, the adjustment package needed to include specific policy actions to reorient Turkey's stabilization and development efforts along the lines of the neoliberal approach, which from the late 1970s to the early 1990s had gained considerable support from researchers and policy makers in the developing world. For the IMF officials, it was just a matter of convincing their Turkish counterparts to develop a package that would comply with the main premises of the neoliberal strategy and then follow up with a typical standby agreement containing the usual and country-specific conditions.

The program design, which was introduced on January 24, 1980, by the Demirel government, included short- and long-term objectives that would build the foundation of an outward-looking free-market economy. A sharp devaluation of the Turkish lira accompanied by steep price adjustments for state enterprise products was expected to lessen the widespread shortages of essential goods. To lower inflation, tight monetary and fiscal policies were also outlined. All of these urgent measures, which were intended to have a shock effect on the economy—plus gradual relaxation of foreign-exchange restrictions, several direct and indirect incentives for export promotion, and gradual liberalization of the import and export regimes—signaled the beginning of a new macroeconomic environment in which major restructuring from inward-looking to outward-looking policies began to take place.

Immediately following the announcement of the program, the Demirel administration went to work to relieve the economy from a severe balance of payments crisis and rising inflationary pressures. A steep devaluation of the Turkish lira and price hikes of the SEE products were introduced and followed by vigorous attempts to raise liquidity from the international community. Overwhelmed by the decisiveness of the Demirel administration and its readiness to deal with the crisis, the IMF further called for interest rate liberalization, a realistic exchange-rate policy, and reforms to remove the heavy burden of the SEEs on the Turkish economy. In a June 1980 letter of intent to the IMF, Turkey vowed to continue its tight monetary policy, raise interest rates, and follow frequent exchange-rate adjustments to achieve a realistic value for the Turkish lira. It also agreed to limit short-term borrowing practices and to establish competitive energy prices. Later that same month, the principal author of the program, Turgut Özal, undersecretary of the prime minister, decided to free interest rates effective July 12, 1980. Interest-rate deregulation, an important milestone in Turkey's liberalization, was expected to ensure positive real interest rates so as to encourage domestic saving.

The Özal Era

In September 1980, nine months after the announcement of the program, Turkish armed forces seized power, dissolved the Parliament and took custody of all party leaders. Chief of the General Staff Kenan Evren became the head of the state, and within a month Admiral Bülent Ulusu formed a new government. To ensure continuity in the implementation of the stabilization and restructuring measures, the military, already familiar with the program through a series of briefings given by Özal before the coup, appointed Özal as the deputy prime minister in charge of the economy.

Özal, who at the time actively participated in the design of the program while serving as undersecretary to the prime minister in charge of the economy, had set the tone of the program. An engineer by training and a longtime associate of Demirel, Özal had grand designs for the future of the Turkish economy. He was a self-educated pragmatic economist who had been impressed with the neoliberal views that had gained popularity during the 1970s. Many of the Western economies were becoming increasingly disillusioned by outdated Keynesian remedies for dealing with the stagflation of the late 1970s and had great hope that the highly advocated new supply-side measures would engender higher productivity and growth. Turkey was also suffering from macroeconomic complications similar to those in other OECD nations. But unlike these nations, the Turkish economy lacked a market orientation and had a structure that was inward-looking and highly protected. The macroeconomic environment in general, and the industrialization strategy in particular, had been the main source of budget and current account deficits for some time and was also responsible for the debt crisis that followed during the second half of the 1970s.

Özal did not question the stabilization role of the state as the new classical economists did. The debate over whether monetary and fiscal policies should be used to fine-tune the economy was not relevant to

Turkey. The supply-side argument to lower taxes and thus stimulate productivity and growth did not make sense for Turkey either. Turkey not only lacked a significant tax base but was also subject to the problems of tax evasion and avoidance. Private and public savings were insufficient, and investors did not have easy access to international loanable funds markets, which most low-risk advanced nations did have. Özal's concern was the size of the public sector and its allocational role in the economy. It was his belief that the state has no business producing goods and services that the private sector could produce. Instead, he believed, it should mobilize society's resources to promote private markets and be active in areas where markets fail or are unable to function efficiently. In a lengthy 1982 interview with *Euromoney*, Özal stressed that he supported government spending on infrastructure but not on industry. Nor did he view support prices favorably, particularly in agriculture. In the same interview, he implied that support prices were a disincentive for higher productivity in agricultural regions where people chose to produce extensively rather than intensively because they are content with the support they get from the state.[9]

It is clear that Özal had confidence in the free-market system. He believed in the private sector and in flexible exchange rates and market interest rates. He also argued that state bureaucracy should not stand in the way of private initiative. When he began his work as the undersecretary to the prime minister in charge of the economy, he was convinced that, in addition to stabilization measures that would restore urgently needed macroeconomic balances, Turkey needed a far-reaching structural adjustment program. If Turkey was going to join the ranks of advanced European nations, then it had to restructure its economy to make it compatible with the economies of those nations, no matter how difficult that may turn out to be.

Özal's tenure in Ulusu's government was short-lived. In 1982, growing opposition to interest-rate liberalization, and an increasing number of bankruptcies that seemed to result from the aggressive liberalization measures, forced Özal to resign. Freeing interest rates was the first step toward financial deregulation. The resulting immediate change in the interest rates was expected to be moderate, in part due to the gentlemen's agreement among major commercial banks with respect

[9] See "A Program to Make Capitalism Work," *Euromoney*, February 1982, 5–10.

to setting deposit rates.[10] As a result of the increased participation of small banks and unregulated brokerage firms in the financial markets, interest rates rose. That led to increased brokerage activity among these firms, which involved marketing corporate bonds, offering their own promissory notes, and buying certificates of deposits at a discount from issuing banks and selling them at a premium to investors. This form of debt financing was highly dependent upon the supply of these types of money-market instruments, and as interest rates continued to increase, it became very difficult to locate new sources of funding that would yield sufficient return to the brokerage houses and service their existing portfolio. The increased volume of refinancing involving nonperforming loans and the upward pressure on interest rates finally led to a loss of confidence in the money markets, an increase in bankruptcy filings, and thus to the ensuing financial collapse of June 1982, which culminated in Özal's resignation a month later.[11]

In 1983, Özal formed the pro-free-market Motherland Party (ANAP in Turkish initials), which he himself described as conservative and nationalistic. Against all odds, he won the general election in November 1983, capturing 45.1 percent of the popular vote and 53 percent of the seats in Parliament. Özal became prime minister of Turkey in December 1983. During his term as prime minister, the economy grew rapidly; inflation remained below the 1980 level, the growth of Turkey's exports was impressive, and even though the trade and current account balances were both in deficit, as a percentage of GNP they continued to improve.

This buoyant economic performance did not last, however, and Özal's popularity started to diminish after the 1987 early general election, which he won with 36 percent of the popular vote.[12] At the top of the list of reasons for Özal's declining popularity as he began his second term as prime minister was the economy. The once-impressive growth was beginning to slow down, real income was shrinking, and due to

---

[10] After 1980, interest rates were determined by banks through gentlemen's agreements, but in 1983, when banks became reluctant to raise rates, the Central Bank was authorized to raise deposit rates and review them every three months on the basis of fluctuations in the inflation rate.

[11] For more on brokerage failures, see Akyüz (1990, 99) and Atiyas (1990).

[12] The *Economist* wrote: "[A]s Prime Minister since 1983, and steersman of the economy for most of the three years under military rule before that, he has done more than any other man in 50 years to shape the Turkey of today and make it ready for Europe tomorrow." See "Half Inside, Half Out," *The Economist*, June 18, 1988, 3.

populist measures such as delaying state price increases and expansionary monetary policies, inflation was edging into its highest level since 1981. These and many other concerns intensified opposition even within his own party, the ANAP. Mehmet Keçeçiler, chief deputy leader of the party, warned its increasingly disillusioned constituents: "If by the end of five years we don't have inflation totally under control, no power in the world can bring us back."[13]

Inflation continued to surge, and the early election held in 1991 did not bring Özal's party back. His old friend, and now his foe, Süleyman Demirel, who had formed a new party called the True Path Party (*Doğru Yol Partisi*, DYP in Turkish initials), was back in power as prime minister. Demirel captured 27 percent of the popular vote, and Özal's ANAP (under the leadership of Yıldırım Akbulut who was appointed prime minister by Özal in 1989 and voted in as chairman of the party during the same year) finished second, with 24 percent of the votes. The election did not mark the end of Özal's legacy, however. The ANAP was out, but not Özal. He had already repositioned himself as president, having been elected to this position in 1989 after Kenan Evren's term in office expired.

The Performance of the Program

During the period 1980–84, GDP growth averaged 3.6 percent annually, and year-end CPI inflation declined from 86.1 percent in 1980 to 49.7 percent in 1984. The budget deficit narrowed (in 1981 and 1982), and as a percentage of GNP, the public-sector borrowing requirement remained steady, significantly below the1980 level (see table 3.2 and table 3.3). During the same period, the current account deficit declined from 4.9 percent of GNP to 2.4 percent of GNP. And despite increased protectionism among the OECD nations, exports managed to rise from about $2.9 billion in 1980 to $7.1 billion in 1984, averaging a 27 percent annual increase (see figure 3.1).

This rapid increase in exports was due to many factors, including growing demand for Turkish products in the Middle East, the Iran–Iraq War, and trade missions promoted by the Turkish government (Şenses 1990, 66–69). Generous export incentives in the form of tax rebates and subsidized credit rates and the availability of substantial excess capacity

[13] "Turkey Puts the Brakes on Rapid Growth," *Wall Street Journal*, August 4, 1988.

Table 3.2 Selected macroeconomic indicators, 1980–1990

Year	GDP growth rate	Inflation rate	Budget deficit	Exports	Imports	Trade balance	Current account
			% of GNP	In million $		% of GNP	
1980	-2.4	86.1	-3.1	2,910	7,909	-6.6	-4.9
1981	4.9	30.3	-1.5	4,703	8,933	-5.3	-2.7
1982	3.6	34.6	-1.5	5,746	8,843	-4.0	-1.5
1983	5.0	37.1	-2.2	5,728	9,235	-4.8	-3.1
1984	6.7	49.7	-4.4	7,134	10,757	-4.8	-2.4
1985	4.2	44.2	-2.2	7,958	11,343	-4.4	-1.5
1986	7.0	30.7	-2.8	7,457	11,105	-3.9	-1.9
1987	9.5	55.1	-3.5	10,190	14,158	-3.7	-0.9
1988	2.1	61.6	-3.1	11,662	14,335	-2.0	1.8
1989	0.3	64.3	-3.3	11,625	15,792	-3.9	0.9
1990	9.3	60.4	-3.0	12,959	22,302	-6.2	-1.7

Sources: TÜRKSTAT, *Statistical Indicators 1923–2005*; Central Bank of the Republic of Turkey, Electronic Data Delivery System; Turkish Treasury, *Economic Indicators*. State Planning Organization, *Economic and Social Indicators 1950–2006*.

Table 3.3 International reserves, external and domestic debt, and PSBR, 1980–1990

Year	International reserves		External debt Total		Short term	Domestic debt	PSBR
	In billion $	% of GNP	In billion $	% of GNP	% of GNP	% of GNP	% of GNP
1980	1.2	1.8	15.7	19.3	3.1	13.6	8.7
1981	1.6	2.2	16.6	20.2	2.6	12.4	3.9
1982	2.0	3.1	17.9	25.1	2.5	12.6	3.5
1983	2.1	3.5	18.8	31.8	3.8	22.8	4.9
1984	3.5	5.9	20.8	35.0	5.4	20.9	5.3
1985	3.3	4.9	25.7	38.1	7.1	19.7	3.5
1986	4.3	5.7	32.2	42.7	8.4	20.5	3.6
1987	5.2	6.0	40.3	46.8	8.9	23.0	6.0
1988	6.4	7.1	40.7	45.0	7.1	22.0	4.8
1989	9.3	8.6	41.7	38.8	5.3	18.2	5.3
1990	11.4	7.5	49.0	32.6	6.3	14.4	7.3

Sources: TÜRKSTAT, *Statistical Indicators 1923–2005*; Central Bank of the Republic of Turkey, Electronic Data Delivery System; Turkish Treasury, *Economic Indicators, Treasury Statistics 1980–2003*.

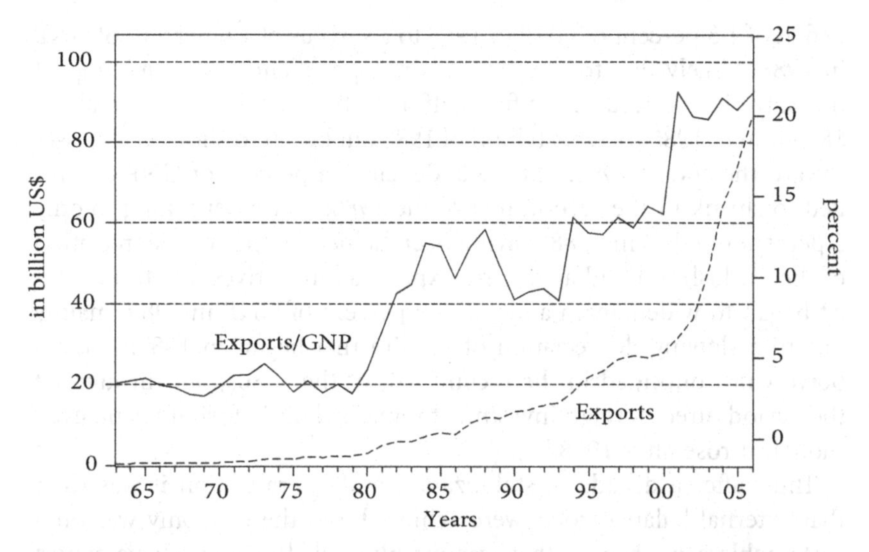

Figure 3.1 Turkish exports, 1963–2006. (Data from Central Bank of the Republic of Turkey, Electronic Data Delivery System; State Planning Organization, *Economic and Social Indicators 1950–2006*; Undersecretariat for Foreign Trade.)

in the import-substituting industries that were created during the last two decades were also factors that contributed to export growth. As a percentage of GNP, exports nearly tripled, from 4.3 percent in 1980 to 12.1 percent in 1984, and continued their upward trend for the rest of the 1980s.

During the period 1985–89, GDP growth averaged 4.6 percent. After reaching its highest level of 9.5 percent in 1987, it dropped to 0.3 percent in 1989 and rose to 9.3 percent the next year. The slowdown in GDP, which started in 1988, occurred despite fairly strong external demand. It was attributed partly to declining real wages and the contraction of output in the manufacturing and transportation industries and partly to the slowdown in total spending caused by contractionary fiscal policies in 1987 and a decline in investment.

The budget deficit as a percentage of GNP continued its decline in 1985, but after 1986 it began to rise, as did the public-sector borrowing requirement.[14] The current account balance improved, rising from a

[14] The variation in the public-sector borrowing requirements, which rose to their highest levels after 1988, seemed to be explained by unsustainable domestic borrowing schemes, such as domestic interest rate shocks and the changes in domestic debt burden. Decomposing the changes in the public-sector borrowing requirements, Boratav, Türel,

deficit of 1.5 percent of GNP in 1985 to a surplus of 1.8 percent of GNP in 1988, largely due to the increase in exports and restrictive import measures introduced in the first half of 1988. Exports rose from about $8 billion in 1985 to $11.6 billion in 1988 but began to show weaknesses toward the end of 1990. The trade deficit as a percent of GNP continued to shrink in the second half of the 1980s. But after falling to only 2 percent of GNP in 1988, having been helped by the real depreciation of the Turkish lira and aggressive export tax incentives, the trade deficit began to widen again and was 3.9 percent of GNP in 1989, mainly due to a slowing depreciation of the lira that began in 1987. Foreign borrowing continued in the second half of the 1980s, but throughout the period direct foreign investment remained fairly insignificant, even though it rose after 1988.[15]

Thus, after a decade of stabilization and liberalization it was clear that external balance goals were achieved and the economy was on a sustainable growth path that was mainly fueled by impressive export performance. Exports were significantly higher than in the pre-1980 years, having been helped by successive devaluations, and most importantly, the normalization of Turkey's creditworthiness eased some of the financial restraints. However, unemployment and inflation continued, and the level of private-sector investment remained far below expectations despite signs of a substantial increase in industrial production toward the end of the 1980s.

Turkish Inflation

The program successfully lowered inflation from 86.1 percent in 1980 to 34.6 percent in 1982 (see table 3.2). Possible explanations for inflation falling so significantly include the anti-inflationary monetary and fiscal policies, rising interest rates, and public-sector pricing policies. A sharp increase in foreign currency inflows as a result of external debt restructuring also reduced the need for inflationary finance during the first two years of the program.[16] But then, in response to declining GDP

---

and Yeldan (1996) reported that for the entire period of 1981–92, two percentage points of the public-sector borrowing requirements were explained by interest rate shocks.

[15] According to Erdilek (1988), Turkey's political and economic environments were the main reasons for the poor performance, and in order to compete for the attention of risk-conscious foreign investors, much was needed to be done to gain credibility.

[16] In addition to tight monetary and fiscal policies, Rodrik (1991) argued that the Turkish public sector had less need for inflationary finance because of positive net resource transfers due to generous inflows from official and multilateral sources.

growth in 1982 and the increase in the Central Bank's foreign assets (due to liberalization of external trade and the payments system), monetary policy was relaxed and remained relaxed until the last quarter of 1985. Consequently, the economy began to grow robustly, with inflation stabilizing at around 30 percent in 1986. But after 1987, populist measures led to excessive spending and rapid expansion of public-sector credits. It was such expansionary fiscal measures that accelerated inflation.[17] High interest rates and exchange-rate adjustments on a daily basis also caused inflation to accelerate.

Throughout the 1980s, the monetary authority did its part, within limits, to combat inflation. Before 1986, the Central Bank used public-sector credits and interest rates as monetary policy instruments. The money supply was determined by total credit expansion, and monetary policy was directed toward controlling private and public spending by setting borrowing limits for the banking system. After 1986, the Central Bank took important steps toward more autonomy. A switch to monetary reserve targeting was accompanied by a series of new laws that allowed the Central Bank to conduct open market operations and monitor a newly established inter-bank market.[18] These reforms were further complemented by accords with the Treasury that limited the short-term credit government could use from the Central Bank. However, despite these measures, which could be interpreted as a move toward greater Central Bank independence, inflation continued to surge after 1990.[19]

Private Investment and Growth

Overall, the investment performance of the 1980s was not impressive. One critical problem was the slow growth of private investment in manufacturing, averaging about 3.6 percent of GNP (see table 3.4).

---

[17] For more on the expansionary fiscal measures during the period 1980–88 see Sayarı (1992).

[18] The new legislation introduced important institutional arrangements. In April 1986, the interbank market was established, and the Central Bank began to use open market operations; in January 1988 the foreign-exchange market began to operate, and in 1989 the capital account was liberalized.

[19] The Central Bank was not independent of macroeconomic policy making. Stabilizing behavior, or the lack of it, was the responsibility of both the fiscal and monetary authorities. The fiscal authority had even more influence on monetary policy during periods of high turnover of coalition governments. For example, during the 1983–86 politically stable period, inflation and inflation uncertainty remained relatively low, but frequent elections and governments that followed after 1987 led to an expanding budget that increasingly relied on Central Bank resources. See Nas and Perry (2000).

Table 3.4 Domestic saving and gross fixed investment, 1975–1990, in percentage of GNP

Year	Domestic saving	Gross fixed investment				
		Total	Public	Private	Manufacturing Public	Manufacturing Private
1975	19.6	22.6	8.0	14.6	2.2	6.3
1976	22.5	25.7	8.9	16.8	2.1	6.7
1977	20.4	27.2	10.0	17.1	2.2	6.6
1978	17.0	24.6	8.4	16.2	1.7	6.0
1979	15.7	21.6	7.9	13.6	1.9	3.9
1980	16.0	21.8	8.7	13.1	2.3	3.9
1981	18.3	19.8	9.0	10.8	2.0	3.7
1982	17.1	19.2	8.2	11.0	1.5	3.6
1983	16.5	20.1	8.7	11.4	1.4	3.7
1984	16.5	19.3	8.0	11.3	1.1	3.7
1985	18.9	20.1	9.2	11.0	1.2	3.5
1986	21.9	22.8	10.2	12.6	1.0	4.0
1987	23.9	24.6	10.0	14.7	0.7	3.7
1988	27.2	26.1	8.9	17.3	0.5	3.7
1989	22.1	22.5	7.5	15.0	0.3	3.0
1990	22.0	22.6	7.0	15.7	0.3	4.1

Source: State Planning Organization, *Economic and Social Indicators 1950–2006*.

Occasional upward trends in manufacturing investment were short-lived; even the change in government investment policy, which was intended to slow the growth of public expenditures to allow increased private investment in manufacturing, did not strengthen the private sector sufficiently for it to take the lead in promoting growth and invigorating the export drive. Private investment, after declining below pre-1980 levels between 1980 and 1985, only began to increase during the second half of the 1980s, reaching its highest level in 1988 (see table 3.4 and figure 3.2). Public investment, on the other hand, averaged roughly 8.5 percent of GNP during 1980–84 and 9.2 percent of GNP in 1985–89. Its structure shifted away from manufacturing and toward infrastructure and remained below private investment levels.

There were several factors that led to this below-expectation investment performance. First, as described in the preceding chapter, Turkey's industrialization policy before 1980 was predominantly one of import substitution—a state-led strategy, a unique state-private sector partnership that lasted almost four decades. The excess capacity remaining from this period was probably the basis of the export growth during

Figure 3.2 Gross fixed investment, 1963–2006. (Data from State Planning Organization, *Economic and Social Indicators 1950–2006.*)

the 1980s. As exports continued to rely on existing capacity, there was little need for new investment.[20]

The second reason for slow growth in manufacturing investment was the existence of an unfavorable policy environment. According to a survey conducted by the Turkish Industrialists' and Businessmen's Association (TUSIAD), 26.7 percent of all businessmen surveyed indicated that economic and political instability had a significant adverse effect on private capital investment.[21] Private investment needed a stable and profitable environment, and for that it was necessary to have lower levels of inflation and nominal interest rates, a slower rate of exchange-rate depreciation, and political stability.[22] However, excessive reliance on

[20] Firms involved in export markets most likely chose to exploit the existing production capacity rather than increasing their real capital base despite the opportunities of expanding export markets. See Şenses (1990).

[21] See Turkish Industrialists' and Businessmen's Association, *1989 Yılına girerken Türk ekonomisi* [Turkish economy at the beginning of 1989]. TUSIAD, İstanbul, 1989, 119.

[22] Analyzing the determinants of investment behavior in Turkey, Conway (1990) reported that private investment had been discouraged by the policy of high nominal interest rates, high inflation, and rapidly depreciating nominal exchange rates.

exchange-rate and interest-rate adjustments and inconsistent monetary and fiscal expansion led to high inflation, high depreciation, and a high nominal interest rate environment toward the end of the 1980s. Real investment was discouraged by frequent real currency depreciation (via increased costs of imported inputs), the uncertainty caused by high inflation, and the high cost of capital resulting from high interest rates.

High interest rates, in particular, created an uncertain environment for those who were accustomed to borrowing at negative real rates. For the most part, real interest rates were negative prior to 1980. After deregulation in 1980 and several other structural measures adopted thereafter, real deposit rates rose significantly, with moderate variations, between 1983 and 1985. A high interest rate was tolerated in order to encourage private saving and raise the availability of loanable funds for capital formation. Although interest rates may have partly explained the rise in private savings as a percentage of GNP in those years, they also may have been the reason for the nearly stagnant private investment after 1980. Firms with low earnings relied more heavily on debt, and in spite of the increased cost of borrowing, they continued to raise their debt-asset ratios mainly to finance "risky survival strategies" such as refinancing nonperforming loans (Atiyas 1990). Hence, investment was adversely affected.[23]

Finally, another situation adversely affecting capital formation was the withdrawal of public investment from the manufacturing industry. Changes in private investment did not compensate for the declining rates of public investment, and that was partly the reason for the erosion of gross fixed-capital formation.[24]

How Successful was the 1980 Program?

Reactions from the academic community were mixed. Several studies on the Turkish experiment did praise Turkey's efforts in increasing exports, lowering inflation from three-digit levels, and normalizing the debt situation. In their quantification of the linkages among fiscal

[23] In addition to the rise in real interest rates, the real depreciation of the Turkish Lira and the introduction of a high value-added tax (over 10 percent) were also perceived as factors contributing to the increased cost of production, which caused financial distress across industries. See Odekon (1992).

[24] Boratav, Türel, and Yeldan (1995) argued that depressed public investments were due to declining rates of public savings and suggest that a growth-oriented public policy should first ensure increased public savings through increased taxation.

policy, investment, and growth, Anand, Chhibber, and van Wijnbergen (1990) explained that capital inflows, the public expenditure program, and interest rate policy were behind Turkey's respectable growth. Rodrik (1988) described Turkey's experience with exports as "astonishingly successful," driven by a combination of export promotion policies (the active real-exchange-rate policy) and good luck. Emphasizing the role of the exchange-rate policy as a dominant factor in export growth, Barlow and Şenses (1995) also found quantitative evidence for the positive effect of external factors such as the recovery of the industrial countries after the mid-1980s.[25] But there were some warnings: export growth and external account improvements were clearly the result of the liberalization of export and import regimes. As Togan (1996) and Aktan (1996) indicated, the policies introduced in the 1980s did not eliminate the bias against exports, and the real exchange rate needed to be reduced further to achieve long-term improvements in the trade account. Baysan and Blitzer (1990) and Şenses (1990) noted the importance of increasing private investment for sustained export performance. But according to Conway (1990), real currency depreciation, high inflation, and high nominal interest rates had discouraged private investment.[26]

The initial reduction of inflation in 1981–82 was remarkable, but inflation persisted thereafter. As Şenses (1988) rightly warned, the failure to control inflation was likely to remain a highly significant and controversial feature of the program, and it did so for the rest of the 1980s and beyond. Inflation persisted not only because of the great impact of exchange-rate adjustments (Öniş and Özmucur, 1990) but also because of the monetization of public-sector deficits (Rodrik 1991). Other factors that made a significant contribution to the inflationary process included lags in price setting and delays in tax collection (Gazioğlu 1986) as well as corrective inflation induced by the liberalization of key relative prices (Öniş 1986).

A number of studies on Turkish liberalization also warned that the financial markets needed fundamental restructuring if they were to perform at the same level of operational and allocational efficiency as

[25] In their regression model, which included 1966–91 annual data, Barlow and Şenses found that during the 1981–89 period real exchange rate depreciation accounted for 42.7–51.7 percent of the agricultural export growth since 1979. For manufactured exports, the increase was above 60 percent; the highest was 102.5 percent, in 1981.

[26] In an earlier study, Conway (1988) reported that while the frequent devaluations of the period and the imported-input liberalization (through tariff reduction) helped the trade balance, they also tended to slow down the economy by lowering investments.

their counterparts did in emerging economies (İnselbağ and Gültekin 1988). Foreign direct investment was necessary to moderate financial pressures resulting from the domestic saving gap, but during the second half of the 1980s Turkey's political and economic environments continued to present shortcomings that were detrimental to attracting foreign capital. Political instability and the risk of a renewed confidence crisis were still posing serious threats, as were the uneven pace of the economy's development and uncertainties surrounding the future of liberalization in Turkey (Erdilek 1988). Clearly, Turkey needed to sustain a steadily growing economy, generate new capacity, and gradually reduce the debt-service burden, and for that it needed continuity in private capital inflows.

Another major concern was related to the deterioration in income distribution during the post-1980 period. Examining income distribution data for 1963, 1968, and 1973, Celasun (1986) detected a relatively high degree of inequality and observed a mild improvement in income distribution thereafter—particularly during the 1973–78 period, when Turkey was following inward-looking policies, with formal planning and a relatively more organized labor market, that led to a notable rise in real wages and favorable support prices and input subsidies for farmers. But during the 1978–83 sub-period, income distribution worsened largely because of the deterioration in the terms of trade for agriculture and the decline in absolute income of lower-income groups relative to average incomes within both agricultural and nonagricultural sectors. According to Celasun (1989), the transition from an inward-oriented to an outward-oriented economic structure, and particularly the abrupt ending of foreign capital inflows, required "a sizable domestic adjustment with an unexpectedly sharp political and social dislocation" (p. 27). Such domestic adjustments, specifically, would necessarily require restrictive policies on real wages and government spending in order to service the foreign debt.

In a lengthy discussion of the distributional outcomes of the 1980 structural adjustment program, Boratav (1990) also emphasized the deterioration in the terms of trade for agriculture and the regression in real wages since the late 1970s, and he associated the decline in the latter to "the overall *anti-labor and pro-capital* orientation of the economic policies of the period" (p. 225). As Boratav concluded, "[T]he transmission of the unstable conditions in the world economy to the Third World has partly been through the kind of externally-imposed economic policy models experienced by Turkey during the last decade and its distributional consequences have been broadly parallel in countries which have passed through the same experience" (p. 226).

In spite of these and other concerns, a complete reversal of the neoliberal strategy seemed unlikely.[27] Challenging the neoliberal orthodoxy that dominated policy making in Turkey during the 1980s, one study in particular raised serious concerns about the prospects for investment and growth. According to Boratav, Türel, and Yeldan (1995), declining rates of public savings, and thus a lack of improvement in the rate of capital formation in the public sector, were not only the cause of lower growth rates in the 1980s but were also possibly keeping Turkey on a lower growth path. A growth-oriented public policy aimed at overcoming future stagnation in capital formation would be necessary, but that, the study claimed, had become much more difficult to achieve due to the "gradual paralysis of the state apparatus" because of the neoliberal policies of the 1980s. The study also pointed out the complications that might arise if such policies were to be introduced in an economic and policy environment that was a creation of the 1980 policies, where compliance with the international financial system's requirements are an issue. It also warned about the high risk of capital flight if measures with longer perspectives, such as those that restrict capital movement in and out of the country, raise taxes for high-income groups, and so on, were to be implemented.

As we continue to assess Turkey's economic and policy environments, it will become clear that during the next two decades there was no reversal of Turkey's liberalization strategy. As predicted by most analysts, the complications that Turkey faced were mostly in relation to the health of the financial markets and the slow pace of economic restructuring during recurring financial crises. Export promotion continued, and as most economists agree, export growth was a success.[28]

[27] As Arıcanlı and Rodrik (1990) stated, "...whatever outcome ultimately awaits the Turkish economy, it is unlikely that there will be a complete reversal from the present strategy: a flexible (nominal) exchange rate has proved too useful a tool to abandon entirely; the almost total neglect of exports in the 1960s and 1970s is unlikely to recur; and for good or ill, some of the financial liberalization will no doubt survive" (p. 7).

[28] The government's export promotion policies were definitely behind the export growth, and the statistics prove that these policies worked, even though the recorded exports appeared to have been significantly inflated due to over-invoicing. For example, according to Rodrik (1988), roughly 21 percent of the recorded increase in exports between 1979 and 1984 were fictitious.

In summary, by the end of the 1980s, Turkey was clearly an exemplary economy that was often cited as having made tangible achievements. Its progress in normalizing the debt situation and increasing exports was impressive, and its restructuring efforts were challenging and full of promise. But its ability to increase the rate of capital formation—both human and physical—and thus achieve sustainable growth was a real concern. Most importantly, in addition to the trade and budget deficits, the problems of unemployment and high inflation continued as potential sources of instability that could complicate and delay the anticipated outcomes of the structural adjustment process. And, as we discuss in detail in the next chapter, it was the policy-making practices since 1987 that led to imbalances in both goods and financial markets and once again required further stabilization and restructuring throughout the 1990s.

CHAPTER FOUR

THE FINANCIAL CRISIS OF 1994 AND THE APRIL 5 AUSTERITY PLAN

A downgrading of Turkey's credit rating by both Standard & Poor's and Moody's Investors Services in 1994 triggered high volatility in Turkey's currency market, which subsequently led to a considerable devaluation of the Turkish lira and a chaotic financing environment. Before this critical downgrading decision, the Turkish economy was in a state of disequilibrium, struggling with persistent imbalances in both goods and money markets. The budget and current account deficits were at unsustainable levels, and excessive reliance on debt financing to meet the record high public-sector borrowing requirement had resulted in high levels of capital inflow, domestic debt stock, and interest rate payments. At the time, the government seemed reluctant to introduce a much-needed stabilization plan to correct the situation. Because of a highly turbulent political environment and the populist tendencies that the forthcoming March 1994 local elections had led to, it made more sense, at least from the politicians' perspectives, to leave the stabilization issue to a more politically favorable date. So instead, in an effort to lower interest rates, the government tried to keep domestic borrowing at a minimum and turned to monetization, extending its short-term advance facility and borrowing heavily from the Central Bank. As markets were adapting to this deceivingly stable but in fact highly fragile and uncertain policy environment, the first warning came from the international rating agencies. On January 14, 1994, both Standard & Poor's and Moody's Investment Services downgraded Turkey's credit rating from investment grade to speculative grade, and that alone prompted intense volatility in both the foreign-exchange and loanable-funds markets.[1]

Subsequent to the downgrading decision, the Turkish lira depreciated sharply against major currencies: the U.S. dollar rose by 13 percent against the Turkish lira, and with no Central Bank intervention in sight, it peaked at 42 percent at one point and closed at 20 percent higher than

[1] Standard & Poor's reduced Turkey's rating from BBB to BBB-, and Moody's reduced it from BAA3 to BA1.

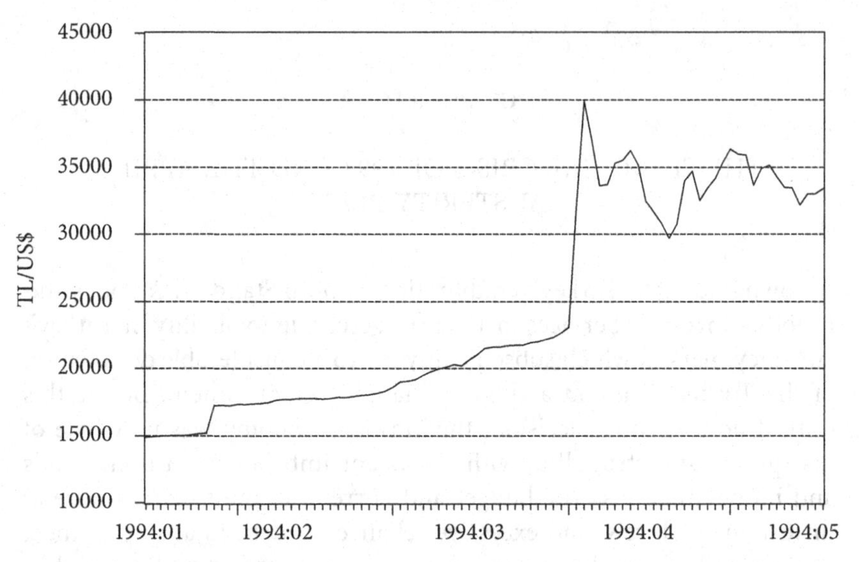

Figure 4.1 Daily official exchange rates, January–May 1994. (Data from Central Bank of the Republic of Turkey, Electronic Data Delivery System.)

its pre-crisis levels.[2] On January 20, the Central Bank finally intervened; it raised overnight interest rates, and the Turkish lira began to stabilize against the U.S. dollar at about 8 percent lower than its January 15 value. But despite the Central Bank intervention, both overnight rates and the value of the U.S. dollar continued to surge. On January 27, the Turkish lira was devalued by 13.5 percent (see figure 4.1).

After the devaluation of the lira, the Central Bank continued to monitor the money markets and the value of the Turkish lira by making frequent changes in overnight interest rates (see figure 4.2). During the following weeks, overnight interest rates fluctuated from about 95 percent to 700 percent, and the interest rate on commercial credit at one point rose to 500 percent. However, despite these highly reflexive daily interest rate adjustments, both interest rates and the value of the U.S. dollar against the Turkish lira continued to rise.

[2] There were several other factors that may have raised the intensity of such volatility. These were: (1) heavy purchases of dollars by the state employees who were on a biweekly payroll, (2) short covering by the commercial banks anticipating devaluation, (3) movement of funds from the stock market to the currency market; and (4) the Central Bank's shrinking reserves and indecisiveness regarding intervention.

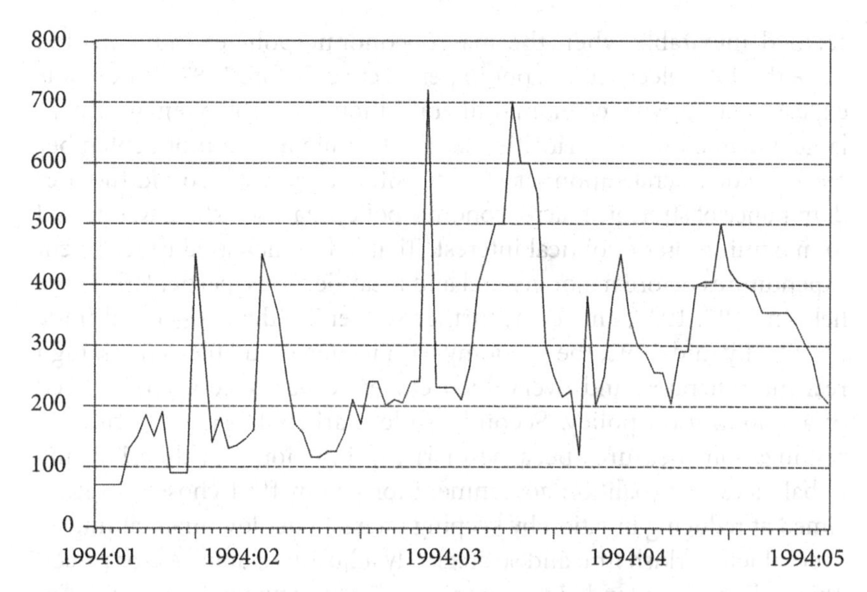

Figure 4.2 Maximum overnight interest rates, January–May 1994. (Data from Central Bank of the Republic of Turkey, Electronic Data Delivery System.)

On March 23, Standard & Poor's once again lowered Turkey's rating, this time from BBB- to BB, and put Turkey on "credit watch" at a politically critical time, just before the local elections. On top of this ill-timed second downgrading decision, the World Bank two days later postponed a $100 million credit earmarked for privatization. As a result of these developments, the Turkish lira continued to lose value. To stop further deterioration in the value of the Turkish lira, the Central Bank intervened numerous times, setting overnight interest rates in the range of 500 to 1000 percent. However, that did not prevent the U.S. dollar from closing against the Turkish lira on March 31 at 60 percent higher than its January 15 value. On April 5, after the local elections, the stabilization package was finally unveiled.

The Causes of the Crisis

There were several explanations for why Turkey greeted 1994 with a financial crisis.[3] First, what occurred during the early days of 1994

[3] See, in particular, Celasun (1998) and Özatay (1996).

seemed inevitable when the macroeconomic policies implemented since the 1987 elections are put in perspective. Before 1987, Turkey was experimenting with economic liberalization in a policy environment largely defined by the priorities set by the military coup of September 1980. As democratization efforts intensified after 1987, so did the predominance of strategic macroeconomic policy making, which was geared to maximization of political interest. That led to increased government expenditures before major general and local elections, particularly those held in 1987, 1988, and 1991, further worsening the budget and trade deficits. By mid-1992, the economy with its unsustainable deficits, high real interest rates, and overvalued currency was once again in need of a stabilization policy. Second, while markets began to anticipate stabilization measures because of rising inflation and deteriorating imbalances, the coalition government formed in 1991 chose a strategy aimed at reducing inflation by keeping interest rates low, maintaining an overvalued Turkish lira, and strategically adjusting public-sector prices. This policy was intended to lower the interest payment component of the budget and to reduce inflation, but instead it led to higher interest rates, higher inflation, and larger deficits.

Third, the destabilizing effect of short-term capital inflows, the so-called hot money, was also a major factor. After 1989 (the year the capital account was liberalized), Turkey's financial markets had increasingly become an attractive destination for short-term portfolio capital, which was invested in domestic currency denominated short-term assets. The inflow of such capital depended on the expected exchange rate movements and real interest rates. When the government began to drive interest rates down and impose a tax on government securities, liquidity first moved to equity markets, and as the expectation of devaluation increased due to widening fiscal and external deficits, the liquidity began to move to the U.S. dollar. Consequently, when the international rating agencies downgraded the Turkish economy on January 14, 1994, excessive short covering became a major factor in the chain of events that led to the financial crisis and the severe downturn in the Turkish economy. A discussion of each of these factors follows.

The Politics of Turkish Liberalization and Macroeconomic Change

As detailed in the previous chapter, Turkey began to pursue an outward-looking and predominantly free-market economic model at the beginning of the 1980s. During the first stage of this transformation, most economic indicators were in line with expectations: inflation was reduced drastically from its three-digit levels, exports showed remarkable growth, Turkey's creditworthiness improved somewhat, and consequently its foreign debt situation normalized. In addition to improvements in the fiscal system and the domestic price structure, important steps were also taken toward the reform of financial markets and the removal of trade and foreign-exchange restrictions.

During the period from 1980 to 1987, many of these reforms were implemented with little political opposition. This was a time of transition from authoritarian rule to an increasingly democratic environment; political stability prevailed, and there was continuity in policy making.[4] However, as Turkey began its gradual move into a politically more liberal setting in 1987, Turgut Özal, who was the prime minister at the time, began to face stiff opposition. The reemergence of inflation during the second half of the 1980s (increasing from 30 percent in 1986 to 55 percent in 1987) and questions over Özal's policy-making style surfaced as two main issues around which the opposition intensified its campaign. According to Sayarı (1992), the "prime minister's highly personalized style of governing" caused "growing resentment and criticism from the bureaucracy, political parties, and the press," and prevented "the government from incorporating constructive criticisms from a wider circle of policy makers into the decision-making process. In particular, middle- and upper-echelon bureaucrats who were left out of policy making, became increasingly embittered over the weakening of their political role and influence" (p. 37). Unable to shield himself from this growing criticism, especially from that which was directed at his unusually pragmatic management style, Özal chose to rely on expansionary fiscal measures. His government increased public spending significantly before the September 1987 constitutional referendum and before the October 1987 general election.[5] Such expansionary policies caused the macroeconomic imbalances to deteriorate, and that required the implementation of another stabilization package, which was announced on February 4, 1988.

[4] For a chronology of political events and a review of the dynamics of competing economic and political interests, see Sayarı (1992).

[5] The referendum issue that Özal unsuccessfully campaigned against was designed to lift the political ban on party leaders and others who were removed from office by the military in 1980. See Sayarı (1992, 38).

Table 4.1 Selected macroeconomic indicators, 1990–1996

Year	GDP growth rate	Inflation rate	Budget deficit	Trade balance	Current account
			% of GNP		
1990	9.3	60.4	–3.0	–6.2	–1.7
1991	0.9	71.1	–5.3	–4.8	0.2
1992	6.0	66.0	–4.3	–5.0	–0.6
1993	8.0	71.1	–6.7	–7.7	–3.5
1994	–5.5	125.5	–3.9	–3.2	2.0
1995	7.2	76.0	–4.0	–7.6	–1.4
1996	7.0	79.8	–8.3	–5.6	–1.3

Sources: TÜRKSTAT, *Statistical Indicators 1923–2005*; Central Bank of the Republic of Turkey, Electronic Data Delivery System; State Planning Organization, *Economic and Social Indicators 1950–2006.*

In the months that followed, the economy improved somewhat. But due to the expansionary fiscal and monetary policies that were implemented to accommodate the forthcoming local and general elections, the Turkish economy continued to experience serious imbalances, which led to the developments that resulted in the financial crisis of 1994. Inflation, which began to accelerate after 1987, remained in the range of 66–71 percent between 1991 and 1993 annually (see table 4.1). The budget deficit also increased from a relatively moderate 5.3 percent of GNP in 1991 to 6.7 percent of GNP in 1993. The GDP growth rate continued to rise; after hitting bottom in 1991, it gradually increased to 8.0 percent in 1993. Trade and current account balances worsened: As a percentage of GNP, the trade deficit rose from 4.8 in 1991 to 7.7 in 1993. During the same period, the current account balance deteriorated from a surplus of $250 million (0.2 percent of GNP) to a record deficit of $6.4 billion (3.5 percent of GNP). The trade deficit was the natural outcome of a high GDP growth rate and an overvalued Turkish lira caused by an inflow of short-term capital, both of which led to higher imports.

On the financial side of the economy, the situation was even more dismal. The total financing requirement reached 10.2 percent of GNP in 1993, and the debt stock, both domestic and foreign, reached record levels (see table 4.2). As a percentage of GNP, domestic debt rose from 15.4 in 1991 to 17.9 at the end of 1993, and during the same period external debt rose from 33.6 to 37.5. Total external debt at the end of 1993 stood at a level of $67.4 billion.

Table 4.2 International reserves, external and domestic debt, and public-sector borrowing requirement, 1990–1996

Year	International reserves		External debt			Domestic debt	PSBR
			Total		Short term		
	In billion $	% of GNP	In billion $	% of GNP	% of GNP	% of GNP	% of GNP
1990	11.4	7.5	49.0	32.6	6.3	14.4	7.3
1991	12.2	8.2	50.5	33.6	6.1	15.4	10.1
1992	15.2	9.6	55.6	35.1	8.0	17.6	10.5
1993	17.8	9.9	67.4	37.5	10.3	17.9	10.2
1994	16.5	12.5	65.6	48.3	8.3	20.6	6.1
1995	23.3	13.7	73.3	41.9	9.0	17.3	4.9
1996	25.0	13.6	79.4	43.2	9.3	21.0	8.6

Sources: TÜRKSTAT, *Statistical Indicators 1923–2005*; Central Bank of the Republic of Turkey, Electronic Data Delivery System; Turkish Treasury, *Economic Indicators, Treasury Statistics 1980–2003*.

Even more problematic were the borrowing practices. The share of domestic borrowing in the total consolidated budget financing requirement declined from 62.2 percent in 1991 to 41.1 percent in 1993, but the share of both external borrowing and short-term credits from the Central Bank increased (see table 4.3). During the same period, external borrowing rose from 5.7 percent to 16.8 percent, and short-term credits increased from 32.1 percent to 42.1 percent. As will be discussed next, one reason for the relative decline in domestic borrowing was the government's desire to lower interest rates.[6] So, as clearly shown by these numbers, the worsening conditions, especially in public finances and in the current account, made the financial crisis almost inevitable. As Üçer, van Rijckeghem, and Yolalan (1998) wrote, there was a heightened probability of such an event since these indicators (such as short-term external debt, international reserves, excess real money balances, and short-term central bank credits) had deteriorated ahead of time.

Macroeconomic Policies in the Early 1990s

In September 1991, Tansu Çiller began her active political career as a state minister in charge of economic affairs in Süleyman Demirel's coalition government. One of the main challenges facing the coalition was to reduce inflation while maintaining a high rate of economic growth.

[6] A new tax on holders of government securities effective at the beginning 1994 was also a contributing factor.

Table 4.3 The proportion of external, domestic, and Central Bank borrowing in the consolidated budget financing requirement, 1987–1996

Year	Financing req.	External	Domestic	Central Bank
	% of GNP		% of total	
1987	3.43	−10.2	96.5	13.7
1988	3.15	7.6	75.9	16.5
1989	3.61	−2.5	97.0	5.5
1990	3.11	0.3	97.1	2.6
1991	5.27	5.7	62.2	32.1
1992	5.39	6.7	64.0	29.3
1993	6.30	16.8	41.1	42.1
1994	3.91	−44.1	110.0	34.0
1995	3.74	−27.7	95.4	32.3
1996	8.46	−10.6	92.5	18.1

Source: State Planning Organization, *Economic and Social Indicators 1950–2006.*

Çiller, a former economics professor, was expected to be instrumental in putting an end to the overly expansionary policies of previous years and moving the economy forward with a long-sought stabilization package to control inflation. The stabilization policy, which became more pronounced after Çiller became prime minister in 1993, was characterized as (1) maintaining an overvalued Turkish lira, (2) keeping the interest rate as low as possible, and (3) strategically adjusting the prices of a wide range of goods produced by the state economic enterprises (SEEs). Under this policy, the Treasury's cash requirement was being satisfied through foreign borrowing and advances from the Central Bank. Domestic borrowing was kept at a minimum to avoid any upward pressure on interest rates and thereby reduce the interest payments category of the budgetary liabilities. To avoid the possibility of higher interest rates, the Treasury borrowed directly from the Central Bank, and the Bank, in turn, re-auctioned these securities through open-market operations to absorb the resulting excessive liquidity.

One apparent justification for such a borrowing strategy was to create an environment that would lead the financial community to form an expectation of declining interest rates. It was soon realized, however, that the strategy of lowering interest rates was counterproductive, especially when the financial markets began to second-guess the outcome of the Central Bank–Treasury alliance. The Treasury's financing priorities, which centered on foreign borrowing and monetization, thus, were no longer workable. This became more apparent when the Treasury failed to deliver the securities to the Central Bank on time, and when they were finally delivered, the Central Bank was not permitted to conduct the appropriate open market operations.[7] Consequently, the increased liquidity began to move to the U.S. dollar, and to prevent the dollar from gaining value the Central Bank ended up selling U.S. dollars and raising overnight interest rates (see figure 4.2). The Treasury's strategy to force interest rates down by restricting the supply of government securities and/or canceling and delaying auctions backfired, causing interest rates to surge instead.[8]

Capital Account Liberalization and the Issue of "Hot Money"

In 1984, in an effort to increase the inflow of foreign currency, the government partially liberalized the capital account; nonresidents were allowed to hold financial assets in domestic markets, and restrictions on residents holding foreign currency and opening foreign-exchange deposit accounts in domestic banks were removed. Restrictions on borrowing from foreign-exchange markets and holding financial assets abroad were also lifted, but only for authorized financial intermediaries, corporations holding investment incentive certificates, and foreign trade companies.[9] In 1989, the capital account was fully liberalized, allowing free inflow and outflow of capital, and with the full convertibility of the Turkish lira officially adopted in 1990, there were no longer restrictions on residents including foreign securities in their portfolios, and nonresidents were allowed to freely trade Turkish securities.

The partial liberalization of 1984 did not lead to a significant change in capital inflow, but after 1990 there was a notable increase in currency

[7] At the time, Bülent Gültekin was the newly appointed governor of the Central Bank; he resigned from his position five months after his appointment. See Gültekin's letter of resignation to President Demirel in Arcayürek (2001, 398–404).

[8] The policy of suppressing the interest rate continued with the next governor, Yaman Törüner, precipitating serious reversals during very delicate situations. For example, on April 7 the Central Bank reduced overnight rates from 120 percent to 90 percent, and consequently the U.S. dollar jumped from 33,000 TL to 40,000 TL, a 24.5 percent devaluation. A week later, the dollar started the day at 37,900 TL and the Central Bank sold U.S. dollars to reduce it to 34,850 TL; but 10 minutes to closing it reduced overnight rates from 280 percent to 180 percent, causing the dollar to move up to TL 37,000.

[9] For the details and the implications of the 1983–84 decrees for the partial removal of capital account restrictions and the 1989 decree, which removed all restrictions, see Altınkemer and Ekinci (1992, 7–24).

substitution and in the volume of short-term capital inflow.[10] During the period from 1990 to1993, rising overnight interest rates and an appreciating Turkish lira (a result of a deliberate policy to keep exchange-rate adjustments below the inflation rate) made currency substitution from major currencies to the Turkish lira and parking the converted funds overnight, an attractive investment opportunity. Private commercial banks, in particular, were holding large short-term positions in foreign currency. After the structural changes in the banking sector that started in 1987, they began to raise the government security investment portion of their assets, increase the volume of foreign currency denominated deposits, and take large short-term positions in foreign currency.[11]

To ensure an uninterrupted inflow of this form of short-term capital, the expected rate of return on deposits denominated in domestic currency must exceed the expected return on foreign currency. Domestic real interest rates may have to be kept high enough to attract foreign capital and there should be low risk of currency depreciation. If interest rates begin to decline and/or the domestic currency shows signs of weakness, the flow of capital quickly reverses itself. Signs of weakness of the domestic currency or speculation of devaluation will likely lead to a massive sell-off of the domestic currency. This is precisely what occurred in 1994: As a result of the Treasury's drive to lower domestic interest rates, maintaining an overvalued Turkish lira was no longer possible. Increased expectations of devaluation led to a surge of the U.S. dollar due to massive short covering as the Turkish lira began to depreciate rapidly and thus followed the outflow of short-term capital (Özatay 1996). One of the major reasons for the financial crisis was the short covering, which began soon after the downgrading was announced by the two rating agencies.

Obviously, the time and the manner in which downgrading decisions were made led to the increased vulnerability of the financial markets and deepened the financial crisis that followed. The economic conditions were fairly critical at the time these rating agencies signaled their first warning early in 1993 and became even worse before the

[10] With the partial liberalization of the capital account in 1984, only authorized banks were allowed to borrow freely in foreign-exchange markets. Total foreign borrowing at the time was medium and long term, amounting to $410 million (Altınkemer and Ekinci 1992, 7).

[11] The volume of short positions increased from $1.8 billion in 1990 to $5 billion in 1993 (Ertuğrul and Selçuk 2001, 20).

delayed downgrading decision that they carried out in two steps. But eventually Turkey's risky interest rate and exchange-rate strategy had to come to an end. As the margin between the official and the market exchange-rate increases, so does the expectation of devaluation. If the decision to devalue were to be delayed, then massive capital outflow and a loss of international reserves would be inevitable. Allowing the domestic interest rates to increase could have narrowed the margin between official and market exchange rates, but this was not the strategy the Treasury wanted to follow. Clearly, maintaining an overvalued domestic currency in a managed floating exchange-rate system, and at the same time administering the nominal interest rate, was not a sustainable strategy.

The Austerity Plan and Beyond

The much-anticipated stabilization package was announced on April 5, 1994. Profiling a classic austerity plan that combines monetary, fiscal, and incomes policies, the package attempted to contract the economy to improve the imbalances in the product and financial markets. Aggregate demand was reduced to slow price increases, and that, through supply-side adjustments, was expected to lower real production costs and bring about an economic recovery led by export expansion.

Some of the measures included in the package were: (1) devaluing the Turkish lira by 38.8 percent with further adjustments based on the average of rates declared by ten banks, including two public banks, (2) gradually reducing short-term credits from the Central Bank, (3) raising taxes by about 9 percent, reducing spending by 12 percent, and lowering the budget deficit by 80 percent for the next three months, (4) removing agricultural subsidies, and (5) raising prices of fuels and tobacco by about 100 percent.[12] After the announcement of these measures, the financial crisis deepened. Deterioration of the Turkish lira continued, despite frequent interventions from the Central Bank to stabilize it. By

[12] During the early days of its implementation, the package was criticized on three points: (1) letting the Turkish lira float freely without establishing a credible monetary policy, (2) no support from international organizations for additional foreign currency, and (3) measures regarding the reforming of the SEEs hardly seemed credible. Also, the markets began to expect a severe recession that was feared to lead to a stagflationary spiral. See the commentary by Salih Neftçi in *Hürriyet*, April 7, 1994.

the end of April, overnight rates soared to about 400 percent and the U.S. dollar appreciated significantly against the Turkish lira.[13]

One serious problem during the next two months was the Treasury's inability to borrow. Monetization was shut off because of the austerity measures, external borrowing was no longer possible, and a lack of confidence halted domestic borrowing. The Treasury was unable to borrow even at rates around 150 percent (295 percent compounded annually); so as a last resort, on May 26, it auctioned 3-month "super bonds" at a 50 percent rate, with an unprecedented annual compounded rate of 506 percent. During the same day, credit markets responded favorably, and interest rates on credit moved up to 461.3 percent, compounded annually.

With this super bond operation and a standby agreement with the IMF, macroeconomic indicators began to improve somewhat during the following months. One important challenge for the government was the task of redeeming these high-yield bonds without reversing the declining rates. This was quite an undertaking, because financing sources were strictly limited. Borrowing prospects from international financial markets looked discouraging, and due to the standby agreement with the IMF, the Central Bank was unable to raise its net assets, so it could not extend credit to the Treasury. The Central Bank, in coordination with the Treasury, attempted to overcome these constraints. To obtain the needed cash requirement, overnight rates were kept low, allowing the banks to borrow from the Central Bank, and these funds were in turn used to purchase Treasury instruments. Bond prices were also forced up in the secondary markets to make new issues attractive at low interest rates, and reserves from the SEEs were used up for financing purposes. By mid-August, overnight interest rates were at about 70 percent and 3-month rates at 22 percent. By the first week of October, the 3-month rate dropped to 19.5 percent.

Thus, interest rates gradually began to fall, nearly returning to levels comparable to those that existed before the crisis. Inflation began to slow down, and the budget, excluding interest payments, showed a surplus during the second quarter of 1994. A budget deficit of 51.3 trillion Turkish liras in the first quarter turned into a surplus of 9.2 trillion

[13] Also, due to short covering, three banks were forced to terminate their operations, which led depositors to lose confidence in the financial system (Ertuğrul and Selçuk 2001).

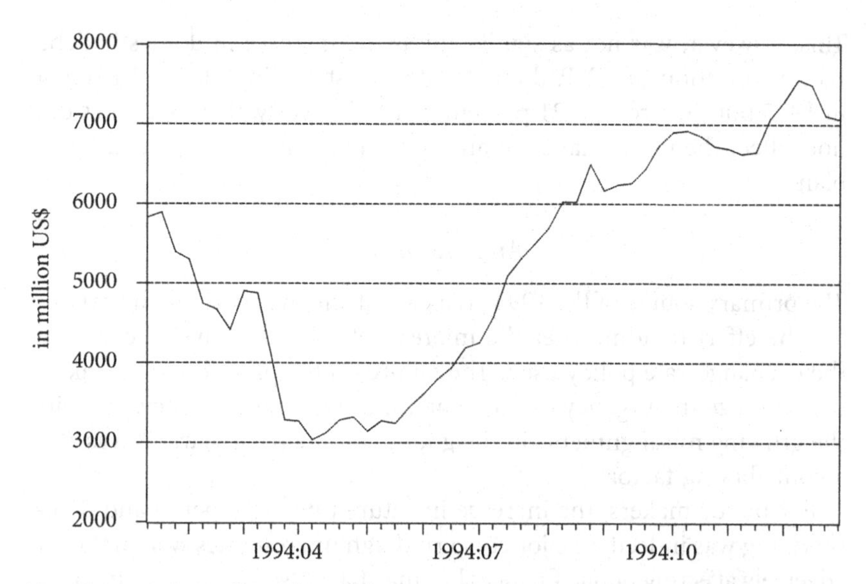

Figure 4.3 Central Bank weekly gross foreign exchange reserves, January–December 1994. (Data from Central Bank of the Republic of Turkey, Electronic Data Delivery System.)

Turkish liras during the second quarter. Also, by the end of July the Central Bank's gross foreign-exchange reserves reached their pre-crisis level of about $5.8 billion (see figure 4.3).

Despite these slight improvements, particularly in the financial sector, markets began to expect a recession followed by a stagflationary spiral. By the end of 1994, the growth rate of real GDP turned negative with a substantial drop of 5.5 percent, and the year-end inflation rate surged to 125.5 percent (see table 4.1). Although the growth rate improved in the next year, reaching an impressive 7.2 percent, inflation remained the top priority despite the anticipated drop that was sought in the package. After surging to 119.7 percent at the end of the first quarter of 1995, it declined to 76 percent by the end of the same year.

Exports continued to grow, but that did not prevent the trade deficit from tripling, rising from $4.2 billion (3.2 percent of GNP) in 1994 to $13.1 billion (7.6 percent of GNP) in 1995. The budget deficit grew as well. Despite notable increases in revenue, expenditures increased at a higher rate, and that led to a deficit of 3.9 and 4 percent of GNP in 1994 and 1995, respectively. The increase in external debt was 11.7 percent. It rose from $65.6 billion in 1994 to $73.3 billion in 1995, but as a percentage of GNP it declined from 48.3 to 41.9 percent (see table 4.2).

This, however, was not as significant as the increase in domestic debt. As a proportion of GNP, domestic debt first declined to 17.3 percent in 1995 but then rose to 21 percent in 1996. Clearly, these statistics did not reflect the performance of an economy implementing an austerity plan.

An Assessment

The primary source of the 1994 crisis was its financial origin, in particular, the effort to administer the interest rate and the adverse effects of the exchange-rate policy used. The failure on the part of policy makers to recognize the urgency of implementing stabilization policies despite the growing misalignments in the goods and financial markets was also a contributing factor.

For policy makers, the increase in future interest expense and debt-servicing was indeed a major concern. High interest rates were not only adversely affecting public finances but may have also contributed to lower investment and an increased cost of working capital, thus adversely affecting inflation and output on the supply side of the economy. Considering that the empirical literature was yet to prove the positive effect of higher interest rates on saving and output growth by efficiently mobilizing domestic resources (see Uygur 1993), for policy makers to attempt to lower interest rates and make that the central feature of their macroeconomic policy making, especially after the October 1991 elections, was not that unexpected. Back then, low interest rates may have been appealing given the burden of high interest costs on the budget, but clearly the low-interest rate policy was not compatible with the external financing policy of the government. Turkey had been under a managed floating exchange-rate system since 1980 and had consistently maintained an overvalued Turkish lira since 1991.[14] As outlined above, the inflow of external capital depended on the expected value of the domestic currency and real interest rates, and attempts to lower interest rates triggered the speculative attack on the domestic currency and contributed to the unfavorable financial environment that led to the crisis of 1994.

---

[14] For an overview of exchange-rate management in Turkey since 1980, see Aşıkoğlu (1992).

In retrospect, the economic events that led to the 1994 crisis clearly show that from the perspective of policy makers, it might have been desirable to have lower interest rates. But it should have been apparent how unlikely that was. Also, if the managed floating exchange-rate system was to continue, then the exchange rate needed to be adjusted in view of market dynamics, but it also should have been clear that exchange rate adjustments could not be delayed because of non-economic concerns.

As an alternative, a pegged exchange-rate regime, which has proven to be effective in reducing inflation in some of the transition economies, including the Czech Republic, Estonia, Hungary, Poland, and Slovakia, for example, might have been considered (Sachs 1996). With a pegged exchange-rate system, it is possible to institute monetary discipline and thus reduce inflation effectively. As outlined by Sachs, with such a system governments become more committed to stabilization plans, and that could help generate a policy environment where lower inflation is expected and households and businesses rebuild their real money balances. It should be pointed out, however, that a pegged (or a less flexible) exchange-rate system could lead to slower growth and higher output volatility (Levy-Yeyati and Sturzenegger 2003) and may not always work well in an economy susceptible to recurrent financial crises. For example, the 1994 financial crisis of Mexico was in essence caused by the December 20–22 devaluation of the Mexican peso, which preceded two severe speculative attacks during the same year. According to Calvo and Mendoza (1996), "[T]he attempt at correcting the misalignment of the exchange rate triggered a deep and protracted economic crisis and caused continued weakness in Mexico's currency and stock markets" (p. 174). Before the crisis, Mexico had fairly strong economic fundamentals with a balanced budget, low inflation, and a widely privatized economy. But a serious financial gap caused mainly by internal political turmoil led to a wide current account deficit, and that was basically what triggered the peso devaluation followed by the decision to allow the peso to float. Thus, in sharp contrast to what happened in 1994 in Turkey, where the crisis was driven by the budget deficit in a politically unstable and high-inflation environment, in Mexico the problem was the current account deficit in a low-inflation and moderate-growth environment. Interestingly, policy making in both economies lacked credibility, and the outcome of both crises was a severe short-term capital outflow, a collapsing currency, and soaring interest rates and recession.

Clearly, during those years neither one of the exchange-rate regimes seemed to be immune to crises. In the case of Turkey, if a pegged exchange-rate system was to be adopted, credibility needed to be established as a top priority, and that could have been achieved through greater autonomy for the Central Bank. Regardless of the exchange-rate choice, however, the sources of high inflation, high interest rates, and volatility of short-term capital were obvious. Without addressing the main issue of the budget deficit and instituting fiscal and monetary discipline and attracting direct foreign investment into the domestic economy, problems faced then were likely to carry into the future, and as we elaborate in coming chapters, they did.[15] It was apparent then, and even much clearer today, that with credible policy making, both money and goods markets can stabilize, and that would likely lead to a policy and economic environment in which necessary structural adjustments can be implemented without further delay.

Turkey took a giant step in its overall liberalization process in 1989 by opening to capital account movements. That decision was prompted by the expectation that somehow the world's liquidity had to find its way to Turkey's evolving financial system, an idea that gained considerable support given Turkey's increased appetite for foreign saving and the difficulties of obtaining that through the official channels of foreign governments and Bretton Woods institutions. Turkey certainly was not alone in its quest for foreign capital: attempts to redirect and attract foreign capital to domestic markets were motivated by similar justifications in many other emerging-markets countries. But as country experiments and empirical evidence thus far clearly show, the flow of capital in and out of an economy has often been disruptive and at times is accompanied by costly adjustments much worse than anticipated, prompted by defaults, bank failures, and speculative attacks.

By the mid-1990s, Turkey had proven that it was not immune to financial crises either, and its exposure to the volatility of the financial markets both internally and externally was likely to continue as long as its growing need for foreign saving continued. The relevant issue at the time, and even now, is not whether it would make sense to argue for the reversal of the financial opening process but how to reduce

[15] Fiscal reform should not be limited to balancing the budget. A comprehensive restructuring involving Turkey's legal, political, and organizational effectiveness will be necessary. See Ersel and Kumcu (1995, 185–87) for specific reform suggestions.

Turkey's vulnerability as a debtor nation to potential currency crashes. Rodrik and Velasco (2000) suggested that nations should monitor the debt composition and the ratio of short-term debt to reserves. Their analysis indicates that countries with short-term debt in excess of their available liquid assets are "three times more likely to experience a sudden and massive reversal in capital flows."

What is also emerging from the recent literature is the view that the sustainability of financial opening may necessitate "a deep fiscal restructuring" (Aizenman 2004). It has been shown, for example, that the impact of liberalizing capital account movements on banking-sector fragility, in particular, appears to be weaker where the institutional environment is found to be strong (Demirgüç-Kunt and Detragiache 1998). Above all, in the opinion of Martin and Rey (2006), what makes emerging markets more vulnerable to a financial crash is the level of "their productivity and income level." They added, "The higher vulnerability is not necessarily due to bad institutions, bad incentives (bailouts), or bad exchange-rate regimes. This is not to say that these problems do not constitute important channels through which financial globalization can make emerging markets more vulnerable to a financial crisis" (p. 1647). Productivity in Turkey has been increasing since 1923, and despite the impressive gains of the 1980s, which were preceded and followed by periods of low productivity growth, it is yet to reach a sustainable high growth level (Altuğ and Filiztekin 2006). When Turkey attains high productivity and high income, undoubtedly the issue of vulnerability will be less of a concern. It will then be more likely for Turkey to also maintain a ratio of short-term debt to reserves and a debt composition that would minimize the likelihood of massive reversal of capital flows. The challenge for policy makers is how to get there, and as we revisit the issue in chapter 6, it will become much clearer that in the case of Turkey, economic restructuring and congruent institutional change in the financial system are two factors that should not have been overlooked.

CHAPTER FIVE

TURKISH INFLATION

It has been over thirty years since Turkey last experienced single digit inflation. After growing fairly mildly in the 1960s, inflation in Turkey registered its last single-digit level in 1972 and rose to its first peak in 1980 at over 86.1 percent. Then it followed a downward trend during the first half of the 1980s before it reached a second peak of 125.9 percent in January 1994. A third peak of 101.6 percent during the first month of 1998 was followed by a sharp decline. After bottoming in the second month of 2001 at 33.4 percent and testing another high of 73.2 percent in January of 2002, it has recently begun to decelerate (see figure 5.1).

What makes Turkish inflation so volatile and distinct? Why has it remained a major macroeconomic problem in Turkey, while in recent years it has hardly been an issue in most other countries, even in those with past records of high inflation? The persistent nature of inflation in Turkey has brought about numerous stabilizing attempts since the early 1970s, but shortly after the implementation of every new austerity package, it resumed its upward trend, raising credibility concerns for both fiscal and monetary authorities. Has inflation remained unresolved for so long because of the lack of credibility of Turkish policy makers, or has it been a policy failure on the part of IMF-sponsored stabilization programs? Attempting to address these and other related issues, this chapter begins with an overview of inflationary dynamics and the inflationary trend in Turkey. A review of possible causes of Turkish inflation is followed by a discussion of stabilization efforts during the last three decades and an outline of possible explanations for Turkey's failure to keep inflation under control.

Inflationary Dynamics

Macroeconomic theory is well-established on the issue of what causes inflation. Based on the monetary neutrality framework (where nominal variables can only be changed by other nominal variables) and the quantity theory of money (which allows for proportional changes in

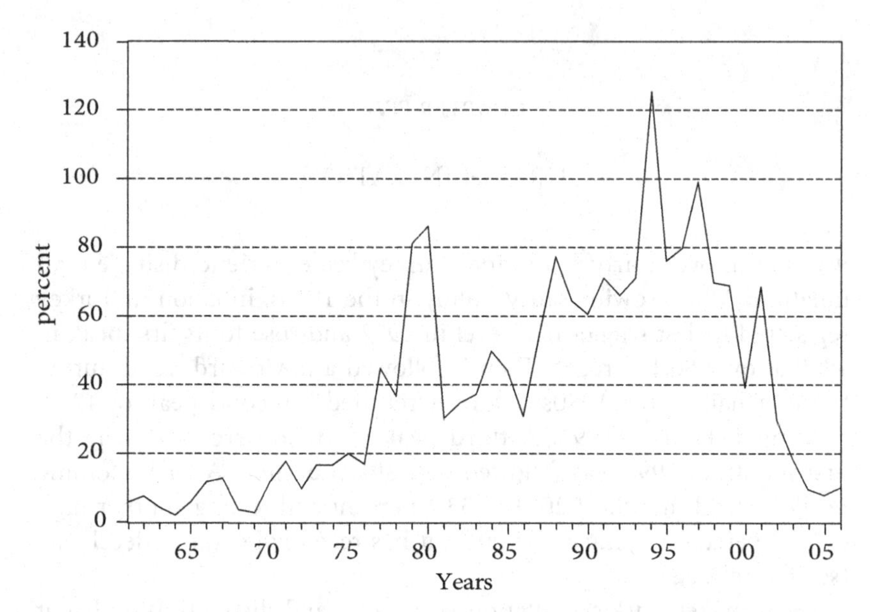

Figure 5.1 Turkish inflation, 1961–2006. (Data from Central Bank of the Republic of Turkey, Electronic Data Delivery System; Global Financial Data, Los Angeles, CA.)

the money stock and the price level), inflation is strictly a monetary phenomenon. The proportional relationship between inflation, π, and money growth, m, holds in the long run and follows from the quantity equation,

$$\pi = m - y + v,$$

where the growth rate of output, y, and the percentage change of velocity, v, are assumed constant or to change steadily.

Monetary neutrality does not hold in the short run, however. Changes in y and v could occur independently of monetary growth or could be induced by an increased money supply via interest rates and aggregate spending, in either case leading to non-proportional changes between monetary growth and inflation. An increase in aggregate demand caused by a monetized fiscal deficit, or any of the demand components, leads to a higher aggregate price level, and when such changes persist, inflation eventually develops.

Inflation can also rise as a result of upward price and wage adjustments accommodated by expansionary monetary policies. An increase in the price of an imported input, for example, causes an upward adjustment in the price level and a decrease in real output. This one-time increase could then trigger inflation when expansionary policies are implemented to restore output to its initial level.

Based on these commonly known inflation dynamics, the most probable disinflation adjustment would be through contractionary monetary policy. A decrease in aggregate demand will set off downward wage–price adjustments, eventually leading to lower inflation and a return to the initial output level. During the self-correcting adjustment process, output losses will be incurred, unemployment will rise, and as expectations of inflation begin to decline, wage–price adjustment will follow, leading to an eventual full recovery of the output loss.

The duration of the adjustment will depend on the degree of price–wage rigidity and the type of expectation formation. A rational expectations-based cold-turkey approach would likely result in lower cumulative output loss and a faster decline in inflation, while an adaptive expectations-based gradualist approach would lead to higher cumulative output losses and a slower reduction in inflation.[1]

Within this general theoretical framework, there does not seem to be ambiguity concerning the relationship between money growth and the inflation rate. According to Dornbusch and Fischer (1991), "There are basically two answers to the question, why is there inflation? One is that inflation is an integral part of a country's public finance. The other is that inflation continues because it is too hard or too costly to stop it" (p. 5). But, within empirical frameworks, the determinants of inflation begin to take varying emphasis. There are country-specific monetary and structural determinants, such as the relative availability of deficit-financing sources, the degree of central bank independence, and external factors such as the degree of dollarization and exchange-rate considerations. There is also inertial inflation that varies in intensity based on country-specific institutional determinants such as indexation, degree of unionization, and so on.

At the applied level, therefore, given the experiences of low, high, and hyperinflation countries, there is no shortage of remedies. To

[1] As an anti-inflationary policy, following a cold-turkey strategy the monetary authority contracts the money supply sharply, creating a deep recession with the expectation that output returns to its natural level. With gradualism, money supply is reduced in small amounts to attain a steady and gradual reduction in inflation, and unemployment does not deviate significantly from its full employment or natural level.

disinflate, countries may implement strict austerity programs involving tight monetary and fiscal policies supplemented by incomes policies; they can then choose to follow one of three possible nominal anchors: monetary, exchange rate, or inflation targeting. Central banks that pursue monetary targeting use operating and intermediate targets, such as monetary base, monetary aggregates (M1, M2, and M3), or interest rates, to achieve price stability. Exchange-rate targeting involves an exchange-rate-based stabilization, which pegs the domestic currency to that of the anchor country or allows a gradual and steady depreciation of the domestic currency. As a third nominal anchor, countries adopt implicit or explicit inflation targeting to achieve price stability. All three forms of nominal anchor have been used in Turkey; before the adoption of a floating exchange-rate system in 2001, Turkey used monetary targeting and exchange-rate targeting, and it adopted implicit inflation targeting afterward.

Inflationary Trends in Turkey

Turkish inflation was relatively mild until the mid-1970s, in spite of rising energy prices and the expansionary effects of Turkey's industrialization, which was driven by import substitution policies. Monetary expansion stemming from export-based, foreign-exchange receipts, workers' remittances, and Central Bank credits to the public sector was moderate, and that kept inflation fairly low throughout the 1960s and early 1970s. Heavy reliance on sterilization during the first half of the 1970s had also eased the expansionary effects of the major funding sources of import-substitution policies.

However, inflation began to increase as foreign-exchange receipts from all sources started to decline during the second half of the 1970s.[2] By the end of that decade, inflationary pressures intensified as foreign borrowing came to a halt, and the debt crisis followed. Despite a major debt rescheduling coordinated by the OECD and the IMF, two major devaluations of the Turkish lira, and two standby arrangements with

[2] From the mid-1960s to 1980 the growth rate of industrial output also fluctuated in a downward trend as inflation rose. During the first half of this period, output growth and inflation rates moved in the same direction. But after the 1973–74 oil crisis, when inflation began its steep rise, output moved in the opposite direction, hitting bottom in 1979 before inflation reached its major peak a year later.

the IMF (in 1978 and 1979), the GDP growth rate became negative in 1979 for the first time in two decades. Inflation rose to a new high of 86.1 percent in 1980. It was then that an orthodox stabilization and structural adjustment program was introduced to relieve the economy from rising inflationary pressures and external and internal imbalances. With this landmark program, Turkey left its import-substitution strategy behind and decisively began a series of reforms to establish an export-oriented, outward-looking free market economy.

After the introduction of the 1980 stabilization and structural adjustment program, inflation began to decelerate, followed by a decline in industrial output. Contractionary monetary and fiscal policies, accompanied by a sharp increase in foreign currency inflows as a result of external debt restructuring, lowered inflation from 86.1 percent in 1980 to 30.3 percent in 1981. During the 1983–86 politically stable period that followed, inflation remained relatively low, fluctuating within the range of 30 to 50 percent.[3]

Inflation bottomed in 1986 but once again began to rise during the following years as a result of fiscal expansion and non-sterilized purchases of foreign reserves by the Central Bank. After remaining within the range of the high 50s to mid 60s throughout most of 1993, it rose sharply in April 1994, mainly due to increases in public-sector prices and the devaluation of the lira, and then it surged to its all-time high of 125.9 percent in January 1995.[4]

After a short period of monetary and fiscal tightening, inflation decreased to 75 percent during the first month of 1997. During that period of political instability, the government followed a policy of "borrowing less than redemption" and relied heavily on short-term advances from the Central Bank. To absorb the excess liquidity that resulted from

[3] As mentioned in chapter 3, the period from 1983 to 1986 was a transition from authoritarian rule to a democratic environment, and during that period many of the 1980 reforms were accomplished with little political opposition.

[4] Industrial output, which began its downward path after 1990, also tested its 1979 lows as inflation reached its highest levels during the 1994 financial crisis and rose sharply as inflation declined the next year. Similar conclusions are reached when inflation uncertainty and output growth rates are compared. At the highest levels of inflation uncertainty, output growth rates were negative and lowest. Although for the most part, rising inflation uncertainty was followed by declining output growth rates, it appears that during the 1979 debt crisis inflation uncertainty followed the decline in industrial output and simultaneously moved in the opposite direction during the 1994 financial crisis. Thus, it is not clear if inflation uncertainty had in fact caused real output to decline overall. See Nas and Perry (2001).

the Treasury's use of short-term advances, the Central Bank conducted open market operations to stabilize the financial markets and in an accommodative fashion tried to control the liquidity level.[5] The policy of borrowing less than redemption was implemented in an effort to lower domestic borrowing and thus reduce the interest burden of the budget. Consequently, interest rates continued their downward trend, which had started at the beginning of 1996, and inflation began to move below its 1995 levels. This policy continued until mid-1997.

After the change of government in June 1997, inflation gradually increased following the upward price adjustments in the public sector. The new government attempted to reverse the policy of borrowing less than redemption and lower the Treasury's use of short-term advances from the Central Bank. But such changes in borrowing practices did not make a difference. Once again, the increase in public-sector prices in the third quarter of 1997 led to higher wholesale and consumer price indexes.

After having reached its third peak in January of 1998, inflation began to decline as a result of a protocol between the Treasury and the Central Bank to keep inflation under control. Other factors that helped inflation to decline during this period included the contraction of domestic demand, a slowdown of public-sector price adjustments, and a significant drop in crude oil prices. Consequently, inflation continued its downward trend throughout 1998 despite the uncertainty in the financial markets caused by the 1997 financial crisis, which started in Southeast Asia and spread to Russia.

The decline in inflation slowed down in 1999, and toward the end of that year inflation began to move upward after the public-sector price hikes and rising average crude oil prices. With sharp increases in the public-sector borrowing requirement, rising interest rates, and a widening budget deficit, inflation remained on a slight upward trend throughout the remainder of 1999 and dropped sharply after the December 1999 standby agreement with the IMF. Early data showed that the IMF agreement worked well despite remaining concerns about the budget deficit and the unsettled issue of central bank autonomy. But as we discuss in detail in the following chapter, the 1999 disinflation

---

[5] During the first quarter of 1997, the Central Bank also continued its sterilization policy by selling foreign exchange. As a result of both open market operations and sterilization, broad monetary aggregates declined in real terms. See *Yapı and Kredi, Quarterly Economic Bulletin* (1997/I, 14).

and fiscal adjustment program, which survived the financial distress of November 2000, had to be abandoned as Turkey began to face one of its worst crises at the beginning of 2001.

Causes of Turkish Inflation

Studies of Turkish inflation from the 1980s and early 1990s associated inflation with inflows of foreign exchange and monetization of budget deficits. When the Central Bank expanded domestic credits and increased the money supply in response to the inflow of foreign exchange, inflationary expectations rose and the budget deficit became larger due to delays in revenue collection and erosion of the tax base. The Central Bank then monetized the budget deficits and monetary aggregates continued to grow, leading to a higher rate of inflation (Fry 1986). The increase in inflation was fairly moderate during the 1960s because of sterilization. But during the second half of the 1970s, pressured by the inadequacy of funding sources and shortages of foreign currency, to meet the growing public-sector borrowing requirement the Central Bank was forced to end the sterilization practice and turn to heavy monetization and short-term foreign borrowing (Celasun 1990). That led to the first major upward trend in inflation, which reversed in the early 1980s.

The inflow of foreign capital in the early 1980s was the reason for the rapid decline in inflation. But subsequently the steady erosion of the monetary base, which resulted from a higher foreign currency demand, caused another upturn in inflation. As the public sector began to consistently rely on revenues from seigniorage and the inflation tax, inflation continued its stepwise increase during the 1980–89 period.[6] In addition, even though there was little evidence of systematic cost inflation, the exchange-rate policies of the period also fueled inflation (Rodrik 1991).

Among possible causes of inflation, exchange-rate adjustment is one determinant that most analysts seem to agree on.[7] Examining the

[6] Seigniorage is the revenue government receives by issuing money. It is also referred to as an inflation tax.

[7] Other inflation-causing factors considered in the studies of Turkish inflation from the 1980s included lags in public price setting (Gazioğlu 1986), the oil crisis, and other supply shocks caused by the worldwide stagflation of the 1980s. Focusing on internal factors that may have destabilizing effects, Ertuna (1986) reported that nonmonetary factors were also behind price increases, with excess demand due to the growing gap between

period from 1973 to 1984, for example, Conway (1988) reported that exchange-rate devaluation accounted for 39 percent of total inflation, reflecting both increases in final-good prices and the increase in the domestic-currency price of imported inputs. Öniş and Özmucur (1990), who argued against a pure monetary interpretation of inflation, also provided evidence of the strong impact of exchange-rate devaluation on inflation.[8]

Another source of inflation that many studies, especially those from the late 1990s, focused on is inertial inflation. Covering the 1985–97 period, the study by Alper and Üçer (1998), in particular, concluded that inflation is inertial and has been nurtured by monetary and exchange-rate policies since the mid-1980s. Akçay, Alper, and Özmucur (1996) maintained that inflation is a process with inertia likely to result from the accumulation of inflationary expectations. Covering the 1988–2000 period, Metin-Özcan, Berüment, and Neyaptı (2004) also found strong inertia for Turkish inflation.

A recent work by Erlat (2002) dealt with the highly persistent nature of Turkish inflation. The study suggested that Turkish inflation has a strong long-memory component and will therefore initially resist disinflationary policies. But the author also argued that if policies turn out to be successful, the results will be long-lived.

Even though there seems to be a consensus on the inflationary effects of exchange-rate adjustments and inertia, the question of whether there is a relationship between budget deficits and inflation still remains, however. Using data from the 1950–88 period, Metin (1998) found a positive relationship between budget deficits and inflation. But, as Akçay, Alper, and Özmucur (1996) and Alper and Üçer (1998) argued, this is a difficult relation to prove empirically. Akçay, Alper, and Özmucur, in particular, maintained that there is a stable long-run relationship between budget deficits and inflation, but the link gets weaker as deficits are financed by alternative sources such as domestic bond financing. As Alper and Üçer noted, for example, in 1997 the only source of deficit financing was bond-finance, which may have been the cause of the weak link between budget deficits and inflation. A similar conclusion

domestic saving and investment raising the inflationary pressures. For a brief summary of these factors and early studies on Turkish inflation, see Kibritçioğlu (2004).

[8] In a recent study, however, using the 1981–98 estimation period, Akyürek (1999) found both changes in the monetary base and nominal currency depreciation as two significant sources of inflation.

was reached in a study by Tekin-Koru and Özmen (2003), which also found no link between inflation and budget deficits and showed that budget deficits did not lead to growth of seigniorage, but they did lead to the expansion of interest-bearing broad money.[9]

The relationship between inflation and fiscal deficits is indeed complicated and difficult to prove empirically. This is likely to be the case not only because of the frequency, volume, and timing of bond financing but also because of dollarization, changing economic and policy environments, and the varying sample periods used in applied work. In order for fiscal authorities to raise seigniorage revenue to finance fiscal deficits, the demand for domestic currency and therefore the monetary base must increase. But if there is ongoing currency substitution, fiscal and monetary authorities may choose to further increase seigniorage or rely on bond-financing and/or external funding. But as Selçuk (2001) wrote, in the presence of currency substitution Turkish fiscal authorities may not be able to collect more seigniorage by increasing the monetary base at a higher rate. Soydan (2003) also suggested that currency substitution limits money creation and that makes the relation between monetary aggregates and inflation weak and ambiguous.

Despite the empirical evidence concerning the weak relation between budget deficits and inflation and the significant inflationary effects of exchange-rate adjustments, inertia, and inflation uncertainty, there still seems to be a consensus on the root cause of inflation as being unsustainable fiscal deficits, however they are measured. As Akat (2000) noted, "[T]he monetization of the often large public deficits is always the 'original sin' from which high inflation emerges, as it did in Turkey in the 1980s and early 1990s" (p. 269). That makes fiscal discipline a necessity in the fight against inflation.

There is an extensive list of other contributing factors included under the demand side, supply side, inertial, and the institutional categories. Kibritcioğlu (2004) included massive investment spending on infrastructure, military expenditures, populist budgeting, increases in actual and expected costs of production due to changes in imported input prices,

[9] In this respect, the suggestion by Akçay, Alper, and Özmucur (2002) that the public-sector borrowing requirement should be a better indicator of fiscal deficits than the consolidated budget deficit obviously makes more sense. This argument found support from Akat (2000), who noted that the official budget deficit is only a small portion of the actual public-sector borrowing requirement. As Akat elaborated, successive governments have found ways to undertake substantial spending outside the budget.

interest costs, and inflationary expectations. Dibooğlu and Kibritcioğlu (2004) also argued that a major component of inflation is demand-driven core inflation, and therefore it is essential that credibility in policy making is restored and structural reforms are implemented to stabilize the economy with effective demand management policies.

Added to this list of studies on the determinants of inflation, there are also the recent works on inflation and inflation uncertainty (Nas and Perry 2000; Nas and Perry 2001; and Neyaptı and Kaya 2001). The results of the Nas and Perry (2000) study provided strong statistical evidence that increased inflation significantly raised inflation uncertainty in Turkey between 1960 and 1998, and Neyaptı and Kaya (2001) confirmed this relationship. Nas and Perry (2000) also found that inflation uncertainty could cause higher inflation in the short run. The study provided statistical evidence that increased inflation significantly raised inflation uncertainty in Turkey between 1960 and 1998 and in various sub-samples. Over the full sample period, increased inflation uncertainty was associated with lower average inflation at all lags. For both the 1986–98 and 1990–98 sub-sample periods, inflation uncertainty was associated with significantly higher levels of inflation.[10] During those periods, inflation uncertainty raised average inflation over lags of a year or less, and led to lower inflation at longer lags of 12–24 months. Thus, stabilizing policy behavior seemed to prevail overall, especially in the long run, since higher inflation uncertainty is also associated with lower average inflation, but opportunistic behavior was evident in the short run in the later sub-sample periods. The study speculated that the problems of time inconsistency, the lack of fiscal discipline, a high turnover of Central Bank governors, and politically motivated monetary expansions were all contributing factors that led to opportunistic behavior and subsequently to periods of high inflation and inflation uncertainty.

[10] This is somewhat interesting since the steps taken toward increased Central Bank autonomy after 1986 should have resulted in stabilization rather than opportunistic behavior. One possible explanation is that the statistical test in the Nas and Perry (2000) study seems to capture the policy motives of both macroeconomic policy makers in Turkey rather than specifically those of the Central Bank. Throughout the sub-sample periods, the Central Bank has in fact tried to stabilize inflation in spite of inflexible fiscal policies.

Why Couldn't Turkey Lower Inflation?

Analysis of the macroeconomic environment in Turkey clearly shows that stabilizing policy behavior appears to have dominated during the last three decades. Yet inflation remained a lingering problem despite the repeatedly implemented anti-inflationary measures. Why was it that while many high-inflation countries in the past managed to disinflate successfully, Turkey did not seem to be able to keep inflation under control?

One possible explanation might be the macroeconomic performance and management style of some of the past coalition governments. With very few exceptions, they all seemed to give top priority to their own political agendas and for the most part followed shortsighted opportunistic macroeconomic policies. Rapid expansion of public credits, public-sector price freezes, and excessive monetization before local and general elections were commonly used measures, and they were always followed by phases of price adjustments and macroeconomic contraction. In most situations, as the swollen budget numbers became public and price indexes turned out higher than expected, financial markets moved in anticipation of higher inflation, followed by the implementation of a stabilization package usually in coordination with the IMF. With few exceptions, stabilization measures were successful, at least in the short run, in restoring confidence and improving the macroeconomic environment. Factors that had led to higher inflation variability were effectively managed for the intermediate term, but the root cause in most cases remained untouched.

This does not imply that policy makers in Turkey were unaware of or unconcerned with the root cause of inflation. Notwithstanding a large pro-inflation constituency that existed as a result of inflation continuing for such a long time, an impatient public, a highly sophisticated media, and an inquiring academic community always felt the need for fiscal discipline and the tradeoffs that it presented. During the politically more liberal period that began in 1987, politicians attempted to disinflate or at least gave the impression that disinflation was a top priority while they were running for office. From the time inflation started its latest upward trend in 1987 until it reached a peak in 1997, all of the nine ruling governments enthusiastically promised lower inflation but, predictably, failed to deliver. After assuming a policy-making role as elected officials, they instead turned to the populist measures mentioned above, and as the situation got out of hand they intervened using their best crisis management skills to normalize the situation.

For example, as discussed in detail in chapter 4, in the hope of fighting off inflation, Çiller's administration followed a policy of maintaining an overvalued Turkish lira and lowering interest rates. It also strategically tried to adjust the prices of a wide range of goods and services produced by the state enterprises. However, this highly ambitious anti-inflationary plan turned counterproductive, and consequently interest rates began to rise and the Turkish lira lost value against major currencies. To avoid upward pressure on interest rates, domestic borrowing was kept at a minimum. But, when the Treasury began to restrict the supply of government securities by canceling or delaying security auctions, the strategy of less domestic borrowing backfired, causing interest rates to surge instead. Also, as domestic borrowing in total budget financing requirements declined, the share of both foreign borrowing and short-term credits from the Central Bank rose.

In addition to the widening budget deficit, the trade deficit began to rise as well. So by mid-1993 financial markets began to anticipate devaluation, a higher risk of further monetization because of rising deficits, and possible implementation of a stabilization package. Çiller's government tried to assure the financial markets that devaluation was out of the question and continued to force down interest rates by relying on Central Bank resources. However, Çiller's desire to keep interest rates low to fight inflation did not work. The Treasury, unable to borrow at lower interest rates, became more dependent on short-term advances from the Central Bank. The outcome was higher interest rates, larger deficits, and higher inflation.

Lowering inflation expectations and changing the nature of the budgeting process have considerable impact on the real economy. A cold-turkey approach could send the economy into a severe recession with serious allocational and distributional outcomes. A gradualist approach could be less costly in the short run, but it usually requires continuity in the political process. For either approach to be effective it is imperative to have an administration in place with a credible agenda and to have one that is willing to assume responsibility in a low-turnover political environment.

Given the realities of Turkish politics since the 1960s, neither option seemed feasible for most administrations. However, the political climate and the economic reality had changed somewhat by the end of the 1990s. First, Turkey's candidacy status for the European Union was upgraded at the Helsinki summit in 1998, so Turkey had to become even more determined to put its house in order. In addition to the Copenhagen criteria that covered human rights and democratic values with which all candidate nations must comply, Turkey also needed to meet the economic criteria to start the process of closing its economic gap with the EU. Second, it was no longer possible to maintain the status quo without additional external financing. Clearly, such financial help was out of the question unless Turkey took credible anti-inflationary measures convincing enough for the international financial community. Above all, Turkey's maturing democracy was certainly becoming more responsive to those politicians who deliver than to those who do not. The Turkish people had grown weary of inflation and were therefore prepared to reward any political formation that would be credible enough to do the job.

Supported by numerical superiority in the Turkish Parliament, Ecevit's coalition government, formed in May 1999, was able to move on with a highly risky disinflation strategy—a strategy, had it been successful, that would have had a high payoff for all members of the coalition government. As described in the next chapter, the program failed, and as the follow-up measures continued and the economy experienced a severe slowdown, Ecevit's government understandably lost its support. Despite some improvements in the economy, it appeared that none of the coalition partners would have been able to secure their position in the Parliament if, at the time, an early election had been held. This specific episode provides a clear explanation for the reluctance of past governments to take serious measures to disinflate the economy.

Inadequacy of Macroeconomic Policies

Even if the policy makers had chosen to disinflate by following either the gradualist or cold-turkey approach, they still would have faced complications in managing the economy due to the absence of, or ineffectiveness of, monetary and fiscal policies. In the past, both fiscal and monetary policies have been ineffective and have rarely been used for macroeconomic stabilization. For the most part, fiscal policy in Turkey has been expansionary, not because it was designed to be so, but essentially because government has consistently assumed an active role in developing the economy. In addition, for the most part the limited tax revenues fell short of the excessive spending incurred by all branches of the government.

Also, from the very early days of the Republic, the monetary authority played a fairly passive role in macroeconomic policy making. Money supply was determined by total credit expansion, and monetary policy was directed toward controlling private and public spending through setting borrowing limits for the banking system. Monetary policy was accommodative. The Central Bank's main objective was to maintain some ratio of private-sector domestic credit to nominal GNP in line with the Treasury's priorities. Essentially, the Bank used public-sector credits and interest rates as monetary policy instruments to back the government's development and industrialization policies and frequently monetized the resulting fiscal deficits.

This type of money management began to change after 1986, however. The Central Bank took important steps toward more autonomy by adopting contemporary central bank practices. A series of new legislation allowed the Central Bank to conduct open market operations and monitor a newly established interbank market. These reforms were further complemented by monetary programs and accords with the Treasury limiting the short-term credit that the government could use from the Central Bank.

Beginning with the 1986 monetary program, the Central Bank attempted to set monetary targets in accordance with the inflation and growth targets of the government's annual programs. Shifting the emphasis from the traditional approach of money and credit expansion, the 1986 program used M2 as a target variable and focused on reserve money and its major components, such as the Bank's net domestic and foreign assets. However, the Bank discontinued M2 targeting in 1988 due to the large discrepancy between the targeted and realized values. In 1990, the Central Bank announced another program that was viewed as an essential step toward central bank independence and monetary stability. This time, the program, which targeted several monetary aggregates from its balance sheet, was successful. However, in the next year, when targets were once again missed, the Central Bank chose not to announce a monetary program for 1991. Instead, it tried to monitor the reserve money and pursued an exchange-rate stabilization policy by managing foreign-exchange reserves through open market operations. During the years 1992–93, the Central Bank failed to meet its monetary targets due mainly to the rapid expansion of public-sector credits, and the excessive monetary growth continued.

During the first quarter of 1994, the Central Bank continued its open market operations to minimize the expansionary effects of public-sector borrowing and kept monetary policy tight during the rest of 1994 and 1995, in line with the April 5 stabilization program. In 1996, in addition to efforts to stabilize the exchange rate, the Bank also began a new policy of reducing the volatility of interbank rates. As we detail in the next chapter, the Central Bank's efforts to achieve monetary stability continued throughout the remainder of the 1990s.

It is clear that especially after 1986 the Central Bank has been making a concerted effort to play its stabilizing role. Even though its monetary programs and its alliance with the Treasury have sought, and to some extent succeeded, to put downward pressure on inflation at least for a short period of time, higher inflationary expectations continued. Despite measures that could be interpreted as a move toward greater central bank independence, inflation and inflation variability continued to surge after 1990. While the attempts to stabilize inflation seemed to work during the politically stable periods of the early 1980s, the political instability in the late 1980s and the 1990s resulted in opportunistic policy behavior. From this brief examination of Turkey's disinflation experiment, it is clear that central bank independence could have accomplished little without fiscal discipline.

As emphasized in Nas and Perry (2000), throughout the three-decade period and particularly during the 1990s, inflation stabilization increasingly suffered from the problem of time inconsistency and also failed to produce a fiscal environment that would have allowed the Central Bank to practice its autonomy. It was concluded that if Turkey was to become a single-digit inflation country, it seemed almost imperative for the fiscal authority to seriously consider policies aimed at moving away from inflationary bias. Then it would have been possible for the Central Bank, as an autonomous entity, to stabilize the economy through sound monetary policies. We will revisit the issue of central bank autonomy in chapter 8, where we re-examine the anti-inflationary programs and follow-up policies of 2000–2004 that have finally led to a dramatic decrease in inflation. The analysis of the anti-inflationary and structural adjustment programs and the highlights of the 2000–2001 financial crises follow next.

CHAPTER SIX

THE CRISIS OF 2001 AND THE PROGRAM FOR THE TRANSITION TO A STRONG ECONOMY

February 19, 2001: As the media were gathered outside the Çankaya Presidential Palace, awaiting the brief statement that was routinely provided after Turkey's National Security Council meeting, the unexpected happened. Prime Minister Bülent Ecevit suddenly left the meeting and astounded the media by recounting the dispute that had just taken place between him and Turkey's President Ahmet Necdet Sezer. Apparently, during the meeting, which was chaired by the president and attended by the prime minister, key members of the cabinet, and high-ranking generals, the president questioned the prime minister and his coalition government's handling of the corruption charges that had surfaced in the banking sector. This unprecedented incident shocked the financial markets, which were already jittery from fresh memories of the November 2000 financial crisis and the widespread speculation about the future of Ecevit's three-party coalition government that followed. As the financial community attempted to adjust to the plunging stock market and surging overnight interest rates, Turkey decided three days later to let the Turkish lira freely float.[1]

Overwhelmed by the turn of events, some commentators, including Turkish and European diplomats, thought this was clearly a political crisis that called for a political solution. The credibility of Ecevit's coalition government was at stake, and a change in government was inescapable. But Prime Minister Ecevit did not consider the situation political, and he hinted that the economy had already been in trouble before this incident. Major players in the financial markets were also expecting difficulties ahead because of the financial distress of November 2000. The dispute between the president and the prime minister (which from

[1] For details of the daily events, see, in particular, "Deepening Political Crisis Rocks Markets in Turkey," *New York Times*, February 22, 2001; "Turkey's Currency Keeps on Tumbling," *Washington Post*, February 23, 2001, p. A-14; "Turkey Floats Currency, and It Falls 25%," *New York Times*, February 23, 2001.

now on will be referred to as the Çankaya incident) became a triggering event with significant consequences for the Turkish economy.

A former lawyer and head of Turkey's Constitutional Court, Ahmet Necdet Sezer had been elected by the Turkish Parliament as the tenth president of Turkey. Prime Minister Ecevit and his coalition partners had nominated Sezer for the presidency. Ecevit's first choice was the outgoing president, Süleyman Demirel, but the Turkish Constitution did not allow a second seven-year term in office, and attempts to amend the Constitution to allow Demirel to serve a second term failed. Ecevit's nomination of Sezer received overwhelming support in the Parliament, and Sezer became president in 2000.

The new president quickly gained the trust of the Turkish people. His adherence to the rule of law and strict compliance with the Constitution was certainly a source of admiration for many. But his attention to legal details and the judicious manner in which he was perceived to be conducting his presidential duties began to create procedural complications. Bülent Ecevit, whose integrity had also never been questioned, soon found himself at odds with the president as disagreements on major legislation began to surface. Ironically, this confrontation between two of Turkey's most trusted leaders had created a political crisis, and oddly enough, what prompted the controversy was the issue of how to handle corruption charges and whether the charges were being handled adequately and expediently by the executive branch of government. Such an incident might have had little impact on the economy under normal circumstances. But Turkey was on a tightrope. Financial markets were yet to recover from the financial turmoil of November 2000. Most importantly, the success of the ongoing disinflation program aimed at bringing down three decades of high inflation largely depended on the government's credibility.

This chapter analyzes the economic events that led to and followed the adoption of a floating exchange rate regime, which was a major departure from Turkey's 1999 Disinflation and Fiscal Adjustment Program. A detailed review of the program outcome and the November 2000 banking crisis is followed by highlights of the events of the 2001 crisis and a discussion of the Memorandum on Economic Policies and various letters of intent that were submitted to the International Monetary Fund.

The Disinflation and Fiscal Adjustment Program

After the three years of economic recovery that had followed the 1994 financial crisis, the economy was once again in need of stabilization. Beginning with the fourth quarter of 1998, the growth rate, which had reached 7.5 percent in 1997, turned negative, and even though the inflation rate had declined from its 1997 level of 99.1 percent it was still at a two-digit level (see table 6.1). As a percentage of GNP, the public-sector borrowing requirement had increased, and both domestic and foreign debt had reached unsustainable levels (see table 6.2). The only

Table 6.1 Selected macroeconomic indicators, 1997–2003

Year	GDP growth rate	Inflation rate	Budget deficit	Primary budget surplus	Trade balance	Current account
			% of GNP			
1997	7.5	99.1	–7.6	0.1	–7.7	–1.4
1998	3.1	69.7	–7.3	4.3	–6.8	1.0
1999	–4.7	68.8	–11.9	1.8	–5.4	–0.7
2000	7.4	39.0	–10.9	5.3	–10.9	–4.9
2001	–7.5	68.5	–16.5	6.8	–2.6	2.3
2002	7.9	29.7	–14.6	4.3	–4.0	–0.8
2003	5.8	18.4	–11.3	5.2	–5.9	–3.4

Sources: TÜRKSTAT, *Statistical Indicators 1923–2005*; Central Bank of the Republic of Turkey, Electronic Data Delivery System; State Planning Organization, *Economic and Social Indicators 1950–2006*.

Table 6.2 International reserves, external and domestic debt, and the public sector borrowing requirement, 1997–2003

Year	International reserves		External debt Total		Short term	Domestic debt	PSBR
	In billion $	% of GNP	In billion $	% of GNP	% of GNP	% of GNP	% of GNP
1997	27.1	14.1	84.2	43.8	9.2	21.4	7.6
1998	29.5	14.2	96.2	46.6	10.0	21.7	9.3
1999	33.7	18.2	103.1	55.7	12.4	29.3	15.5
2000	34.2	17.1	118.5	59.3	14.1	29.0	11.8
2001	30.2	20.7	113.6	78.0	11.2	69.2	16.4
2002	38.0	21.0	129.7	72.0	9.1	54.5	12.7
2003	45.0	18.8	144.9	60.7	9.6	54.5	9.3

Sources: TÜRKSTAT, *Statistical Indicators 1923–2005*; Central Bank of the Republic of Turkey, Electronic Data Delivery System; Turkish Treasury, *Economic Indicators*.

improvement was in the trade and current account balances, both of which were in deficit but were declining from their 1997 highs (see table 6.1).

Thus, as expected, on December 22, 1999, Turkey signed a three-year standby agreement with the IMF amounting to a $4 billion credit to support its disinflation and fiscal adjustment program.[2] The program, which was formulated after lengthy discussions with the IMF, aimed at lowering the inflation rate, restoring macroeconomic balances, accelerating privatization, and introducing radical structural reforms in the economy. Accordingly, fiscal and monetary policies were to gradually reduce inflation from a projected 65.4 percent in 1999 to 25 percent in 2000, 12 percent in 2001, and 7 percent in 2002.[3] During the three-year period, the rate of growth of real GNP was projected to increase from –2.1 percent to 5.8 percent, and the current account deficit was expected to increase from 0.5 percent to 1.5 percent of GNP. The program also predicted a primary surplus of the public-sector budget of about 3.7 percent of GNP in 2002, a respectable increase from a projected deficit of 2.7 percent in 1999.

The top priority of the program was to reduce Turkey's double-digit inflation. As described in detail in chapter 5, a combination of internal and external factors dating back to the late 1970s were responsible for Turkey's chronically high inflation. Excessive spending that had created fiscal imbalances, exchange-rate adjustments, and strategic public-sector price adjustments, were key determinants. Delays in stabilization, particularly in the early 1990s, also fueled higher inflation. Rather than implementing a credible stabilization package, the coalition governments introduced populist measures, such as maintaining an overvalued Turkish lira, lowering interest rates, and strategically adjusting the prices of a wide range of goods and services produced by the state economic enterprises (SEEs).

Throughout most of this period, Central Bank policies were generally accommodative, backing the government's development and growth policies and frequently monetizing the fiscal deficits that resulted. Inflation, therefore, continued to rise, and as a historical analysis of Turkey's record shows, the future course of inflation became much

[2] See IMF *Press Release No. 99/66*, December 22, 1999.

[3] See IMF *Letter of Intent*, December 9, 1999, and *IMF Press Release No. 99/66*, December 22, 1999.

more difficult to predict during the episodes of high inflation, leading to a close link between the level of inflation and inflation uncertainty. After surging to 125.5 percent in 1994, year-end inflation declined to 76 percent in 1995 but rose again to almost 100 percent by 1997.[4]

Clearly, the program needed to include measures to minimize uncertainty and lower inflation expectations. Hence, in addition to tight fiscal and monetary policies, which had been implemented and subsequently failed many times in the past, the program incorporated a disinflationary exchange-rate design. With this exchange-rate system, known as the *crawling peg regime*, exchange-rate adjustments are declared in advance, and with a built-in feature of pre-announced exit strategy from the system the exchange-rate policy was designed to be predictable. Accordingly, the December 9, 1999, letter to the IMF outlined a pre-announced exchange-rate path, which held the rate of depreciation at 20 percent during 2000. Rate adjustments were to be made gradually on a monthly basis, starting with 2.1 percent during the first quarter of the year followed by 1.7, 1.3, and 1.0 percent monthly devaluations in the second, third, and fourth quarters, respectively. During the first 18 months, there was no band around the exchange-rate path, but then gradually the band was set to widen to 22.5 percent by the end of 2002.

Monetary policy in this system was designed to be rather passive; it would remain tight and include a no-sterilization rule. The money supply could only change in response to variations in the foreign-exchange reserves. Short-term liquidity changes, however, were allowed. The December 1999 net domestic asset level of the monetary base was to be kept constant, but short-run fluctuations during the quarter were allowed within 5 percent of the monetary base. This feature was added to provide flexibility to monetary policy so that excessive volatility in overnight rates could be avoided. Domestic interest rates were to be determined through market dynamics, and the Central Bank's role was limited to adjusting the interbank interest rates daily in accordance with changes of the overnight money market rates.

[4] An analysis of the historical data also indicates a close association between inflation, inflation uncertainty, and real output. Before 1980, a decline in inflation was followed by a decline in output, but thereafter, as inflation began an upward trend during the 1980s and 1990s, output growth fluctuated for the most part in the opposite direction. At the highest levels of inflation uncertainty, output growth rates were negative and at their lowest levels. See Nas and Perry (2001).

During the second half of 2001, the monetary framework, which mimicked a relatively softer version of a "currency board," was expected to allow a gradual shift from the exchange-rate-based monetary management to a monetary-aggregates-based monetary policy with inflation targeting. In this system, the currency market sets the exchange rate and the management of domestic liquidity belongs to the central bank, thereby allowing the bank more flexibility in pursuing inflation targeting.

One other important aspect of the program was its emphasis on structural reforms. Since 1980, when Turkey began the implementation of its liberalization program, most governments either overlooked the prospective long-term gains or chose not to face the immediate complications and the distributional costs of restructuring. Almost all of the stabilization and structural adjustment programs introduced since then had promised change, but governments always dragged their feet, and by doing so the task inevitably became an impossible one. Over the years, fiscal adjustments had become more and more unsustainable, and deficits in public finances continued to raise public debt to unmanageable levels. In a nutshell, the 1999 Disinflation and Fiscal Adjustment Program emphasized the structural reforms needed to make the fiscal adjustment sustainable, improve economic efficiency, and accelerate the privatization of SEEs. That and an exchange-rate-based monetary policy that was an important aspect of the program were expected to lower interest rates and inflationary expectations.

The Program Outcome and the November 2000 Crisis

One year after its implementation, the disinflation program was on track.[5] Monetary and exchange-rate policies had been put in place in accordance with the program, and fiscal targets had been largely met. The primary public-sector balance improved to a surplus of 5.3 percent of GNP from a projected deficit of 1.9 percent a year earlier, inflation dropped to its lowest levels since 1986, interest rates declined considerably, and the economy began to show signs of recovery. However, there were some lingering problems. In addition to delays in privatization and structural reforms that were specifically called for in the program, ris-

[5] See IMF *Letter of Intent*, June 22, 2000, and IMF *News Brief No. 00/52*, July 6, 2000.

ing oil prices created an extra burden on the performance of the SEEs. Rising interest rates on emerging market debt also began to adversely affect the economy in the second half of the year.

Most importantly, however, domestic interest rates fell rapidly at the beginning of 2000. Because the program did not allow sterilization, the inflow of short-term capital caused high liquidity; that led to lower interest rates and an increase in domestic demand, adversely affecting inflationary expectations in the second half of the year. Furthermore, the surge in domestic demand led to the deterioration of the external balances and heightened expectations of a much wider current account deficit by the end of 2000, an increase to 4.9 percent from 0.7 percent of GNP in 1999 (see table 6.1).

Thus, as a result of deteriorating external balances, financial markets began to anticipate sharp currency depreciation. That, and increased speculation about a liquidity crunch in the banking system, triggered capital outflow and created further liquidity problems for the entire banking sector.[6] Accelerated outflow of foreign reserves led to a steep rise in overnight interest rates and a sharp decline in the bond market, followed by a nearly 50 percent fall in the stock market. To restore confidence in the financial markets, the Central Bank reluctantly added liquidity to the system, exceeding the limits allowed by the IMF standby agreement. On December 7, 2000, the IMF also provided additional resources under the Supplemental Reserve Facility (SRF) in the amount of US$7.5 billion to alleviate the balance of payments difficulties stemming from this unexpected crisis.[7]

The financial turmoil appeared to recede at the end of the first week of December 2000, after the news that Turkey and the EU had finally ironed out their differences concerning Turkey's accession to the EU.[8] Financial markets responded positively to the announcement of the new IMF aid package and the soothing words from the U.S. administration and financial organizations. The stock market, after plunging 50 percent during November, recovered most of its losses after the announcement of IMF liquidity injection.

---

[6] For the details, see Alper (2001), Alper, Berüment, and Malatyalı (2001), Ertuğrul and Selçuk (2001), and Tükel, Üçer, and Van Rijckeghem (2006).

[7] See *IMF Press Release No. 00/80*, December 21, 2000.

[8] A compromise was reached by the EU ministers on December 4, 2000, in Brussels to modify the Accession Partnership Accord to include Turkey's sensitivities regarding the Cyprus issue and the territorial disputes with EU member Greece.

In the letter of intent of December 18, 2000, the Turkish authorities assured the IMF that they stood "ready to take additional measures, if necessary, to keep the program on track, consulting regularly with the Fund." To achieve the program's key macroeconomic goals, Turkey was to implement revenue-enhancement measures and keep the growth rate of government expenditures below the GNP growth rate. Regarding monetary policy, efforts were made to rebuild foreign-exchange reserves and absorb the excess liquidity created during the November crisis as well as accelerate structural measures to restore confidence in the banking system. Most importantly, they renewed their commitment to privatize key areas, such as telecommunications and energy, and to take decisive steps toward the liberalization of tobacco and sugar markets.

In their request for the completion of the fifth review under the standby agreement, Turkish authorities further assured the IMF of their compliance with the strengthened policies outlined in the December 18, 2000, letter of intent.[9] For the return of full market confidence it was important for the Turkish authorities to clearly state their commitment to the pre-announced exchange-rate system and to manage a disinflationary monetary policy. On February 5, 2001, the IMF approved the fifth review, enabling Turkey to draw up to $1.4 billion, bringing the total to about $3.7 billion.[10] Once again, the IMF reminded Turkey that "[s]trict adherence to the monetary, fiscal and the structural reform program" was necessary "for the return of full market confidence and for the success of the authorities' ambitious disinflation program."

Causes of the Crisis

Before the November 2000 crisis, economic data did not show the symptoms of a country in financial distress. The economy was growing robustly, and fiscal performance was strong and on target. Most importantly, interest rates, even though they were moving downward, remained high enough to attract foreign capital to finance the current account deficit and meet the Treasury's foreign borrowing needs (Akyüz and Boratav 2002, 15). There was some concern about the government's commitment to the disinflation program, however; the inflation rate was coming down significantly but was still above the program target

[9] Also see an updated *Letter of Intent*, January 30, 2001.
[10] See *IMF News Brief No. 01/13*, February 5, 2001.

of 25 percent, due in part to an unexpected increase in world energy prices.

When the crisis began, it was initially attributed to nervousness about the banking sector, which was a situation viewed as temporary by Central Bank Governor Gazi Erçel.[11] One cause of the liquidity problem could have been the seasonal factors of capital outflow known as the January effect, which was ruled out by the Central Bank of Turkey.[12] Perhaps volatility in the currency market was a little higher than normal, but very few suspected that the sudden increase in the overnight interest rate would cause an outflow of foreign reserves to the extent that it would to lead to the questioning of the program's future. So what was behind the sudden reversal of capital flow and the liquidity crisis?

The traditional view would point out the overvalued exchange rate as a likely factor that triggered a sequence of events leading to increased exchange rate risks: increased capital inflows lead to higher growth, currency appreciation, current account deficits, and then to high exchange-rate risks.[13] In the case of Turkey, with increased exchange risk came erosion of confidence, and consequently, as Akyüz and Boratav (2002) noted, "[F]oreign creditors refused to roll over their contracts with local banks or sold assets to exit" (p. 18).

Ekinci and Ertürk (2007) provided an alternative explanation of the crisis based on portfolio dynamics driven by speculative asset price expectations. In their view, "Once the expectations of asset price increases cease for whatever reason capital flow reverses regardless of whether devaluation risk and foreign exchange reserves are high or low." Pointing out that net portfolio investment had already been declining during the months preceding the November crisis, they suggested profit taking as the real cause of the capital reversal: investors holding Treasury bonds and unloading their portfolios when they no longer anticipated the exchange rate to remain at its current levels.

---

[11] See "Central Bank Says Moves in Harmony with IMF," *Turkish Daily News*, November 25, 2000.

[12] "January effect" is a stock market term used in reference to abnormally high stock returns in January because of year-end tax-related equity transactions. Investors tend to sell some of their stocks (mostly the shares of small companies) to take capital losses before the end of the tax year, usually in December, and then buy back stocks in January. So it is possible that as Alper (2001, 69) indicated, such selling might have increased during the last quarter of 2000 and led to the capital outflow from emerging markets.

[13] For a detailed discussion of this view, see Akyüz and Boratav (2002) and Alper (2001).

Özatay and Sak (2002) did not dismiss the possibility of strong capital reversals stemming from current account deficits and currency appreciation, but they still argued that "without a fragile banking system and triggering factors, high current account deficit and real appreciation of the lira would not be enough to precipitate the 2000–2001 crisis." The cause of the crisis, according to Özatay and Sak, was a combination of "a fragile banking sector" and a set of "triggering factors." Providing evidence of increased open foreign exchange positions in the banking system, maturity mismatches (high ratios of liabilities with short-term maturities and assets with long-term maturities), and significant increases in the ratio of nonperforming loans during the pre-crisis period, they identified triggering factors such as delays in structural reforms of the banking sector, rumors of possible bank failures, criminal investigations, and takeovers by the Savings Deposit Insurance Fund (SDIF), a unit of the newly formed Banking Regulation and Supervision Agency (BRSA or BDDK in Turkish).[14]

The fragility of the banking sector as a likely explanation of the events that may have led to the crisis appears to have been a shared observation in most studies on the topic. An ongoing corruption investigation of 10 small banks that were under the BRSA led to speculation of a widened investigation and rumors of possible bank bailouts. A sell-off of government securities by a medium-sized private commercial bank that was in financial difficulty elevated such concerns.[15] In addition, because the Turkish lira was grossly overvalued and the current account deficit was expected to increase, there was a growing expectation of devaluation. That, as expected, led to a massive capital outflow estimated at about $6 billion.[16] In need of liquidity and having no prospect of obtaining

[14] The BRSA was an autonomous new supervision authority established with the banking law that was introduced in June 1999. It assumed the regulatory and supervisory roles of the Treasury and the Central Bank with regard to the banking sector and became operational in August 2000. Some of BRSA's functions included monitoring the banks through off-site and on-site examinations of bank balance sheets and income reports as well as taking the necessary actions to strengthen the banking sector and minimize the cost of bank failures. The SDIF, originally run by the Central Bank of Turkey, was transferred to BRSA in August 2000. For more on the SDIF and the BRSA, see IMF *Letter of Intent*, December 9, 1999 and December 18, 2000, Ertuğrul and Selçuk (2001, 24–27), and Pazarbaşıoğlu (2005, 163–64).

[15] This mid-size bank was holding a large portfolio of mostly long-term government debt instruments used as collateral against foreign-currency borrowing and was heavily dependent on overnight funds (Özatay and Sak 2002).

[16] For details of the daily events as the financial turmoil deepened, see "Turkish Crisis Deepens," *BBC News*, December 4, 2000; "Döviz Çıkışı 5.2 Milyar Düzeyine Çıktı,"

credit in international markets, Turkish banks began to unload their bond holdings, causing bond yields and overnight rates to increase. The Central Bank intervened to ease the reserve requirements and through open market operations raised the liquidity level. Domestic institutions reacted by short covering their foreign-currency positions, and that led to an increased demand for foreign currency. Working in harmony with the IMF, the Central Bank intervened first by lowering banks' liquidity ratios and reserve requirements. But then, as a result of the Central Bank announcing a return to initial monetary expansion policies that were constrained by the disinflation program, the crisis deepened during the first week of December 2000.

Could the crisis have been avoided? Not according to Akyüz and Boratav (2002). The 1999 Disinflation and Fiscal Adjustment Program failed to deliver, not because it was incorrectly implemented, but simply because of the shortcomings in its design. It was necessary for interest rates to come down for the fiscal adjustment, but that adversely affected the banking sector, which was heavily dependent on high interest rates and inflation. The program also failed to achieve its inflation targets despite the tight fiscal and monetary policies. Inflation declined at a much slower pace than was expected under the program, at about 15 percentage points above its target level.

A major shortcoming of the disinflation program was the no-sterilization rule, a "design flaw" in the program, initially leading to interest-rate undershooting (Alper 2001), and the program's dependence on short-term capital inflows as a source of "the liquidity generation mechanism" that led to increased likelihood of speculative runs (Ertuğrul and Yeldan (2003). The reduction in real interest rates leads to a higher GDP growth rate prompted by consumption and investment. That in turn adversely affects the current account due to an increase in imports. International reserves consequently decrease unless supplemented by further capital inflows, which leads to speculative attacks and to abandoning the exchange rate anchor.

Alper (2001) suggested that the crisis transmission of an exchange-rate-based stabilization program could be explained by the following steps:

Milliyet, December 1, 2000; and "4.3 Milyar Dolar Gitti, Faiz 202'ye Çıktı, Bürokratlar Alarma Geçti," *Hürriyet*, Nov. 29, 2000.

> Due to seasonal or some external factors as well as "reform fatigue" or delayed stabilizations, an outflow starts, liquidity in the system is reduced, repo and the interbank market rates increase, signifying a drop in the value of the assets in the commercial banks' balance sheets.
>
> The increase in the overnight rates leads to sales of government securities by banks who are desperately seeking funds and are not able to obtain them from the interbank market because their credit lines are cut due to an increase in vulnerability.
>
> The prices of the government securities fall and the monetary authorities cannot intervene since there is a ceiling on the net domestic assets of the Central Bank. This leads to margin calls putting upward pressure on the short-term funding needs. The vulnerability of the whole banking system increases, the interbank market becomes dysfunctional. A liquidity crisis occurs.
>
> Since the banks that are financially distressed are regarded as a liability to the government budget, the sovereign risk rises.
>
> Capital outflow leads to a reduction in the international reserves causing an upward pressure on the exchange rate risk, prompting a speculative attack.
>
> The monetary authority has to abandon the exchange rate anchor. (p. 75)

In retrospect, based on this most likely sequence of events that led to the expectation of devaluation and thus the outflow of capital, it appears that the sudden and unexpected decline in interest rates was the root cause. If that was the case, then a more flexible monetary policy could have prevented the massive outflow of capital if the monetary authority had been able to strategically absorb the excessive liquidity stemming from the inflow of short-term capital in the first place. Furthermore, the liquidity crisis could have been avoided if, in anticipation of lower interest rates, the program had also set targets for interest rates just as it did for the exchange rates and other indicators.

Another question is whether the design flaw of the stabilization program was the cause, or if the crisis was already in the making irrespective of the stabilization program, however it was designed. Take, for example, the 1994 crisis, which was triggered by a downgrading by the international rating agencies in a deteriorating macroeconomic environment due to delayed stabilization. Policy makers' interference with market dynamics aimed at lowering interest rates was the primary cause of the events that led to the speculative attack on domestic cur-

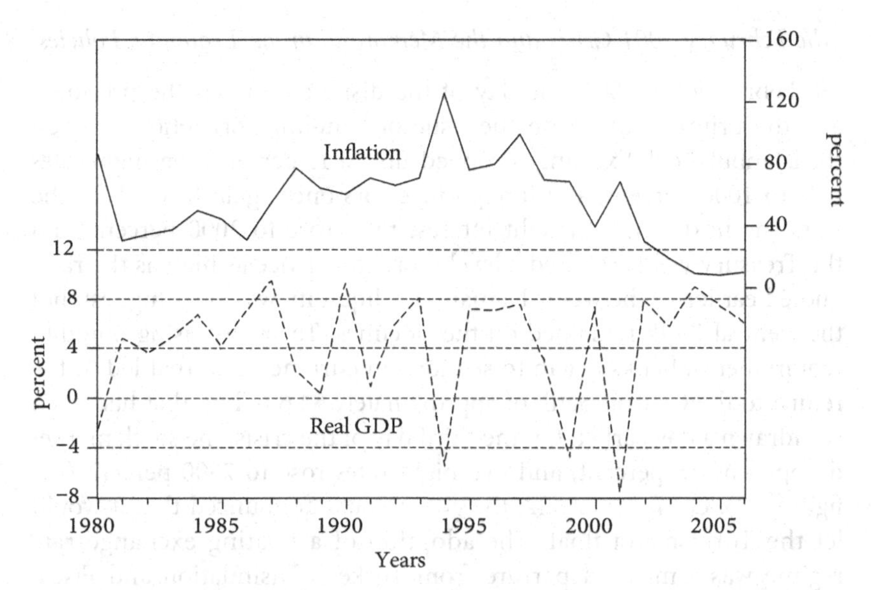

Figure 6.1 Inflation and real GDP, 1980–2006. (Data from Central Bank of the Republic of Turkey, Electronic Data Delivery System.)

rency and thus the resulting massive outflow of short-term capital. Six years later, the Turkish economy again experienced a massive outflow of short-term capital, and the primary cause once again was declining interest rates, but this time it was the stabilization design in place that led to the lower interest rates. In fact, one striking similarity between the January 1994 crisis and the November 2000 crisis was the trend in the financial indicators. Before the onset of both crises, changes (as a percentage of GNP) in the public-sector borrowing requirement and external and domestic debt ratios were on an upward trend. International reserves were on the rise, as well. But key macroeconomic indicators were changing in opposite directions. Before 1994, both GDP growth and inflation rates were increasing, and the trend was upward, but before the November 2000 crisis both were moving in a downward trend (see figure 6.1). During the post-crisis period, output in both cases resumed its growth, and inflation fell significantly. Output loss was only temporary, and short-term foreign capital quickly returned. In both situations, then, the costs of disinflation appear to have been the adverse effects of rapidly moving short-term capital, loss of international reserves, and the resulting increase in foreign debt.

The February 2001 Crisis and the Memorandum on Economic Policies

On February 19, 2001, the day of the dispute between the president and the prime minister on the issue of handling corruption charges, the Istanbul Stock Exchange dropped almost 15 percent, overnight rates rose to 1000 percent, and foreign investors once again headed for the exit. The next day, overnight interest rates rose to 3000 percent, and the Treasury yields reached a level more than twice as high as the rates quoted earlier in the week. Demand for liquidity was at its highest, but the Central Bank remained on the sidelines. To satisfy rising liquidity requirements, banks began to sell foreign currency, and that led to the return to the Central Bank of approximately $4.6 billion that had been withdrawn a day earlier. On the third day of the crisis, the stock market dropped by 18 percent, and overnight rates rose to 7500 percent (see figure 6.2). On February 22, the government announced that it would let the Turkish lira float. The adoption of a floating exchange-rate regime was a major departure from Turkey's Disinflation and Fiscal Adjustment Program, which had been keeping the Turkish lira crawl in a pre-announced path since December 1999. Consequently, the lira lost 28.4 percent of its value in one day (see figure 6.3).

Officials from the U.S. Treasury and the International Monetary Fund publicly expressed support for Turkey's decision to let the lira float. But according to the *New York Times*, "[I]n private these officials were much more critical. American officials noted that in the autumn, before the IMF worked out a $7.5 billion emergency loan deal to support economic change in Turkey, many at the Treasury thought the effort to maintain a fixed exchange rate was doomed. And a senior IMF official said: 'There was a lot of doubt that they could make the reforms stick, and that they were playing with global markets they didn't entirely understand. They didn't have the political cohesion to make it work.'"[17] The official statement from the IMF, however, supported Turkey's decision to float the lira.[18] The first deputy managing director of the IMF, Stanley Fischer, who happened to be in İstanbul at the time for the G-20 meeting, reassured the financial community of his full support, reemphasizing the need to continue to reduce inflation and ensure

[17] See "Turkey Floats Currency, and It Falls 25%," *New York Times*, February 23, 2001.

[18] See IMF *News Brief No. 01/21*, February 21, 2001.

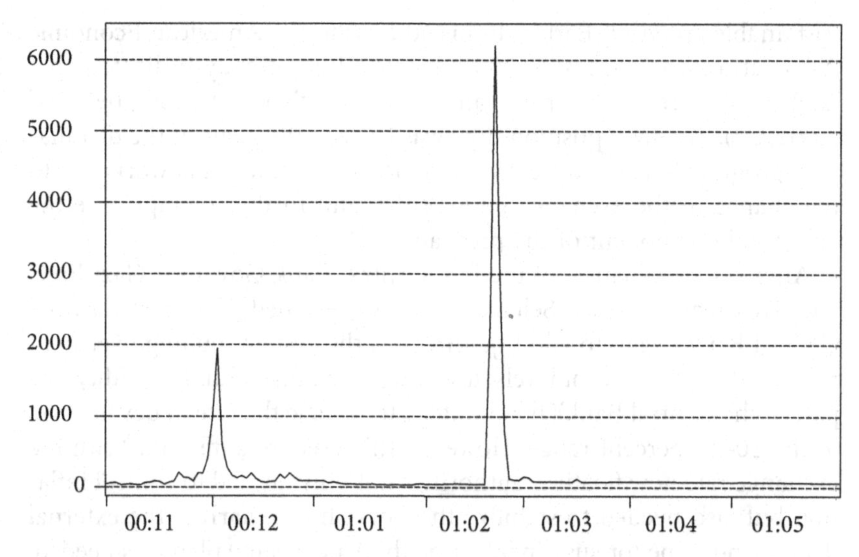

Figure 6.2 Maximum overnight interest rates, November 2000–May 2001. (Data from Central Bank of the Republic of Turkey, Electronic Data Delivery System.)

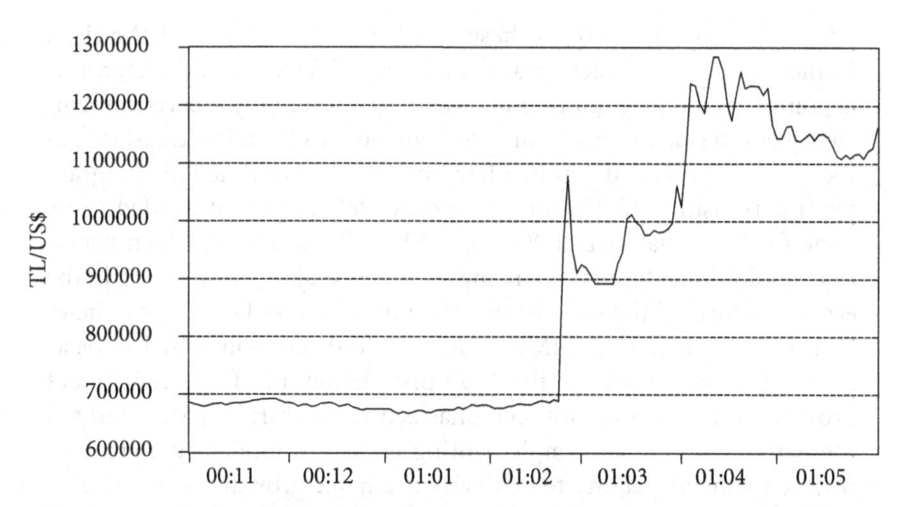

Figure 6.3 Daily official exchange rates, November 2000–May 2001. (Data from Central Bank of the Republic of Turkey, Electronic Data Delivery System.)

sustainable growth.[19] Earlier, in his address to the American Economic Association on January 6, 2001, Fischer had already indicated that "soft pegs" were "crisis-prone" and were not "viable over long periods" (2001, 22). The IMF position now was to keep the goals of the disinflation program unaltered, revise the macroeconomic framework due to the change in the exchange-rate regime, and further reemphasize the structural component of the program.

After the devaluation of the lira, Central Bank Governor Gazi Erçel and Treasury Secretary Selçuk Demiralp resigned. The next day, the Central Bank began to add liquidity into the system, pulling overnight rates to 100–150 percent levels. It was reported that adding liquidity was part of the Central Bank's new strategy to reverse the rate of devaluation to the 10–15 percent range. However, this was not sufficient. With the exchange rate now floating, authorities not only needed to control inflation but also needed to stabilize the Turkish lira, narrow the external deficit, and hope for sustainable growth. A new game plan was needed, but no one seemed to know what to do next.

The Memorandum on Economic Policies

After the resignations from these two key positions, Kemal Derviş, a former economics professor and a longtime World Bank director, was appointed as the state minister in charge of the economy. Derviş immediately went to work with a team of top bureaucrats from the Treasury and the Central Bank, and within a few weeks he had outlined his Program for the Transition to a Strong Economy, detailing what needed to be done for the remainder of 2001 and 2002. The program, which necessitated additional foreign financing as well as major restructuring in the economy, formed the basis of the Memorandum on Economic Policies that was presented to the IMF on May 3, 2001. Described by Derviş as a strengthened version of the 1999 disinflation and fiscal adjustment program, the new program reemphasized restructuring, particularly in the banking sector, and implementing fiscal and monetary policies to restore financial stability to achieve sustainable growth.

The program included banking law reform, financial restructuring, and a complete reorganization of public banks to bring the banking sector closer to EU standards. It allowed for the privatization of state

[19] See IMF *News Brief No. 01/66*, July 28, 2001.

banks through mergers, sales, and liquidations, and aimed at strengthening small banks, developing the legal and institutional framework to increase supervision and auditing in the banking sector, and making the sector more competitive. The banking-sector reform specifically gave priority to the elimination of portfolio losses and liquidity problems of the state- and SDIF-owned banks, some of which had incurred substantial losses due to their required lending at subsidized levels and reliance on overnight funding to cover their losses.[20] These banks were to be given government securities to be sold to the Central Bank, and the proceeds from the sale of the securities were to be used to cover their overnight liabilities. A set of guidelines was also established for setting uniform deposit rates on a daily basis and limits on overnight borrowing from commercial banks.

Under the new program, empowered by an amendment that has given operational independence to the Central Bank since May 2001, an active monetary policy was going to be pursued. In contrast to the previous program, monetary policy was to be conducted by keeping the growth level of the monetary base in accordance with the inflation and GNP growth projections of the program. The Central Bank would monitor money-market interest rates and raise them, if necessary, to alleviate inflationary pressures. It would also carry out foreign-exchange transactions, not to stabilize the exchange rate, but to restore stability in financial markets and lower interest rates if necessary.

With respect to fiscal policy, the new program allowed for significant revenue-enhancement measures, including increases in the petroleum consumption tax and the value added tax. In addition, several measures on the expenditure side, such as reducing SEEs' operating expenses, limiting the volume of support purchases of cereals, and keeping support-price increases in 2001 at targeted inflation, were highlighted. Efforts to privatize key markets, including telecommunications, electricity, natural gas, tobacco, and sugar were also viewed as being essential. These and many other fiscal details were outlined in the program to reduce the government's borrowing requirement and ensure the long-term sustainability of public debt.

The Memorandum set targets for the primary surplus of the public sector at 5.5 and 6.5 percent of GNP in 2001 and 2002, respectively. Inflation rates were estimated at 52.5 percent and 20 percent for 2001

[20] The SDIF, which was established in 1983, has taken over 13 banks since 1997.

and 2002. GNP growth was projected at negative 3 percent in 2001 and was expected to grow annually by 5 to 6 percent in 2002 and 2003. The current account balance was projected to improve, and real interest rates were expected to decline.

After major legislation that was required for the program was passed in the Turkish Parliament on May 15, 2001, the IMF decided to support the program with an additional $8 billion, bringing the total standby credit to $19 billion, of which $3.8 billion was made available immediately.[21] Turkey continued to pass key legislative measures proposed in the new program. However, disagreements began to surface among the coalition partners, particularly with regard to the appointment of the Board of Türk-Telekom. Derviş publicly warned some of the ministers about the necessity of complying with the requirements set out in the Memorandum. The IMF continued its contact with the Turkish government as this legislation was debated, rescheduled a meeting because of the uncertainty concerning the status of the Türk-Telekom Board, and finally approved the eighth review on July 12, 2001, enabling Turkey to draw about $1.5 billion immediately.[22]

As talks continued before the ninth review, adjustments were made in the overall macroeconomic targets.[23] The projected growth for 2001 was changed to a decline of 5.5 percent from a 3 percent decline. Inflation turned out to be higher than expected by about 6 percentage points; it was revised to 58 percent by the end of 2001 and 30–35 percent in 2002. The external balance was expected to have a surplus of $5 billion, due mainly to strong export performance and a decline in overall domestic demand.

After the ninth review and approval of an additional $1.5 billion standby credit on August 3, 2001, macroeconomic indicators began to improve.[24] By late summer, inflation and interest rates on government securities were declining, and the balance of the current account was showing a surplus. Considerable progress was also made in restructuring. Encouraged by these developments, authorities decided to adopt inflation targeting in the fourth quarter. The crisis was coming to an end.

---

[21] See IMF *Press Release No. 01/23*, May 15, 2001.

[22] See IMF *Letter of Intent*, June 26, 2001, and IMF *News Brief No. 01/57*, July 2, 2001.

[23] See IMF *Letter of Intent*, July 31, 2001.

[24] See IMF *News Brief No. 01/73*, August 3, 2001.

The Tragedy of September 11, 2001

The tragedy of September 11 complicated the Turkish efforts. In reaction, the Istanbul Stock Exchange dropped sharply, the depreciation of Turkish lira accelerated, and interest rates rose considerably. Authorities estimated that real GNP would decrease by 8.5 percent in 2001, which was a sharp decline compared to the earlier projection of a decline by 5.5 percent.[25] They also lowered the growth projection by one percentage point to 4 percent in 2002. The introduction of inflation targeting was postponed until 2002, and inflation projections were once again revised from 58 to 65 percent in 2001 and set at a target of 35 percent in 2002. In addition, initially anticipating a surplus of $2.25 billion in the 2001 current account, the authorities projected a deficit of $2 billion for 2002. And they expected to meet the public-sector primary surplus target of 5.5 percent of GNP.

The IMF hinted that additional financial support might be needed for Turkey to achieve its goals. This was noted in the tenth review on November 28, 2001, which also released another $3 billion, bringing the total funding used by Turkey to $11.7 billion.[26] The tenth review took note of Turkey's strong fiscal balance and emphasized that it was critical for the authorities to continue their efforts to achieve the targeted public-sector primary surplus of 6.5 percent of GNP in 2002. Anne Krueger, the IMF's newly appointed first deputy managing director and acting chair, agreed with the Turkish decision to postpone the introduction of inflation targeting until 2002. In the November 28, 2001 IMF news brief, Krueger stated, "As current conditions are not conducive to the successful introduction of formal inflation targeting, the Fund agrees that a delay until 2002 is warranted. The authorities should use this additional time to extend the necessary technical work, further strengthen the fiscal position, bring down inflation, and resolve the remaining problems in the banking system, so that a successful launch of inflation targeting can take place at an early date. In the meantime, the program will continue to be anchored by base money, with firm implementation of the program providing a good basis for a reduction in interest rates."

Turkey's vital statistics at the end of 2001 were as follows: Real GDP had declined by 7.5 percent, inflation had risen to 68.5 percent, and the

[25] See IMF *Letter of Intent*, November 20, 2001.
[26] See IMF *News Brief No. 01/121*, November 28, 2001.

average nominal Treasury bill interest rate stood at close to 100 percent. As a percent of GNP, the primary budget surplus had increased to 6.8 percent, the public-sector borrowing requirement (PSBR) had increased to 16.4 percent, and the current account balance had increased to a surplus of 2.3 percent. At the end of 2001, real GNP was projected to fall by 3 percent, inflation to decline to 52 percent, and the Treasury bill interest rates to fall to 81 percent. As a percent of GNP, the primary surplus of the public sector was expected to rise to 5.5 percent, the PSRB to change to 17.1 percent, and the current account balance to become negative 0.6 percent.[27] As Derviş indicated, "We have had a tough year, but through stringent fiscal policy, the new floating exchange rate regime, and extensive structural reforms, wc have come out of the intensive care unit."[28]

Turkey attempted to lower inflation with exchange-rate targeting under the crawling-peg exchange-rate system, and the outcome was an unforeseen disaster. At the end of 2001, it decided to move on with inflation targeting under the floating exchange-rate regime along with an ambitious agenda of restructuring. The new plan had to work. If it were to fail, the implications for the Turkish economy would have been fairly significant, which would have required a larger volume of financial support to rectify the situation, and no doubt, the credibility of IMF supported stabilization was going to be at stake.

Our assessment of the outcome of the floating exchange rate system and the discussion of the ongoing restructuring efforts will continue in chapter 8. However, first we highlight the economic and policy environment before the 2002 general election in Turkey, which we turn to next.

---

[27] See IMF *Press Release No. 01/23*, May 15, 2001.
[28] *BBC News*, February 4, 2002.

CHAPTER SEVEN

ECONOMIC AND POLICY ENVIRONMENT BEFORE THE 2002 GENERAL ELECTION

"We have committed political suicide," conceded outgoing Prime Minister Bülent Ecevit on November 3, 2002, in response to the results of the parliamentary election. Discontented with the consequences of two consecutive economic crises and weary of the unfulfilled campaign promises of the previous decade, voters had finally spoken out and, as daily *Milliyet*'s front-page headline read, Turkey's inflexible political establishment was finally "red carded." Ecevit's three-party coalition obtained only 14.71 percent of the vote, and none of the parties forming the coalition could make it beyond the 10 percent threshold that was needed to win parliamentary representation. The Justice and Development Party (*Adalet ve Kalkınma Partisi*, abbreviated as AKP in Turkish) won 34.29 percent of the vote, securing a two-thirds majority in the Parliament, and the incoming opposition, the Republican People's Party (*Cumhuriyet Halk Partisi*, CHP), received only 19.38 percent, gaining the remaining third of the seats.

The overall outcome of the election was indeed remarkable, even though the result was not unexpected; it was clearly predicted by most polls conducted in the months leading up to the election. What began to sink in, however, was that a party still perceived to be Islamic by Turkey's strong secular establishment had gained a majority in the Parliament by an incredibly wide margin and was to rule Turkey for the next five years, an outcome that had been inconceivable until then. More striking was that during the campaign, the AKP's alleged religious aspirations were not openly disclosed, but despite the ambiguity, the party appealed to the majority of voters, only a small fraction of whom might have had deep religious inclinations. During the campaign, incumbent Prime Minister Ecevit had repeatedly warned the electorate about the risks and likely complications that might endanger Turkish democracy if a party with a religious agenda were to take over. But the voters were not impressed; Ecevit's calculated warning and a highly inspiring campaign by the CHP and others were hardly enough to block the AKP.

Interestingly, however, a sense of relief and optimism began to prevail as election results were finalized, and both the outgoing and incoming members of the Parliament greeted the outcome in a manner much like that of their contemporaries in Western democracies. The conciliatory tone between the leaders of the AKP and the CHP was unusually cordial, as were the commentaries in the national media, signaling the beginning of a new political era hailed as a requisite for true democracy. A political party that was allegedly religious and perhaps alarmingly radical to some won the election, and all formations within the political spectrum, including Turkey's strong secular establishment, acknowledged the results as the will of people.

The Advancement of Political Islam and the AKP

Since the establishment of the Republic of Turkey, the Islamic movement has always faced resistance from Turkey's rooted secular establishment. Formed in 1970, Turkey's first official Islamic formation, the National Order Party (*Milli Nizam Partisi*, MNP), managed to survive only two years before it was driven out of politics by a Constitutional Court decision. The movement's second attempt was more fortunate and longer-lived. Within two months it gained legitimacy with the creation of a new party labeled the National Salvation Party (*Milli Selamet Partisi*, MSP). During the period 1974–77, the MSP participated in successive coalitions as a junior partner that had significant influence on Turkey's internal and external policies. But the MSP did not survive, either. In September 1980, it was banned from politics along with all other political parties. This time the party closing was ordered by Turkey's pro-secular military, which seized power in September 1980, dissolving the Parliament and taking custody of all party leaders, including the head of the MSP, Necmeddin Erbakan, one of the early leaders of Turkey's modern Islamic movement.

It was more than three years before Erbakan was able to return to active politics, but due to his banned status he had to do so indirectly. Through a former aide, Recai Kutan, he formed the Welfare Party (*Refah Partisi*, RP) in 1983 and four years later assumed the party's leadership. After remaining in opposition for nearly seven years, Erbakan won the December 1995 general election with over 21 percent of the popular vote. On June 28, 1996, he formed a coalition government with former

Prime Minister Tansu Çiller's center-right True Path Party (*Doğru Yol Partisi*, DYP) and was forced out of office one year later.

On January 16, 1998, Turkey's Constitutional Court closed down the Islamist Welfare Party and imposed a five-year political ban on its leaders. This decision, which was mildly criticized at home and in Europe, came after close investigation of actions allegedly committed against the secular state by Erbakan and several of his aides. Prior to and during his controversial term in government, Erbakan was heavily criticized for his anti-secular stand. His macroeconomic management style, perceived to be based on Islamic norms, and his emphasis on shifting Turkey's alliance from the West toward the Islamic world, left little room for tolerance among Turkey's military, which has been the guardian of the secular state since the inception of the Republic.[1] Because of growing skepticism about Erbakan's true intentions, public support for his administration, irresolute for the most part, was also on the decline. His rhetoric was viewed as provocative, uncompromising, and exceptionally intolerable to many who had been nurtured by Atatürk's vision of modernity, secularism, and Western way of life.

While in office, Erbakan's economic policies were received with skepticism. His populist measures, such as raising the wages and salaries of public employees, accelerating investment spending, and lowering interest rates, were less than reassuring in an inflationary environment. But as Erbakan began to unveil parts of the economic program and cautiously follow a neutral rhetoric, public sentiment toward the RP gradually changed. The RP's macroeconomic management appeared much the same as the management style of a centrist party and gave the impression that, despite their Islamic agenda, the Islamists were unlikely to meddle with the dynamics of the free-market system.

Surely, the RP represented Islam-based values, and it was definitely a party that once thrived on a core constituency with various degrees of Islamic indoctrination. However, as a democratically elected party, the RP also seemed reluctant to ignore the priorities and expectations of

---

[1] His proposal for a Just Economic Order (*adil düzen*), summarized by Gülalp (1995, 56), was based on "Islamic principle of justice." Entailing "spiritual development, protection of environment, elimination of corruption, decentralized administration, promotion of individual enterprise, and withdrawal of the state from all economic activities," this economic order, Gülalp suggested, "surpasses both capitalism and communism, in that it includes their positive aspects (profit, free competition) but excludes the negative ones (interest, monopoly, central planning)." For more on political Islam and the Welfare Party, also see Yavuz (1997), Gülalp (2001, 2002), and Öniş (2006).

the populace at large. True, the RP had a strong moral foundation based on Islamic values, but as a party in power it was Turkey's party and was compelled to embrace even those who find comfort at the opposite end of the political spectrum. So this was the message from Erbakan and his party elite. Despite continuing skepticism about his true intentions, the emergence of this fairly moderate and compromising side of the RP, combined with somewhat effective public debt management, raised hopes for a new period in Turkish politics and inspired cautious yet optimistic reviews among commentators.

The Turkish economy, however, needed more than the assurance of a new perspective and heightened expectations. As explained in chapter 4, since 1987, the period when populist policies began to dominate Turkey's political landscape, Turkey had been suffering from extreme macroeconomic imbalances. Excessive government expenditures before major general and local elections put a strain on the budget and drove public financing requirements to uncontrollable levels. The macroeconomic policies followed by Demirel's coalition government, and later continued under the Çiller administration, also led to higher interest rates, higher inflation, and larger deficits, causing the total financing requirement to reach record levels. Consequently, the unusual increase in both foreign borrowing and short-term credits from the Central Bank and the resulting worsening conditions in both public finances and the current account led to the financial crisis in 1994. The austerity plan that was introduced in 1994 by the Çiller government improved GDP growth in the following years but did not eliminate the financial troubles. The negative growth rate of 5.5 percent in 1994 turned positive, rising 7.2 percent in 1995 and 7 percent in 1996. The year-end inflation rate, after surging to 125.5 percent in 1994, managed to decline to 79.8 in 1996. The consolidated budget-financing requirement resulting from the austerity program decreased in 1994 and 1995, but as the economy began to improve the financing requirement also increased, and the budget deficit as a percentage of GDP reached 8.3 percent in 1996.

Thus, when the RP came to power in June 1996, the Turkish economy, with high inflation and persistent budget deficits, was once again in serious need of a stabilization package. This is precisely what was expected of the RP. Yet, the RP had little to offer except for measures to raise revenues from untapped sources with highly publicized resource packages and lengthening the maturity of government debt securities. This was done in an effort to lower domestic borrowing and thus reduce the interest burden of the budget. Consequently, interest rates continued their downward trend, which had started at the beginning of 1996, and inflation also began to move below its 1995 year-end levels. A close examination of the budget between June 1996 and June 1997 shows that the RP administration was particularly successful in lowering the interest burden, but other items in the budget indicate that the government's populist style led to increased expenditures in the non-interest categories of the budget. Even though total expenditures rose by 3.5 percent in real terms, interest expenditures declined by 22 percent, and non-interest budget expenditures rose by 25 percent.[2] So it seemed that there was nothing new other than a commitment to lowering the interest burden in the budget and introducing some ways to accomplish that without exerting destabilizing pressures in the financial markets.

As a politician and senior coalition partner, Erbakan's style at first appeared conciliatory; he not only managed to compromise with the secular establishment, especially during the first eight months of his administration, but he also continued to promote traditional non-secular Islam-based economic and social goals for the satisfaction of the RP's fundamentalist audiences. To the surprise of many, however, the RP suddenly changed its strategy. At a time when independent commentators began to praise some of the RP's macroeconomic performance, the party leadership suddenly moved the economic agenda to the background and renewed the "just order" rhetoric, to the irritation of the secular establishment. Unable (or reluctant) to rein in its more radical party elements, it resorted to a wide range of anti-secular activities, raising serious concerns about the party's congruity with the traditions of a modern centrist party.[3] That finally led to the chain of events resulting in the forced resignation of Prime Minister Erbakan on June 18, 1997, and seven months later to the interruption of this highly controversial Islamic movement.

[2] Thus, a decrease in the primary budget surplus once again raised the question of the sustainability of budget deficits. See "The New Government, Budget Performance and Revised Economic Forecasts for 1997," Yapı and Kredi Bank Occasional paper, no. 2, 1997, 5.

[3] For example, while in power, Erbakan used every opportunity to extend the influence of Islam in both education and the judicial system. He also actively campaigned to build a mosque in Istanbul's Taksim Square, a location with symbolic value for Turkey's secularists. According to a commentary in the *Wall Street Journal*, this was the "rough equivalent of Bill Clinton saying he was replacing the Jefferson Memorial with a Baptist Church." *Wall Street Journal* (January 20, 1998, A18).

The Rise of the AKP

Within a few months, however, the Islamists formed another party called the Virtue Party (*Fazilet Partisi, FP*). Even though the new party was fairly guarded and appeared to be distancing itself from Erbakan,[4] from the secularists' viewpoint, the new party leadership had shown no detachment from Welfare's pro-Islamic "just order" aspiration, which was still radiating hope for Turkey's Islamists. Very few among the secular establishment were convinced that the FP would be a fresh start for this highly determined and disciplined movement. Its members seemed to be willing to embrace democracy and be more cautious in their rhetoric, but that was not sufficient for the skeptics.[5] However, with public opinion polls still showing strong support for the party leadership, there was little doubt that the FP would forgo the opportunity to join future coalitions. But, again, the inevitable happened, and on November 17, 2000, the FP was banned.[6]

Two groups of the banned FP immediately went to work on new formations. The traditionalists, led by the former FP leader Recai Kutan, formed a new party called *Saadet* (SP), which means happiness. A few months later, the modernizers who identified themselves as reformists announced the formation of the Justice and Development Party (AKP), led by former mayor of Istanbul, Tayyip Erdoğan.

Before the November 2002 general election, both formations were represented in the Turkish Parliament, having inherited their seats from the FP. As the continuation of the FP, the traditionalists were determined to build on Erbakan's legacy. But the reformists seemed eager to prevail at a different plateau. Rather than pursuing a political agenda limited to only a core Islamic constituency, they appeared more interested in targeting the wider population by building on the more compromising side of their conservative agenda, hoping to eventually become a centrist party.

---

[4] See Gülalp (2001, 434).

[5] Compared to the Welfare Party, Virtue placed more emphasis on human rights, relied on market mechanisms, and was much more balanced in foreign policy matters. See Öniş (2006, table 7.1).

[6] Two years before Virtue was banned, the *Economist* (May 30–June 5, 1998, 53), wrote: "Virtue, the latest Islamic movement, talks a lot about democracy in general terms. But this may be only because it wants more freedom for its supporters to be demonstratively religious." The same article asked, "[C]an Virtue be compared to the Christian Democrats of Western Europe?" Its response was not different than one would have anticipated from the majority of Turkish democrats: "Not quite, not yet."

By the end of the year 2000 it was still unclear what the future would bring for Turkey's Islamists. Two offspring of the Virtue Party, the SP and the AKP, were busy trying to bring Virtue's loyal followers into their own ranks and to appeal to the masses by communicating the modern Islamist image and the vision of democracy that they claimed to follow. Obviously, to form a legitimate democratic centrist party the Islamists needed to move closer to the median voter within the existing Western-style democratic structure. It was certainly evident that to advance their cause it was no longer possible to follow Erbakan's agenda and thus attract the median voter to their own ideals. It was also becoming increasingly clear to all concerned parties that such a strategy would both delay Turkish democracy from maturing and raise the risk of pushing the system off its course.

Yet the SP chose to remain entrenched in opposition, still guided by the vision and the directives of Erbakan and other loyal party elite. The party's official leader, Recai Kutan, tried to enhance both his own credibility and that of the party by promoting calculated and balanced politics, but that did not completely conceal his position as caretaker of the party and the interminable role that Erbakan continued to play in party politics. For the AKP, on the other hand, it was a fresh start. Energized by its charismatic leader, Tayyip Erdoğan, and rising public support, the party began its broad-minded, sanguine, but yet very calculated campaign to distance itself from Erbakan and at the same time secure an abiding place in Turkish politics. The message that needed to be conveyed was that the AKP was a conservative centrist party and was in no way in conflict with Atatürk's vision of modernity, secularism, and westernization. Certainly, the AKP had chosen to move to the center and represent the median voter, as contemporary politicians would do in matured democracies, rather than hoping to convert the median voter as its pro-Islamic fundamentalist predecessors had tried and failed to do.

To many observers, including Turkey's pro-secular media, academics, and foreign observers, it was becoming very clear that the party's future depended on compromise rather than collision, and most of all, it was essential for the party leadership to distance itself from the outdated, damaging, and confrontational ways that had led to several party closings in the past. The AKP seemed determined to break away from the familiar pattern that proved to be fruitless. Its leaders claimed that the party had changed and aggressively began to pursue public campaigns to prove that that was in fact the case. But the secular establishment had a long memory, and the party's leader, Erdoğan, in particular, had a lot of convincing to do. Many of the public statements that he made in the past were similar in tone to those of his former leader Erbakan.[7] Erdoğan claimed that he had changed, and before the November 2002 general election the polls showed that his followers, who included potential voters from all walks of life, seemed to believe that he had. Skeptics were yet to be convinced, however.

The November 2002 General Election

The November 2002 general election was the defining moment for both formations. The traditionalists lost and the reformists won. The traditionalists' drive for power, and thus the Erbakan legacy, was definitely coming to an end. But the reformists' stunning victory not only seemed to ensure a secure position for the Muslim democrats in the political spectrum but also raised hopes for a more promising and challenging era in Turkey's maturing democracy.

Throughout the campaign, the AKP tried to deliver a message of change and to focus on the economy, transparency, and the rule of law. In doing so, the party leadership, which successfully distanced itself from radical Islam, skillfully targeted the median voter, leaning toward the preferences and priorities of an ordinary citizen. Moreover, unlike its predecessors that had found comfort in Erbakan's vision of Islam, the AKP showed sensitivity toward Turkey's secular heritage and campaigned in compliance with the rule of law and principles of democracy.[8]

---

[7] For more on Erdoğan's political background, see "Erdoğan Predicts Victory as He Tries to Keep Politics Separate from Religion," *Financial Times*, October 30, 2002, p. 19; "How Islamic is Turkey's New Political Star?" *Washington Post*, November 11, 2002; "Eyes on Turkey; the Government is Collapsing. The Economy is a Mess. Voters are Fed Up. The Stage is Set for an Islamic Party to Take Power. Should Europe—and the World—Worry?" *Newsweek*, August 5, 2002; "Well Along Road to Secularism, Fears Detour to Islamism" *New York Times*, January 8, 2002; and "Recep Tayyip Erdoğan: Charlemagne," *Economist*, September 22, 2001.

[8] Öniş (2006) wrote that "in certain respects, the AKP appeared to be more of a European style social democratic party of the third way, compared to its main rival in the November 2002 elections, the Republican People's Party (the CHP). With its emphasis on the benefits of the market, the need to reform the state in the direction of a post-developmental regulatory state, its concern with social justice issues, its commitment to multiculturalism and extension of religious freedoms and its trans-nationalism as exemplified by its commitment to EU membership and the associated set of reforms more than any other political party in recent Turkish society, the AKP projected the image of a political party of the third way more so than the CHP which appeared a

The election results certainly raised the probability of the AKP becoming a centrist party, especially as potential new members began to diversify and broaden the representation of the party's constituents. Now that the AKP had gained a decisive majority, the prevailing view was cautiously reassuring: the party leadership would have no choice but to respond to the political preferences and expectations of the median voter.

During the campaign, the CHP also seemed conciliatory on the contested issues of religion and secularism. As an incoming party and the only opposition in the Parliament, the CHP gained a key advantage in becoming a potential haven for other social democrats and left-leaning formations and strengthened its position as a primary center-left party.

The post-election composition of the Parliament was certainly a source of optimism for Turkish democracy. For the first time since the two-party period that characterized Turkey's evolving democracy dating back to the 1950s, the Turkish Parliament once again was going to house two parties.[9] This was a welcome change for the majority of Turkish voters, who had been disillusioned in the past by inert political fragmentation and the narrow coalitions that it led to. In the past, Turkish voters went to the polls to choose among many parties campaigning on political platforms at or near the center, and in most cases such fragmentation failed to mandate a clear winner. To the dismay of the Turkish voters, the coalition governments that had been formed one after another failed to govern effectively, and to some extent they were all blamed for the economic misfortune and the populist measures they chose to follow.[10] Even to the most critical minds, the differences between Çiller's True Path Party (DYP) and Yılmaz's Motherland Party (ANAP), two parties that claimed a firm position at center-right, were inconsequential and largely personality-based, and thereafter neither

---

much more inward-oriented and in certain respects far more conservative judged by the standards of European style third way politics."

[9] Excluding two short-lived attempts to establish opposition to the ruling CHP in 1924 and 1930, Turkey had a single-party system until 1946. The newly established Democrat Party (DP) formed in 1946 gained strength in the polls and became the ruling party after the 1950 general election. Since then, a multiparty system gradually evolved, and the number of political parties included on the ballot reached 18 parties from a wide political spectrum in the 2002 general election.

[10] Beginning with the 1991 general election, the Turkish people went to the polls three times, and with the exception of a short-lived minority government under the leadership of Bülent Ecevit, about eight different coalitions were formed within a decade.

party was able to convince the voters that it should be the one preferred over the other.

The situation was very much the same among the social democrats. The Republican People's Party, the Democratic Left Party (DSP), and many other smaller parties on the left had caused the partition of left-leaning votes in previous elections. Even in this latest election it did not make sense that the DSP, the CHP, and the newly created New Turkey Party (YTP), a breakaway party from the DSP formed under the leadership of former foreign minister İsmail Cem, failed to join forces. Such a united front could have raised the likelihood of larger social democrat representation in the Parliament and most likely would have changed the overall outcome of the election. Clearly, Turkish voters sent a strong message in the November 2002 election, as they had repeatedly done in the past, hoping that new alliances both in the center-left and in the center-right would lead to lasting political and economic stability.

Why the AKP?

The question in the minds of many observers was whether the election results truly favored the AKP because of its Islamic roots, even if such an affiliation was gently presented during the campaign, or if the failure of the established parties was simply due to deteriorating economic conditions and ineffective policy making during the last three decades. The consensus view of both domestic and foreign media was the latter. As the *New York Times* wrote, "[T]hese elections were not about Islam or whether Turkey would turn its back on modernization and secularism. These elections were about realigning Turkey's politics; they were the eruption of popular wrath against established parties." The article also declared that "[f]rom this perspective, the Justice and Development Party has spoken for the angry, downtrodden, impoverished and excluded masses that have borne the burden of the economic crisis and Turkey's integration with global markets."[11]

During the campaign, the AKP vigorously tried to underscore the economic policy failures of previous regimes and capitalize on its image as a mainstream new political party, willing and able to deliver what the outgoing government allegedly failed to achieve. The outgoing coalition government, shaken by recent economic crises, extremely disadvantaged

[11] See "Islam Takes a Democratic Turn," *New York Times*, November 5, 2002.

because of the heavy short-term costs of the stabilization measures, and in disarray because of heightened concerns about Ecevit's health, had lost credibility and was hardly in a position to be convincing.[12]

In retrospect, Ecevit's coalition had truly committed political suicide, not only by implementing an exceptionally risky stabilization program that no other government had dared to attempt in the past, but also by calling for an early election at a time when the economy was poised to recover from two successive crises. The 1999 program was beyond doubt an ambitious one with a heavy anti-inflationary emphasis, and had it appeared to succeed, it could have been politically rewarding. As inflation began to fall, however, growing political uncertainty and economic complications both internally and externally raised serious questions about the economic outlook, the applicability of the program, and the rapidly diminishing credibility of the Ecevit government. The Çankaya incident between Ecevit and the president, which was fueled by corruption accusations the government seemed less than eager to investigate, compounded the situation. Furthermore, as the economy began to recover from one of its most severe recessions, concerns about Ecevit's health and an increasingly deteriorating political environment captured the headlines, warning about the resulting authority gaps at the top and renewing calls for early elections. Differences within the DSP regarding who might assume responsibility after Ecevit and about the status of the party's future leadership had also surfaced. And while workable political alternatives could have emerged to allow Ecevit's government more time, miscalculation on the part of the coalition partners, particularly the leaders of both the Nationalist Action Party (MHP) and the ANAP, led to an early-election decision nearly 18 months ahead of schedule.

The Economic Factor

The severity of economic conditions was certainly a determining factor, just as it had been during the previous election held nearly four years prior. When the Ecevit coalition was formed after the May 1999

---

[12] Providing evidence in support of the view that economic voting is likely to penalize the incumbents was at the time present in Turkey, the study by Başlevent, Kirmanoğlu, and Şenatalar (2005) identified the AKP's electoral base as consisting of relatively younger voters who have been negatively affected by the economic conditions. The electoral base also included those who were against Turkey's prospective membership in the EU and elimination of the death penalty.

parliamentary elections, economic indicators were dismal and deteriorating. The first quarter GDP growth rate was negative 8.2 percent, and inflation was around 63 percent and increasing. Naturally, combating inflation and promoting growth were used by all political parties as a campaign promise that led to prematurely heightened expectations. However, during the campaign, none of the political leaders other than Ecevit seemed convincing enough. Tansu Çiller, who had served three times as prime minister, was at a great disadvantage because of a highly criticized coalition that she had formed with the Islamist Virtue Party in 1996. Accusations of wrongdoing against the ANAP's Mesut Yilmaz were in the headlines, and his constant bickering with Tansu Çiller had alienated voters. The Virtue Party was severely bruised because of Erbakan's mismanagement while serving as prime minister and the so-called February 28 warning from the National Security Council that subsequently led to his resignation. Finally, the CHP, still vulnerable and in disarray because of internal party divisions, was also far from having a strong showing in the election.

Thus, as expected, Ecevit, who had campaigned on promises of low inflation and transparency, emerged as a winner in 1999 with 22 percent of the counted votes, as did the MHP, coming in second with 19.45 percent. The Islamist Virtue Party shed most of its gains from the previous election, and the ANAP and the DYP came in fourth and fifth with the biggest losses. The CHP, one of the winners of the previous election, failed to obtain the 10 percent minimum vote for gaining representation and thus remained outside the Parliament. However, Ecevit's victory was not adequate to form a majority government. With only 136 of 550 seats gained, the DSP fell far short of the margin needed to form a majority government. Even so, given the post-election composition of the Parliament, Ecevit managed to gain a comfortable majority by forming a three-party coalition with the far-right nationalist MHP and the center-right ANAP.

Post-election public opinion polls showed solid support for the new government, not just for the political stability it represented but also for Ecevit himself—for the fifth time. Ecevit was prime minister in 1974 when Turkey intervened in Cyprus in response to the coup staged by Greek extremists on the island who were backed by the military junta in Greece.[13] As the leader of Turkey's first center-left movement, Ecevit

[13] At the time, Ecevit was in a coalition with the Islamist National Salvation Party, and Erbakan was serving as deputy prime minister.

had won the 1973 election and formed a coalition government with Erbakan. After his brief tenure in government, Ecevit led another coalition with two other center-right parties during 1978–79, when Demirel's first and second National Front governments failed due to heightened economic problems and escalating terrorism. Ecevit's modesty, impeccably clean record, and above all, his genuine respect for human rights, democracy, and the rule of law definitely left a lasting impression in the minds of many Turkish voters. So it was not surprising that after serving three terms as prime minister during the 1970s and then remaining in opposition both in and outside the Parliament for nearly two decades he made a comeback as the head of Turkey's fifty-sixth and fifty-seventh governments.[14]

In 1999, Ecevit was once again the nation's hope. A newcomer, the MHP's Devlet Bahçeli, and the ANAP's experienced leader, former Prime Minister Mesut Yılmaz, were also welcomed as two well-deserving partners in the government despite rooted ideological differences that had kept their parties apart in the past.[15] The coalition government's first major undertaking was the disinflation program that included tight fiscal and monetary policies and an anti-inflationary exchange-rate design. The disinflation program, supported by the December 1999 standby agreement with the IMF, also emphasized the structural reforms needed to make the fiscal adjustment sustainable, improve economic efficiency, and accelerate the privatization of state economic enterprises. As described in detail in chapter 6, both the restructuring efforts and the exchange-rate-based monetary policy that were proposed in the program were expected to lower interest rates and reduce inflationary expectations.

Within the first six months after the implementation of the program, macroeconomic indicators began to improve. The GDP growth rate turned positive in the first quarter of 2000, and inflation began to decelerate to its lowest level a year later. But sharply declining interest rates and deteriorating external balances raised concerns about the sustainability of the program. Rumors of possible devaluation of the

[14] Before the formation of the coalition government, Ecevit also served for about six months as a prime minister in a minority government formed after the resignation of Mesut Yilmaz, who had been the prime minister since July 1997.

[15] During the 1970s, Ecevit's social democrat supporters and the National Action Party sympathizers, a highly organized ultranationalist group known as the Gray Wolves, were at odds, frequently clashing during the political violence of the 1970s.

Turkish lira and bank bailouts, heightened by speculation concerning the liquidity levels in the banking sector, led to massive capital flight and thus to the November 2000 crisis. The situation was contained quickly and returned to normal through effective crisis management. Inflation continued to decrease during the early months of 2001 but resumed its upward trend after the February crisis; GDP also fell throughout 2001. Even though 2002 was a year of recovery, the economic upturn was not reflected in the living conditions of the larger population.

In summary, when the Ecevit government took office in 1999, the macroeconomic environment was in need of serious stabilization and structural adjustment measures. As has been the case in the past in Turkey and elsewhere, if such measures had been successful, they would have been likely to have led to a beneficial outcome in the long run at the expense of adverse output and income distribution effects, at least in the intermediate term. Yet Ecevit's government went to work, and as the economy began to suffer from the pains of the recovery, additional measures, more painful, were required and carried out. Most of the structural reforms that were necessary for the improvement of the macroeconomic environment, and, moreover, to prepare Turkey for the future membership in the EU, were being adopted at a speed not common in the recent history of the Turkish Parliament. It was the tremendous cost that the Turkish people were bearing, and later the lack of leadership due to Ecevit's alleged health complications, that led to a highly uncertain political environment, which made early elections unavoidable. In retrospect, one more year for the Ecevit administration could have changed the outcome of the November election.

The Corruption Factor

Corruption was another consideration that may have swayed voters in the November 2002 election. Political parties in Turkey tend to capitalize on the misconduct of their opponents, perhaps more intensely than their contemporaries do in other democracies, and during political campaigns they intensify their rhetoric, generously offering promises of transparency, the rule of law, and an effective agenda against corruption. With almost no exception, such promises take less priority once the campaigns are over and new governments are formed. Even at times when incoming governments seem overly eager to fulfill their promises, they quickly find the task impossible and thus choose to either maintain the status quo or apply individual-level deterrence as a means of reducing corruption.

What helped social democrats to emerge as winners in the previous parliamentary election held in 1999 were the trust and the confidence that the Turkish voters had vested in Bülent Ecevit. His integrity and an unblemished political career were great assets throughout the campaign, and while in office not one incident that would tarnish his impeccable record either directly or indirectly was linked to him. Yet during his administration, corporate and political corruption prevailed, despite serious attempts to alter the inefficient structural (bureaucratic, legal, and political) conditions that continued to nurture corrupt behavior. Structural alterations, which intensified after the Çankaya incident, the investigation of corruption charges that fueled the controversy between the president and the prime minister, had little positive impact on the image of the traditional politician, who had increasingly become credibility-deficient. That image grew over time not only because of a corrupt few that would be present in any parliamentary system but also because of highly publicized corrupt practices that seemed to be the tip of the iceberg to many, especially when government and the Parliament failed to pursue effective policy responses.

Causes of Corruption

The causes of corruption and how to deal with it have not been different in Turkey than in any other country at a similar level of development. Corruption results from a collaborating effort between public officials and private parties, and it is a product of interacting individual variables (greed, unethical temptations, etc.) and structural inefficiencies (bureaucratic, legal, and political). Deterrence based on the likelihood of detection and prosecution, as has been the traditional approach to corruption control in many instances, is a necessity both on moral and legal grounds, especially when the corrupt act is a result of individual variables. But it is of limited effectiveness if corruption results from structural inefficiencies. Bureaucratic impediments, such as red tape and procedural details, for example, impose additional time and resource costs on potential violators, who rationally resort to some form of corruption in return for an accelerated economic transaction. Due to bureaucratic obstacles, private entities attempt to avoid the formal channels through illegitimate means to achieve desired social outcomes. The degree of vagueness or lack of property rights concerning the ownership of societal resources is another source of corrupt practices. A public official who is expected to safeguard the public's interest may be tempted to enforce rules and regulations in exchange for private benefit.[16] Also, low political participation, rational ignorance, and the absence of political pressure groups vary with the level of corruption. For example, as Nas, Price, and Weber (1986) argued, "Nepotism and patronage as methods of awarding governmental jobs and contracts are practices that are difficult to maintain under intense public scrutiny" (p. 115). Under such circumstances, an appropriate policy response may have to be oriented toward structural changes: improving bureaucratic effectiveness, introducing legal changes to clarify property rights, and initiating political reforms aimed at increasing political participation.

In Turkish politics, such structural inefficiencies, which prevailed throughout the post-World War I period, had fashioned a type of politician and citizen accustomed to rationalizing how and when to expedite a business transaction, especially when it involved the public sector. Over time, violating some of the rules and procedures that created obstacles for the efficient conduct of business had become an expected response, a sort of rationalization that overlooked the immoral and illegitimate nature of such transactions. Seemingly, increasing deterrence in such an institutional setting did more harm than good. Both the unethical public official and private participants retreated when corrupt practices were in the spotlight, usually after a national scandal; then they reemerged to continue business as usual. By attempting to uncover the recurring corrupt practices, society at times faced the risk of forgoing productive transactions, thus creating likely negative effects on the nation's output. Thus, it was not unexpected when politicians who first showed great enthusiasm to fight corruption later dismissed the issue, especially when confronted with adverse income and output effects.

Of course, corrupt practices, no matter how they are rationalized or whatever their output effects might turn out to be, should not be overlooked. Deterrence should not be viewed as a policy of last resort, either. As a second viable option, society could effectively fight corruption by pursuing organizational, legal, and political restructuring. For that to be effective, the credibility of public officials needs to be restored, and

[16] Another form of corruption concerning the legal system may occur when there is a lack of congruence between social demands and political outcomes. Society's preferences may dictate a resource allocation, but the legal structure does not authorize such an alteration. See Nas, Price, and Weber (1986).

individuals must be encouraged to conduct business within a corruption-free environment. Both options, however, remained a challenge for most Turkish governments in the past, and none of them managed to make any significant progress in fighting corruption. The Ecevit government was no exception.

The Failure of the Traditional Politician

The November 2002 election penalized more than just the members of the ruling coalition parties. It was the traditional politician—regardless of party origin—who seemed to have been voted out. The outgoing members of the Parliament, as a group, were considered productive. Yet public sentiment toward the parliamentarians was still negative and became much worse as a result of untimely and miscalculated actions that they attempted before the election. In the midst of Turkey's worst economic crisis, for example, populism should have been avoided. As the Turkish people anxiously hoped for economic recovery, Kemal Derviş's efforts to turn the economy around continued to receive a cool reception from some of the coalition partners, who resisted the IMF-imposed structural reforms, fearing possible adverse effects on the well-being of their constituents. The media, the business world, and major participants in the financial markets grew restless. Public dissatisfaction grew even more pronounced when several parliamentarians, sensing a likely defeat in the forthcoming elections, tried to revoke their early-election decision. Furthermore, seemingly indifferent to the fact that the economy was struggling with severe resource constraints, the deputies' repeated attempts to legislate a salary and benefit package to better ensure their future certainly did not bode well. While the standard of living of the majority of Turkish people continued to deteriorate, the growing dissatisfaction with lawmakers turned into resentment.[17]

Since the early days of Turkey's multiparty electoral system, the disconnect between voters and politicians has been a weakness in the nation's maturing democracy. True, Turkish voters always went to the polls and revealed their political preferences, freely casting their votes

---

[17] Referring to Turkey's traditional policy makers as "political grandees," the *Financial Times* wrote, "The fate of this self-obsessed group, whose bickering, incompetence and corruption did so much to create the economic and financial turmoil of recent years, was richly deserved, they had disconnected from ordinary Turks whose lives they did so little to improve." See "Leader: Turkish Delight," *Financial Times*, November 5, 2002.

for the party of their choice. Faced with a myriad of constraints and political imperfections common to all democratic societies, including those resulting from rational ignorance, short-sightedness, and special interest effects, they freely expressed their preferences, casting their votes out of either self-interest, civic duty, or both. Politicians also complied with the basic rules of collective decision making. Beginning with the 1950 parliamentary election, most governments became increasingly more responsive to voters' preferences. It is reasonable to assume that Turkish democracy, in spite of its short history, performed fairly well, particularly from the demand (voters') side of the collective decision making process.

Yet, one of the major influences on Turkish politics has been the unique role of the state in Turkish society. None of the centrist parties made it clear to their constituents to what extent the state was a factor in economic and social life, other than endorsing an interventionist state that would pursue economic development and growth and also promote the interests of their electoral coalition. Rather than building their platform on issues relevant to the traditional allocation, distribution, and stabilization functions of the state, as is the case in most modern democracies, mainstream political parties in Turkey have instead emphasized their ideological differences.[18] The existence of the governing parties either on the left or the right was therefore highly dependent on public expenditures to maintain a minimal winning electoral coalition.[19] In the latest election, Turkish voters may seem to have sent a clear message that such traditional politics needed to change. It has also become clear that in order for Turkish democracy to gain strength, the collective decision-making process must evolve along the lines of contemporary institutions, organizational efficiency, and public policy making.

To summarize, this chapter highlighted some of the economic and political factors that might have led to the AKP's strong showing in the 2002 parliamentary election. Among likely factors that may have

[18] The realization of a politician as a public goods supplier in the collective decision-making context is a relatively recent phenomenon, and hopefully it will begin to make a difference.

[19] For example, referring to Özal's period, Waterbury (1992) stressed patronage politics and the interventionist character of Turkey's public sector. In addition to programs designed to "enhance economic efficiency and state fiscal strength," governing parties also rely on discretionary expenditures for "coalition maintenance through state patronage" (p. 49).

underscored the defeat of Ecevit's coalition government and thus brought Turkey's alleged Islamists to power, the chapter focused on economic hardship, the declining credibility and influence of traditional politics, and the weak public policy responses to corrupt practices in the past. Despite occasional bickering and highly publicized disagreements within the coalition, the outgoing Ecevit government made an attempt to overcome some of the critical economic issues that no government in the past had dared to tackle. However, time was not on its side. Turkey's recent economic problems were definitely the doing of governments dating back to the late 1980s, Islamist and secular alike, and none of the previous administrations had a clear mandate or the opportunity to initiate the needed stabilization and structural adjustments. The economic literature is full of explanations regarding the hardship society may have to bear during serious and committed austerity programs. Moreover, it is an undeniable fact that what a country in a position similar to Turkey's needed to do was consistently implement and monitor austerity measures in spite of their high costs. That requirement was there each time a new government was formed during the last decade or so. Also, Ecevit, a man of high principles, might have appeared stubborn at times, especially during the controversy regarding his replacement when the status of his health was at issue. One can hardly argue, though, that he was the focal point of public resentment toward the traditional politician's image. When it comes to the issue of fighting corruption, although Ecevit may not have been as aggressive as he could have been, very few in Turkey would question his integrity or claim that his administration accomplished less in this area than any other government had in the past. Ecevit's government implemented an economic recovery and restructuring plan with long-term rewards and short-term costs, and in the short run it had to pass the torch to the AKP. Will the AKP continue with follow-up policies, move on with the recovery that started during the post-2001 crisis, and keep the economy on a more stable and policy environment? This is the question we address next.

CHAPTER EIGHT

MACROECONOMIC POLICIES AND OUTCOMES DURING THE POST-2002 ELECTION PERIOD

In December 2002, the European Council Presidency promised Turkey the start of accession negotiations for full membership contingent to Turkey's full compliance with the Copenhagen political criteria.[1] Turkey had applied for full membership in 1987, formed a customs union with the Community in 1996, and obtained candidacy status in the 1999 Helsinki summit. And with the December 2002 decision, it was given conditional assurance for starting the accession talks. Considering that the membership goal had been a driving force for Turkey's modernization for nearly three decades, the conditional decision was rather disappointing for Turkey, but on the positive side the seemingly affirmative and somewhat promising resolution was not all that insignificant. Despite the strong European opposition to Turkish membership and a growing tendency among the member states to lean toward granting Turkey special status instead of full membership, the Council did in fact reconfirm Turkey's eligibility to become a candidate, an outcome that was inconceivable a few years earlier.

During the 1990s, Turkey's prospective membership had become a lesser priority for the EU. With the emphasis of EU enlargement gradually shifting toward East Europe, particularly after the end of the Cold War, the Council was pushing its agenda toward building the foundation of a future Europe by expanding to the East but not necessarily including Turkey, at least not yet. To most Europeans, Turkey was too large and culturally different to integrate with, but at the same time strategically too important to ignore. So, given the geopolitical reality of the time, the EU was prepared to welcome any justification or initiative to put Turkey on hold while keeping its European perspective alive. At the conclusion of the Union's 1997 Luxembourg summit, the EU launched its historic enlargement process, which included three Baltic nations, five Central

[1] The Council of the European Union, *Presidency Conclusions*, December 12–13, 2002, Copenhagen.

and East European applicant states, Cyprus, and Malta.[2] The best the EU could do in Luxembourg was to point out the conditions that Turkey needed to satisfy in order to gain candidacy status, conditions that at the time seemed unattainable, at least in the medium term.

However, despite the discriminatory tone of the Luxembourg decision, Turkey determinedly took the necessary steps for the introduction of the needed reforms and began to lobby intensely to improve its status, consequently changing it from eligibility to candidacy for full membership. It obtained the candidacy status in the 1999 Helsinki summit, and thus was promised in 2002 a conditional date for starting accession negotiations, with the expectation that Turkey would fulfill the Copenhagen criteria.

Turkey had already been in the process of restructuring its economy and its judicial system along the lines of the Copenhagen criteria for more than a decade. The Ecevit government, in particular, instituted key economic reforms that made the mark, but still more had to be done to bring Turkey closer to its European destination. The new government formed by the AKP leadership also seemed eager to proceed with the restructuring process, firmly committed to easing the way toward full membership in the EU. In the past, irrespective of the EU membership, the Turkish people had been anxious to enjoy the fruits of a modern democratic society. However, mindful of the prevalent political dynamics, most governments seemed hesitant to expedite the restructuring process, partly because there was no clear signal from the EU regarding the prospect of full membership. Now that the EU's historic decision had finally been made, Turkey had a much clearer vision of its future, and therefore the AKP seemed in a much better position to further Turkey's reforms and move forward with the EU project. With diminished political uncertainty in Turkey, the EU's almost certain commitment to start accession negotiations, and the majority of Turkish people backing EU membership, further restructuring had clearly become a top priority.

This chapter focuses on Turkey's restructuring efforts and the reform process that gained renewed urgency after the EU's affirmative December 2002 decision, which immediately followed the general election. Recapitulating the main highlights of the economic developments before the

[2] The Council of the European Union, *Presidency Conclusions*, Press Release, Nr: SN400/97, December 12, 1997, Luxembourg.

decision, the chapter examines macroeconomic policies and outcomes during the post-election period and briefly examines some of the major reforms that have been introduced since then.

The Economy before the 2002 Copenhagen Summit

Turkey had already experienced two consecutive financial crises and consequently had undergone a major revision of the anti-inflationary program that was introduced in 1999. The program had been designed to lower inflation, accelerate privatization, and emphasize restructuring. But due to external factors, such as higher oil prices and rising interest rates on emerging market debt, and internal factors, such as delays in privatization and restructuring, as well as increased domestic aggregate demand resulting from rapidly declining interest rates, the economy's vital indicators deteriorated. An ongoing corruption investigation in the banking sector and an overvalued Turkish lira also led to heightened speculation of devaluation, and thus short covering of foreign currency positions; a liquidity crunch followed.

The liquidity crisis was quickly contained through Central Bank intervention. Financial markets also responded favorably to the news of improved Turkish-EU relations and additional financial support from the IMF. However, as the economy was set to recover from the distress of the November 2000 crisis, a second debacle followed two months later. An unprecedented political mishap led to a severe financial crisis and thus to a major revision of the 1999 disinflation program. Turkey unexpectedly abandoned the crawling peg exchange-rate system in favor of a floating exchange-rate system. And with a strengthened new version of the 1999 disinflation program, the role of monetary policy was changed to pursuing disinflation by relying on the monetary base rather than the exchange rate as an anchor. In addition to this new policy of implicit inflation targeting, the program also reemphasized restructuring and adopting tight fiscal policy to restore stability in goods and financial markets and thus achieve sustainable growth.

The 2001 program, further complicated by the tragedy of September 11, remained on track. But it continued to be a source of anxiety for the remainder of 2001 as economic growth first stalled, inflation rose, and—during the early part of 2002—both indicators began to improve significantly. The GDP growth rate, after dipping to its lowest level in the fourth quarter of 2001, was just beginning to recover. The inflation rate was also falling, but any increase in expectations of inflation was still carrying the risk of quickly reversing the trend. Furthermore, the total outstanding external debt, after declining throughout 2001, was also rising.

The economic and financial conditions of 2001 pretty much reflected the tone of the January 28, 2002, letter of intent to the IMF, which outlined the request for a new standby agreement for 2002–2004.[3] The objectives of the 2002–04 program were to restore confidence in financial markets through greater interest-rate and exchange-rate stability, improve the resiliency of the economy against future crises, and move forward with inflation targeting and sustainable economic growth. The emphasis this time was on structural reforms, which included the completion of banking and public-sector restructuring and privatization, and the enhancement of fiscal transparency.

The IMF executive board responded favorably. Under the new agreement, signed on February 4, 2002, Turkey agreed to continue to implement the strengthened program and receive an additional $16 billion in standby credits to compensate for the projected financing gap due to the September 11 shock. Obligated to strictly comply with the standby agreement, Turkey was in no position to tolerate any shock to its economy that could once again lead to financial turmoil. The economic and social costs of financial crises were enormous, and any further complication that would have delayed the recovery could have been even more costly.

War in Iraq

War in Iraq increasingly became a possibility during the early months of 2003, and to enter Iraq from the north, the United States wanted access to both Turkish airspace and military bases, and to have the option of deploying a significant number of U.S. ground forces through Turkey. Overwhelmed by the extent of the U.S. request, the newly formed Turkish government was facing its first foreign policy crisis and was forced to make critical decisions that were to potentially impact Turkey's strategic alliances. The majority of the Turkish people opposed the war, as did the EU. Yet denying strategic support to a longtime ally that seemed determined to attack Iraq and remove Saddam Hussein from power undoubtedly was going to have consequences. Having just

[3] See IMF *Letter of Intent*, January 18, 2002.

experienced two consecutive crises that had distressed its financial markets, a war in Iraq, or even the prospect of it, was a major setback for Turkey in its effort to stabilize its economy and speed up its reforms.

Starting in the second half of 2002, the U.S. administration began pressuring the Turkish government to dispatch the authorization motion to the Parliament, expecting an outcome that would have paved the way for troop deployment through Turkey. Despite differences on issues of national interest to both sides, it was inconceivable for the United States to anticipate that Turkey would not comply. Unable to withstand the U.S. pressure, Turkey was also aware that it had to eventually yield. Hoping to find a mutually acceptable middle ground, the Turkish government continued negotiations with the United States and finally sent the motion to the Parliament on March 1, 2003. Surprisingly, the vote in the Parliament fell short of approval by a narrow margin.

Because the outcome was so close, the United States was convinced that the Turkish government would reconsider, so it further increased the pressure. It was vital for the United States to secure the northern front in its plan A, the most preferable strategy for invading Iraq. But the Turkish government, also disappointed by the outcome, seemed more concerned about the likely political fallout in the event that the motion was resubmitted and rejected for a second time.

During the days leading up to the war in Iraq, which began on March 20, 2003, Turkey was still indecisive. Months of hard bargaining and negotiations were inconclusive, and as far as the U.S. administration was concerned, the Turkish deal seemed to be over. Not unexpectedly, therefore, the United States put plan B into action and suddenly Turkey was out of the equation. Secretary of State Colin Powell informed Foreign Minister Gül that it was too late for the troop deployment from the north and that overflight rights alone would do. In view of this last-minute change in U.S. strategy, the Turkish Parliament met once again behind closed doors and overwhelmingly approved Powell's reduced request.

In the early post-invasion period, despite Powell's visit and his much-needed soothing words to mend relations, the strain between the two countries continued but did not last long.[4] As the United

[4] The U.S. administration continued to distance itself and seemed hesitant to involve Turkey in the post-invasion restructuring of the region. And that led to the growing impression in the Turkish media that Turkish sensitivities on critical issues of northern Iraq were no longer a priority for the United States. See Taha Akyol, *Milliyet*, June 4, 2003.

States continued to face setbacks in Iraq, especially during late 2003 and early 2004, commentaries on the future of the alliance began to surface, pointing out that as long as the geopolitical realities of the region remained, the alliance should continue, and it did. Both sides began to show a strong will, not only to mend the relationship but also to deepen the alliance on the basis of shared democratic values and common economic interests.[5]

Post-Invasion Macroeconomic Environment

The motion incident with the United States did not create lasting complications in the economy. The manner in which the AKP handled the situation with the United States was certainly a source of uneasiness, but the outcome did not appear to be as damaging as some had feared. The volatility in financial markets while the motion was being debated in Parliament was short-lived, and thus the impact on the economy was inconsequential.

During the period after the invasion, Turkey's vital statistics began to show large improvements. GDP, which had been declining since the last quarter of 2002, rose in the third quarter of 2003 and continued its robust growth during the rest of the year. Behind this strong performance was an impressive increase in total factor productivity; its contribution to GDP growth nearly doubled during the period 2002–2005 compared to the 1996–2000 period, rising from 24.5 percent to 42 percent annually. Also, during the period 2002–2005, the contributions of capital accumulation and employment to GDP growth were 51.7 percent and 6.3 percent, respectively.[6] Inflation was also decreasing. After the announcement of the 1999 disinflation program, it was already on a downward trend. But after hitting a low of 33.4 percent in February 2001, it began to climb once again, reaching another high a year later and from then on began to decrease to a low of 26.4 percent during the first month of 2003. After rising to 30.7 percent two months into the Iraq conflict, it then began to decline steadily to a single-digit level in May 2004 for the first time in more than three decades.

---

[5] See, for example, two commentaries by Recep Tayyip Erdoğan, "My Country is Your Faithful Ally and Friend," *Wall Street Journal*, March 31, 2003, and "A Shared Strategic Vision," *Washington Post*, April 21, 2003, p. A-23.

[6] State Planning Organization, *Ninth Development Plan, 2007–2013*, 24.

Other indicators, including the current account deficit, the primary budget surplus, and the overall budget deficit also improved, with slight deviations from their projected levels. Government tax revenues increased and expenditures declined as a result of a drop in domestic interest payments and a minor decline in public investment. That led to a primary budget surplus of 5.2 percent of GNP and an overall budget deficit of 11.3 percent of GNP in 2003, both deviating from their targeted levels. One possible reason for the failure to meet the targeted primary budget surplus was the acceleration of public spending at the end of 2003.[7] The current account deficit was 3.4 percent of GNP in 2003, fractionally above its projected level, largely due to the real appreciation of the Turkish lira and the expanding trade deficit. The rise in imports was the result of the high rate of growth in industrial output, growing domestic demand, and the increase in crude oil prices.[8]

By the end of 2003, despite the risks of accelerating domestic demand, a widening current account deficit, and domestic debt and its composition, the economy remained on a sustainable low-inflation and high-growth path.[9] And the recovery that started after the 2001 crisis continued paving the way for a more stable economic and policy environment. Fiscal discipline also continued with revenue enhancement programs, and monetary policy became much more effective as the Central Bank increasingly became independent and credible. With a gradual move toward formal inflation targeting, and by relying on the monetary base and short-term interest rate cuts, monetary policy proved effective in bringing inflation down significantly.

Restructuring of the Turkish Economy

Economic restructuring has been an ongoing process since the early 1980s, with the expectation of a gradual reduction in the state's resource-allocation role and its impact on the Turkish economy. Before 1980, the

---

[7] Because of under-spending, the primary surplus through November was over the projected level, but the accelerated spending in December eliminated the over-performance. See IMF *Country Report No. 04/227*, 14, July 29, 2004.

[8] Ministry of Finance, *Turkish Economy in 2004*, 160. Also see the Central Bank of the Republic of Turkey, *2003 Annual Report and Monetary Policy Report 2004-I and 2004-II*, and the IMF *Country Report No. 04/227*, 11, July 29, 2004.

[9] On July 30, 2004, after concluding the Article IV consultation with Turkey, the IMF specifically noted that "vulnerabilities remain." In addition to short-run challenges, major concerns included the size and composition of the domestic debt, exchange rate and interest rate shocks, the quality of fiscal adjustment, and the pace of restructuring. See IMF *Public Information Notice No. 04/87*, August 10, 2004.

allocation functions of the state had been centered on promoting growth and development, providing goods and services in key industries, and encouraging investment and the formation of private capital. Throughout the period, which started during the protectionist years of the 1930s and continued through the planning decades of the 1960s and the 1970s, the state developed a unique partnership between the public and private sectors and had become the driving force behind the inward-looking growth strategy. That lasted more than four decades, during which time the state advocated heavy industrialization and strategically increased its presence in the economy through the formation of state economic enterprises (SEEs), producing a wide range of production and consumption goods, both public and private.

However, by the end of the 1970s, the inward-looking strategy was no longer sustainable because of the deteriorating economic and financial conditions. As detailed in chapter 3, Turkey's heavy foreign debt and supply-side shocks prompted by the energy crisis of the 1970s led to high inflation, shortages of foreign currency, and unsustainable budget and current account deficits. Consequently, a dramatic change in industrialization strategy and restructuring followed, which was designed to promote an outward-looking competitive economic and financial structure.

Economic and financial restructuring intensified during the 1980s and has continued to date with the introduction of key political and economic reforms in the hope of modernizing the Turkish economy. Through liberalization, deregulation, privatization, and public-sector reforms, government policies were aimed at aligning Turkey to the forces of an open market economy, thus promoting long-run growth through trade and financial-sector liberalization and increased efficiency in both public and private sectors.

The outcome was not always as expected, however. At times there was tension between stabilization and restructuring efforts, and usually the latter intensified during periods of high growth, which Turkey experienced throughout the 1980s.[10] Yet restructuring continued during the 1990s and beyond, despite recurring economic and financial crises. The

[10] The sustainability of these reforms was endangered due to excessive public-sector dissaving (Conway 1988). The outcomes of the reforms were also far below expectations because of the patronage politics and interventionist character of Turkey's public sector (Waterbury 1992).

restructuring during the 1980s and early 1990s, in particular, focused on restoring competitiveness in external markets and stimulating aggregate supply through trade liberalization and improved market conditions. The economic environment also improved through reforms in the financial sector. However, the policy environment, dominated by an institutional setting partly incompatible with competitive-market forces, continued to allow intervention.

After the two consecutive financial crises in 2000 and 2001, various reforms were front-loaded in order to promote economic efficiency. These included legislative acts to phase out state-supported purchase programs and price-support mechanisms, reduce monopolistic practices and increase the pace of the SEE privatization program, and develop measures to enhance efficiency in the sugar, tobacco, telecom, electricity, and natural gas sectors.[11]

SEEs, in particular, were in need of restructuring. During the 1980s, growing losses and inefficiencies of the SEEs had led to major reform ideas, including measures to grant administrative autonomy, promote competitive pricing and output policies to increase profitability, and ultimately proceed with privatization. But for most of the 1980s and early 1990s there was not much effort expended to increase the efficiency of the SEEs nor a willingness to relinquish control over public resources, mainly because of political constraints (Öniş 1996, 164–68). Privatization did not become a serious consideration until the late 1990s, as Turkey's efforts of aligning its economy with the EU intensified, and it was later incorporated as a top priority in the 2001 stabilization program. Thereafter, with increased privatization efforts, the state gradually began to withdraw from basic industries that should have traditionally been attended to by the private sector, and it took the necessary steps to return to its primary public functions.[12]

After 2001, many reforms were introduced to improve fiscal transparency and management, including the elimination of several budgetary and extra-budgetary funds and legislation of a new public procurement law and a new law on public finance and debt. Before 1999, there were

[11] As stated by Kemal Derviş, the main architect of the 2001 program, intensive restructuring was intended to demonstrate the strong will of the administration and thus establish credibility. See Derviş (2003).

[12] As of the end of 2004, about 70 percent of 241 companies had already been privatized through either public-share or asset sales, and there were 39 SEEs, of which 19 were included in the privatization program. See State Planning Organization, *Pre-Accession Program, 2004*, 64–66.

13 extra-budgetary funds, accounting for 15 percent of the central government's primary expenditures, and none of them were subject to parliamentary review. There were also a large number of budgetary and revolving funds belonging to off-budget institutions.[13] As part of the 2001 restructuring package, between December 2000 and April 2002, a number of the budgetary and extra-budgetary funds were closed and the revolving funds were consolidated.[14]

Among other legislative acts, the public procurement law was introduced in order to set technical and financial criteria for contractors in line with EU standards and to establish an independent agency to enforce the new standards. The new law on public finance and debt mandates that the Treasury, as the single borrowing authority, is to be endowed with the responsibilities of formulating public debt strategy, assessing risk, and coordinating the management of domestic and foreign debt portfolios.[15]

In 2003, various further reforms were introduced to decentralize the economy, attain a public- and private-sector output mix that was congruent with a contemporary market economy, and achieve overall efficiency in resource allocation. Most of these measures were specifically introduced to eventually downsize the state sector, make the Turkish economy less vulnerable to internal and external shocks, and improve internal dynamics of the economy to make Turkey more compatible with the EU nations that it hoped to join in the future. A direct tax reform (January 2004) was passed to gradually transform free-trade zones into export-processing zones, reduce income tax holidays, and align tax benefits with international practices. The reform also introduced subsidies to stimulate employment in poorer regions.

Most of these expeditiously introduced measures were old initiatives, but because of political constraints, complications stemming from the political fragmentation, and the resulting coalition governments that dominated the 1990s, they were not finalized. Given the patronage-

[13] IMF *Report on the Observance of Standards and Codes*, June 27, 2000.

[14] As of April 2002, one budgetary and five extra-budgetary funds were remaining. See IMF *Update Report on the Observance of Standard Codes*, April 4, 2002. Also, as stated in the Public Financial Management and Control Law, which was approved in December 2003 and took effect in 2006, budgets of the remaining extra-budgetary funds and revolving funds were to be included in the budget of relevant administrative units. See State Planning Organization *Pre-Accession Program, 2004*, 90, and *Pre-Accession Program, 2006*, 79.

[15] IMF *Letter of Intent*, April 3, 2002.

oriented politics that characterized coalition governments and the adverse real output and income distribution implications of restructuring in the short run, it is understandable that previous governments did not aggressively pursue such public-policy responses. The benefits of such restructuring are long run and, therefore, it was not unusual for public response not to be immediate and rewarding. But after being hit by a series of economic and financial crises, many of these structural reforms had to be introduced in response to conditions set by the IMF as part of standby agreements. So they were hastily introduced and approved by the Turkish Parliament before the November 2002 election. With these important legislative acts, Turkey took an important step in not only modernizing its economy and bringing it closer to its European contemporaries but also paving the way to an economic and policy environment where the state's allocation and stabilization functions became more significant, as they are in modern democratic societies.

It should be noted that the stable political landscape after the November 2002 elections and the commitment of the new government to intensifying the already-implemented stabilization measures were indeed major contributing factors to the improved economic environment. The upward trend in GNP growth had already begun after the economy suffered its two financial crises in 2000 and 2001, and inflation had been on a downward trend since then. But with the new government, Turkey's vital statistics were showing signs of continued recovery and significant improvements.

Central Bank Independence and Bank Restructuring

Before 1986, the monetary authority had a passive role and lacked independence. Money supply was determined based on total credit expansion, and public-sector credits and interest rates were the two main monetary policy instruments that were used to back the government's growth and development policies. After 1986, despite a series of legislation that allowed the monetary authority to adopt contemporary central bank practices, monetary policy continued to be accommodative, frequently monetizing the public-sector deficits that resulted. The Central Bank thus lacked both instrument- and goal-independence, and it took more than two decades for it to finally gain its autonomy. With the passage of Article 4 of the Law on the Central Bank of the Republic of Turkey (as amended by Law No. 4651) in April 2001, the Central Bank's role was finally redefined as one of price stability, bringing Turkey's monetary policy a bit closer to the policies practiced in contemporary economies. With this major step toward Central Bank independence, Turkey also moved much closer to adopting formal inflationary targeting, which in 2004 helped to bring down its three-decade-old high inflation.

Beginning in 1980, Turkey gradually removed restrictions on interest rates and capital flows and established the convertibility of the Turkish lira. Turkish banks quickly adapted to this evolving and increasingly liberalized financial environment by changing the structure of their balance sheets. After the 1990s, as the means of financing the public-sector deficits tilted toward bond financing and short-term foreign capital, banking business practices began to change, as did the composition of banks' balance sheets. In an environment of high inflation, high interest rates, and delayed exchange-rate adjustment that led to an overvalued domestic currency, the banking sector began to operate by increasing its exposure to government securities and open short positions in foreign currency. This highly profitable but risky banking practice, which developed at the expense of a decline in the traditional financial intermediation role of banking, was unsustainable and quickly came to an end as a result of the 2000–2001 crises. The majority of commercial banks incurred huge losses, losing their net worth, and some even ended up being liquidated (see Ertuğrul and Selçuk 2001). Public banks incurred substantial losses due to their required lending at subsidized levels, which in a high-inflation and rising interest-rate environment led to accumulated losses and erosion of their assets. The capital support to eliminate the losses of public banks alone amounted to $21.9 billion.[16] Additional funding was also provided through SDIF to strengthen the capital structure of private banks by matching private contributions of new equity to meet the capital shortfalls of these banks.[17] In 2001, the total cost of restructuring added up to $48.5 billion, approximately 34 percent of 2001 GDP (Pazarbaşıoğlu 2005, 163). As a result of this requisite financial restructuring program and a series of regulations (and amendments to the Banking Law) that were introduced since 2001 to ensure sound banking practices, the financial condition of the banking sector improved considerably.[18]

---

[16] State Planning Organization, *Ninth Development Plan 2007–2013*, 33.

[17] IMF *News Brief No. 02/1*, January 11, 2002.

[18] As a result of the operational and financial structuring, the numbers of banks in existence were reduced from 61 in 2001 to 50 in 2003, and during the same period the

Political Reforms: Meeting the Copenhagen Political Criteria

In addition to these and other restructuring measures, on October 3, 2001, Turkey adopted 34 constitutional amendments to improve human rights in Turkey. The amendments included improvements in basic individual rights, such as freedom of thought and expression, freedom of association and the press, the protection of privacy, and gender equality. In addition to redefining the status of the National Security Council as an advisory body, the reforms also took the first step in abolishing the death penalty by limiting it to crimes linked to terrorism and war. In August 2002, despite the resistance to the EU-related political reforms from the two dominant parties of Ecevit's coalition government, the reforms continued in compliance with the Copenhagen political criteria, the most significant of which was the complete abolition of the death penalty.[19] Measures were also introduced to improve individual language rights in education and broadcasting, ease restrictions on religious foundations and foreign associations, and accept the right of retrial in Turkey of European Human Rights court cases.

After 2003, Turkey was compelled to refocus and rework its restructuring efforts, this time to comply with the EU Copenhagen political criteria. The political reforms continued, with the new government further strengthening cultural rights, including broadcasting in local languages, which made it possible for Kurdish to be used in broadcasting, additional improvements in the area of religious freedom, and easing of restrictions on the ownership rights of minority foundations and religious communities. Perhaps the most significant changes were the transformation of the National Security Council into an advisory body and the appointment of a civilian as the secretary general of the NSC.

In October 2004, Turkey's compliance with the Copenhagen criteria was assessed and confirmed by the Commission of the European Communities:

---

overall profitability increased from a loss of $8.2 billion to a profit of $4 billion. See State Planning Organization *Pre-Accession Economic Program, 2004*, 71–77.

[19] As Keyman and Öniş (2004) wrote, there was considerable opposition within Ecevit's coalition government. They also noted that Turkey's political parties lagged behind the civil-society organizations in their support of EU membership.

> Following decades of sporadic progress, there has been substantial legislative and institutional convergence in Turkey towards European standards, in particular after the 2002 elections. The political reforms are mainly contained in two major constitutional reforms in 2001 and 2004 and eight legislative packages adopted by Parliament between February 2002 and July 2004. Civil-military relations are evolving towards European standards. Important changes have been made to the judicial system, including the abolition of the State Security Courts. Public administration reform is underway. As regards human rights, Turkey recognizes the primacy of international and European law. It has aligned itself to a large extent with international conventions and rulings, such as the complete abolition of the death penalty and the release of people sentenced for expressing non-violent opinion. Although some practical restrictions still exist, the scope of fundamental freedoms enjoyed by Turkish citizens, such as freedom of expression and assembly, has been substantially extended. Civil society has grown stronger. Cultural rights for the Kurds have started to be recognized. The state of emergency has been lifted everywhere; although the situation is still difficult, the process of normalization has begun in the Southeast. Finally, on the enhanced political dialogue, Turkish foreign policy is contributing positively to regional stability. (*Recommendation of the European Commision on Turkey's Progress Toward Accession*, October 6, 2004, p. 3)

The Commission also made reference to six additional items of legislation that it expected Turkey to fully implement, of which the last three were yet to be adopted by the Parliament. These included the Law on Associations, the new Penal Code, the Law on Intermediate Courts of Appeal, the Code of Criminal Procedure, the legislation establishing the judicial police, and the Law on execution of punishments and measures. The Commission concluded:

> In view of the overall progress of reforms, and provided that Turkey brings into force the outstanding legislation mentioned above, the Commission considers that Turkey sufficiently fulfils the political criteria and recommends that accession negotiations be opened. (*Recommendation of the European Commision on Turkey's Progress Toward Accession*, October 6, 2004, p. 3)

Clearly, all these reforms changed Turkey's judicial system and brought Turkey closer to the EU. But is the EU ready for Turkey? This is the question we turn to next.

CHAPTER NINE

TURKEY AND THE EU

"The European Council recalled its previous conclusions regarding Turkey, in which, at Helsinki, it agreed that Turkey was *a candidate state destined to join the Union on the basis of the same criteria as applied to the other candidate states* and, subsequently, concluded that, if it were to decide at its December 2004 meeting, *on the basis of a report and recommendation from the Commission, that Turkey fulfils the Copenhagen political criteria, the European Union will open accession negotiations with Turkey without delay*." The 16–17 December 2004 Brussels European Presidency Conclusions then continues with the anxiously awaited recommendation, "It invited the Commission to present to the Council a proposal for a framework for negotiations with Turkey, on the basis set out in paragraph 23. It requested the Council to agree on that framework with a view to opening negotiations on 3 October 2005."

This was a historic decision irreversibly reconfirming Turkey's longstanding bid for full membership in the European Union. As an official candidate since 1999, Turkey has been rigorously reforming and restructuring its economy in compliance with the Copenhagen criteria for starting the accession talks. The reform process intensified during the months before the 2004 Brussels Summit, and after intense negotiations and last-minute bargaining Turkey was finally able to get a firm date for the talks. The main question now is whether Turkey will be able to successfully complete the negotiation process, and beyond that, if doing so will be possible in the foreseeable future. The EU, hesitant of a full-membership commitment, is still hoping for a prospect short of that, leaning toward some form of special status as an alternative. At issue are not only the alleged cultural differences and size but also the future of the European Union, which could become uncertain and lead to instability, as argued by those opposing eventual Turkish membership. Will Turkey ultimately join this elite club of Western democracies? The response is unnecessarily ambiguous and not very encouraging despite the 2004 Brussels European Presidency decision to open the talks. As far as the EU treaties dating back to 1963 and the Union's decision-making bodies are concerned, the answer is clearly affirmative. But oddly enough, an overwhelming majority of EU citizens, unaware of the binding treaties that had allowed for the prospect of full membership, are skeptical, and predictably, their political leaders wonder. The majority in Europe questions whether Turkey is European and above all if it is fit for membership because of perceived economic, political, and cultural differences. And this perception exists despite the fact that for over half a century Turkey has been institutionally and politically part of Europe.

This chapter provides a few observations and some qualified generalizations based on major events that have been redefining Turkey's EU membership prospects since the 1963 Ankara Treaty. It begins with a narrative of the European enlargement and a brief history of Turkish-EU relations, followed by a discussion of developments since Turkey's application for full membership in 1987. Highlighting principal aspects of the customs union since 1996, the chapter ends with a summary of the events before the 2004 Brussels Summit and an analysis of its outcomes.

The European Enlargement

In a speech at Zurich University on September 19, 1946, when Winston Churchill alerted his audience about what he was going to say, probably very few imagined they would hear the words that eventually led to the evolution of a radical project on the future European integration.[1] "I am now going to say something that will astonish you," Churchill said. "The first step in the re-creation of the European family must be a partnership between France and Germany. In this way only can France recover the moral leadership of Europe. There can be no revival of Europe without a spiritually great France and a spiritually great Germany." At that point in history, very few ever imagined that this grand project that had evolved through the contributions of French visionaries Robert Schuman and Jean Monnet would lead to today's elite club of democracies that many European nations have aspired to join.[2] It was also unimaginable that

[1] For Churchill's complete speech and the summary of the efforts of early visionaries of a united Europe, see Nelsen and Stubb (1998).

[2] Robert Schuman (1886–1963), France's foreign minister, and Jean Monnet (1888–1979), French civil servant and diplomat, were instrumental in the establishment of the European Coal and Steel Community that led to the formation of the European Economic Community. See Nelsen and Stubb (1998).

nearly half a century later both France and Germany would take the job upon themselves and press forward toward "the United States of Europe or whatever name or form it may take," as described by Churchill. A process that began in Rome on March 25, 1957, by the six founding members has continued to the present, evolving into an enlarged union of 27 member nations in 2007, with the prospect of two or more new entrants by the end of the next decade.

When Turkey first applied for associate membership in 1959, the European Economic Community (EEC) included only six nations: France, Germany, Italy, and the three Benelux countries, Belgium, Luxembourg, and Netherlands. Even though Churchill's vision of a united Europe was the reasoned doctrine behind the formation of the Community, at the time economic progress was clearly the main driving force, but certainly not the only objective. There were other impelling aspirations as well. In the preamble to the Treaty of Rome, the six founding nations also stated their determination to strengthen and preserve peace and liberty, and called upon other peoples of Europe to join in their efforts. According to the Treaty of Rome, joining the Community was possible in two ways. One option was to gain full membership through article 237 of the Treaty of Rome. This was what prompted the Northern enlargement, the Community's first, which included the United Kingdom, Ireland, and Denmark. The other option was through article 238, allowing for the establishment of an association agreement with eventual full membership. This is the route Greece and Turkey chose. Greece became an associate member in 1962, applied for full membership in 1975, and became the tenth member of the Community in 1981. Turkey also became an associate member in 1964, and by the time it applied for full membership in 1987, the Community had already expanded to include Spain and Portugal. And in 1995, two years after the signing of the European Union Treaty of Maastricht, the EU's membership had increased to fifteen, with its fourth enlargement including Austria, Finland, and Sweden.[3] With the fifth enlargement in May 2004, the Union added the following 10 countries: Cyprus, the Czech Republic, Estonia, Hungary, Latvia, Lithuania, Malta, Poland, Slovakia,

[3] In all of these enlargements, the same rules of accession were applied, although each enlargement had a different length of negotiation. For more on this, see Redmond and Rosenthal (1998).

and Slovenia. And finally in 2007, with the admission of Romania and Bulgaria the EU became a union of 27 member states.

The official criteria for becoming a full member during the first three enlargements were those based on the Treaty of Rome, and the fourth enlargement adhered to the full-membership conditions laid out in the Maastricht Summit. Subsequently, all membership applications and admissions to the Union had to observe the Copenhagen political criteria that were agreed upon in 1993. To become a candidate for full membership, it was required that the applicant state "has achieved stability of institutions guaranteeing democracy, the rule of law, human rights and respect for and protection of minorities, the existence of a functioning market economy as well as the capacity to cope with competitive pressure and market forces within the Union."[4] In addition, the candidate states must accept the Union's Common Foreign and Security Policy, subscribe to the long-term objectives of the EU, and be able to implement EU policies through a compatible legal and administrative system.[5]

Turkey as an Applicant for Full Membership

The 1963 association agreement with Turkey had allowed for the possibility of full membership as the final objective, and in line with the additional Protocol, which was signed on November 13, 1970, and became effective in 1973, Turkey was to pass through a transitional stage scheduled to last for 22 years. The transitional stage was designed to allow adequate time for Turkey to gradually eliminate its tariff protection vis-à-vis the EEC and enter the full customs union. To that end, Turkey was to eliminate custom duties on 55 percent of its imports (most manufactures) from the EEC over a period of 12 years, and for the remaining manufactures over a period of 22 years. In return, the EEC agreed to fully withdraw its restrictions on all Turkish industrial goods, except textile and petroleum products, and grant preferential custom duties on the majority of Turkish agricultural exports to the Community. During the transitional period, Turkey was expected to

---

[4] The Council of the European Union, *Presidency Conclusions*, June 21–22, 1993, Copenhagen.

[5] For a discussion of these conditions, see the introduction in Redmond and Rosenthal (1998).

take the necessary steps for the unification of policies in preparation for the prospect of full membership.

Full membership, which was the ultimate objective of the association agreement, was not an extensively debated issue at the time. Opinions in favor of or against Turkey joining the Community were based on lengthy descriptive accounts and had limited policy implications. There were a few studies quantifying the effects of Turkish entry into the EEC, however. One study in particular found that Turkey would have a comparative advantage in its traditional exports, which were mainly agricultural, and in some nontraditional industrial exports such as food processing, clothing, textiles, and knitting industries (Baysan 1974). Carried out to analyze the impact of the Turkish-EEC association on the volume and the direction of Turkey's trade, another study compared actual trade flows with those that would have taken place under the hypothetical case of Turkey remaining outside rather than joining the Union as an associate member (Aktan 1972). The study found that trade diversion among Turkey's suppliers would take place only with respect to the United States, and estimates based on changes in market shares favored the EEC.[6] One other study, which focused on the trade effects of the Turkish-EEC association, concluded that the effect of association on Turkish exports would be moderate, while the effect on imports would not be significant in the earlier years of the association but might be greater after the 1980s.[7] The main finding of this particular study was that the association of Turkey with the EEC would not seriously affect the trade pattern in the short run. But in the long run the effects would be detrimental in the absence of actions taken to improve industrial performance, institutional reforms, and new economic policies. The focal point in most of these and similar studies was the formation of the customs union and its impact on the Turkish economy. None of the mentioned studies looked into the evolving dynamics of the Community and how they might have impacted Turkey as an associate member. The full-membership status that Turkey has been striving to achieve was not in the making, at least during the first half of the 1970s.

[6] The major effect of the EEC tariff reduction was found to be on the exports of tobacco, raisins, and crude materials, which did not receive preferential tariff reduction from the EEC in the first place. See Aktan (1972).

[7] See P. A. International Management Consultants. *The Turkish Economic Development in View of Joining the Common Market*, 1972, İstanbul.

On March 25, 1981, Turkey decided to begin the application process for full membership, but that did not materialize due to the EEC's decision to freeze relations with Turkey in 1982, a policy that lasted more than four years.[8] And in 1987, when Turkey applied for full membership, the Community's response was less than enthusiastic. The Commission specifically stressed the fact that Turkey needed to further its economic, social, and political development before it could be considered for full membership. It also stated that the Community was not ready to accept a new member before the complete integration of internal markets, a process that was expected to continue until 1992.[9] The European Community was clearly focused on its eastward expansion, and therefore Turkish membership was not a priority. Not only was Turkey's prospect of becoming a full member very dim, but any attempt to improve relations or renew talks that would lead to a greater likelihood of full membership was also being rebuffed by either a Greek veto or the expectation of it. In reassessing Turkey's prospects for becoming a full member, the majority of the member states seemed to take a non-committal and usually non-affirmative position. As was written in the *Economist*, for example, "The Community, not wishing to be accused of racial and religious bias, mumbles that it will think about it later. But the sentiment of most Europeans is plain: those Turks do not belong with us."[10]

The Community was "mumbling," simply because on one hand it was aware of the binding treaties that had already established Turkey's eligibility for full-membership candidacy, and on the other hand, it was politically infeasible to overlook European public opinion, which disapproved of possible Turkish membership. In private, the Community leaders were in agreement that Turkey should develop a European perspective, at least for the next two decades. In public, however, the reaction to Turkey's membership aspiration was much more discouraging, particularly during the 1990s, hinting that Turkey was not ready, and a long list of reasons followed for why that was the case.

---

[8] At the time, Turkey was under military authoritarian rule, and the 1980 Financial Protocol, the fourth of the financial aid packages from the Community that were intended to financially support Turkey in its preparation for the customs union in accordance with the Association Agreement, was tabled after the 1980 military coup in Turkey. See Kramer (1996, 206–7).

[9] Commission Opinion on Turkey's Request for Accession to the Community, December 18, 1989.

[10] "The matter of Europe," *Economist*, December 14, 1991.

At the top of the list were human rights violations, which had grown partly because of a decade-long Kurdish terrorist campaign that took the lives of thousands of innocent people. The Turkish public perceived the campaign as a separatist movement, but Europe had a different view. Europe was much more concerned and vocal about the day-to-day violence and viewed the conflicts largely as desperate acts for gaining cultural and democratic rights.[11] The Turkish public was also disturbed by the frequency of human rights violations, but at the same time it was becoming increasingly suspicious of the Europeans' intentions. Not only did Europe seem less vocal when the separatists themselves committed violations, even when they were against those with Kurdish ethnic background, but it also continued to put pressure on the Turkish authorities without showing interest in the root cause of the conflict. Thus, in the middle of this unfortunate period, human rights violations allegedly committed during the conflict captured the headlines in Europe, and there was growing opposition to the heavy-handed approach of the Turkish military and the state. Under those circumstances, it was inconceivable for Turkey to make progress in its quest of candidacy status for full membership.

Yet, despite the Europeans' concerns with Turkey's human rights record and many other issues that had been voiced by European officials, the Community decided to pursue the formation of the customs union, as was promised in the 1963 Ankara Treaty and reconfirmed in the 1970 Additional Protocol.[12] In January 1996, Turkey completed its 22-year transitional period and entered into the customs union with the Community.[13]

[11] Even as of 2004, as Kramer (2004) noted, "A certain re-evaluation after 9/11 notwithstanding, there is still much unqualified sympathy for the Kurdish case in large sectors of the EU public."

[12] See *Establishing an Association between the European Economic Community and Turkey*, Ankara, September 12, 1963 and *Bulletin of the European Communities 3(9/10)*, September/October 1970.

[13] A customs union is a form of economic integration that combines free trade with protectionism. Member nations remove tariffs on trade among themselves and impose common external tariffs against others. Following Viner (1950), the theory of customs union was developed through the theoretical contributions of Meade (1955), Lipsey (1960), Humphrey and Ferguson (1960), and Vanek (1962). For the details of the Turkish-EU customs union agreement, see the EC-Turkey Association Council's *Decision No. 1/95 on Implementing the Final Phase of the Customs Union (96/142/EC)*, December 22, 1995.

The Turkish-EU Customs Union

During the 1970s, Turkey (a semi-industrialized economy at the time) and the EEC (highly industrialized) appeared to be potentially complementary economies.[14] Being relatively more developed in both agriculture and industry, the EEC had an absolute advantage over Turkey. Turkey, on the other hand, seemed capable of competing in the production of some industrial goods, such as clothing and textiles, and several traditional agricultural goods. More significantly, the proportion of Turkish trade with Europe was higher than with the rest of the world or other regions, and thus Turkey's entry into the customs union with the Community was expected to create short-term static welfare effects, such as trade diversion or trade creation.[15] It was also hoped that it would generate dynamic effects that included the impact of a larger common market on efficiency through economies of scale, external economies, more competitive market structure, and improved investment.[16]

Beginning in 1971, the Community abolished tariffs and all quantitative restrictions on Turkey's manufactured goods. Turkey, in return, agreed to adopt the common external tariff against third-country imports

---

[14] Welfare gains would be greater if the economies of the countries forming the union are actually substitute but potentially complementary economies. Countries with similar structures may enjoy increased welfare gains since they would tend to produce goods in which they have a comparative advantage. Early studies defined substitute economies to be ones with similar cost structures, and complementary economies to be ones with dissimilar ratios. If a union creates trade, the gains will be larger when the goods involved in the trade creation are more complementary. That is, these gains will be greater the larger the differences between the costs of the same commodity produced in the two countries. Meade (1955) argued that following protection policies, countries might develop some high-cost domestic industries so that their actual structures become similar. If they form a customs union, then they may cause increases in welfare gains since countries would tend to produce goods in which they have a comparative advantage. This implies that they are potentially complementary economies.

[15] Trade diversion takes place when imports from a lower-cost source are changed to a higher-cost source, whereas the trade creation follows as a result of shifting the imports from a higher cost to a lower cost source.

[16] The empirical work from the early 1970s had some backing for Turkey's entry into the customs union, although the net effect on Turkey's well-being was not as certain. In free trade with the Community, Turkey was modeled to have a comparative advantage in its traditional exports (mainly agricultural) and in some nontraditional exports, which were industrial, such as food processing, clothing, textiles, and knitting industries (Baysan 1974). Exports to the Community were expected to increase in product groups for which Turkey had high demand elasticity and high comparative advantage rankings (Nas 1977). Trade diversion among Turkey's suppliers was also predicted to take place with respect to the United States, and estimates based on changes in market shares favored the EEC (Aktan 1972).

and gradually reduce trade restrictions on industrial products from the Community within 22 years. The removal of trade restrictions by the Community (completed in 1973) excluded textiles and clothing, and the Association Council decided in 1980 to completely remove restrictions on agricultural imports by 1987. There were some rough spots along the way, however. One key provision of the Ankara Agreement, the free movement of workers, which was expected to start in 1986, did not materialize. After abolishing tariffs on imports from the Community in 1973 and 1978, Turkey also put its forthcoming prescheduled tariff rate reductions on hold. However, the process did resume in 1988, one year after Turkey applied for full membership. Even though the response to the Turkish application was not affirmative, the Community did in fact show interest in intensifying relations on the basis of existing agreements and accordingly introduced a comprehensive package to improve relations with Turkey, which ultimately led to the formation of a customs union.

The customs union agreement, which went into effect in 1996, allowed for the adoption of EU's commercial policy toward third countries, harmonization of agricultural policy, implementation of intellectual property rights, and elimination of all quantitative, non-quantitative, and technical barriers to trade between Turkey and the Union. Even though Turkey had completed most of the procedures required by the agreement and had fully aligned its legislation by 2004, there were still a few exemptions and exclusions outstanding in agriculture and in areas related to trade defense measures and safeguards. Moreover, the customs union was yet to evolve into the next phase, which would eventually allow for the adoption of the common agricultural policy, trade liberalization in services, and the free movement of workers (Ülgen and Zahariadis 2004).

As of 2006, based on the latest trade data, it appears that the customs union with Europe had a positive impact on Turkey's trade volume and broadened its diversification, both in exports and imports. During the three-year period before and after 1996, total exports as a percentage of GNP averaged 11.6 percent and 13.6 percent, respectively (table 9.1). For the same period, the volume of imports as a percentage of GNP increased from 18.4 to 23.1 percent. The EU's share in the total exports inched up slightly from 49.5 percent to 50.2, and imports also rose from 47.1 to 52.1. Over time, however, both total exports and imports as a percentage of GNP increased significantly from 12.6 and 23.8 in

Table 9.1 Annual total exports and imports, 1993–2006

Year	Total exports			Total imports		
	In billion $	% of GNP	EU share	In billion $	% of GNP	EU share
1993	15.4	8.4	49.5	29.4	16.5	47.1
1994	18.1	13.8	47.7	23.3	17.6	46.9
1995	21.6	12.6	51.2	35.7	21.0	47.2
1996	23.2	12.6	49.7	43.6	23.8	53.0
1997	26.6	13.5	46.6	48.6	25.2	51.2
1998	27.0	13.1	50.0	45.9	22.2	52.4
1999	26.3	14.2	54.0	40.7	22.0	52.6
2000	27.8	13.8	52.2	54.5	27.3	48.8
2001	31.3	21.7	51.4	41.4	28.4	44.2
2002	36.1	19.7	51.2	51.5	28.5	45.2
2003	47.2	19.8	51.8	69.3	29.0	45.7
2004	63.2	20.9	54.5	97.5	32.6	46.6
2005	73.5	20.3	52.3	116.8	32.4	42.1
2006	85.5	21.4	51.6	138.5	34.7	39.3

Sources: State Planning Organization, *Economic and Social Indicators 1950–2006*; Undersecretariat for Foreign Trade.

1996 to 21.4 and 34.7 percent in 2006, respectively (figure 9.1). Clearly, the Turkish–EU customs union affected Turkey's trade volume, with a major impact on imports rather than exports. The share of EU-destined exports continued to increase, rising from 49.7 percent in 1996 to 51.6 percent in 2006, and during the same period the share of imports from the EU in total imports declined from 53 percent to 39.3 percent (see figure 9.2).

These statistics certainly find support in recent empirical work on the subject. The Neyaptı, Taşkın, and Üngör (2003) study, for example, provided evidence that positively linked Turkey's trade performance to the custom union agreement. An earlier study by Harrison, Rutherford, and Tarr (1997) predicted a gain of 1 to 1.5 percent of GDP stemming from Turkish access to third markets through the EU's reciprocal preferential access agreements. Also, according to Utkulu and Seymen (2004), the increase in trade volume may have been the result of an increase in demand in the EU, in addition to Turkey's trade and exchange-rate liberalization policies.

In addition to increasing the trade volume, a customs union may cause alterations in both the production techniques and production

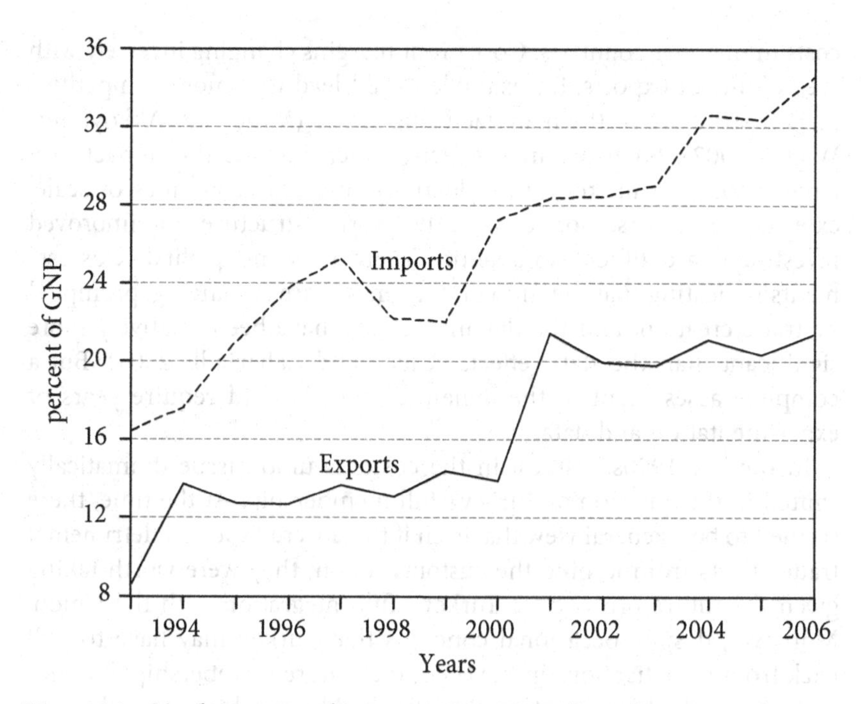

Figure 9.1 Total exports and imports, 1993–2006. (Data from State Planning Organization, *Economic and Social Indicators 1950–2006*; Undersecretariat for Foreign Trade.)

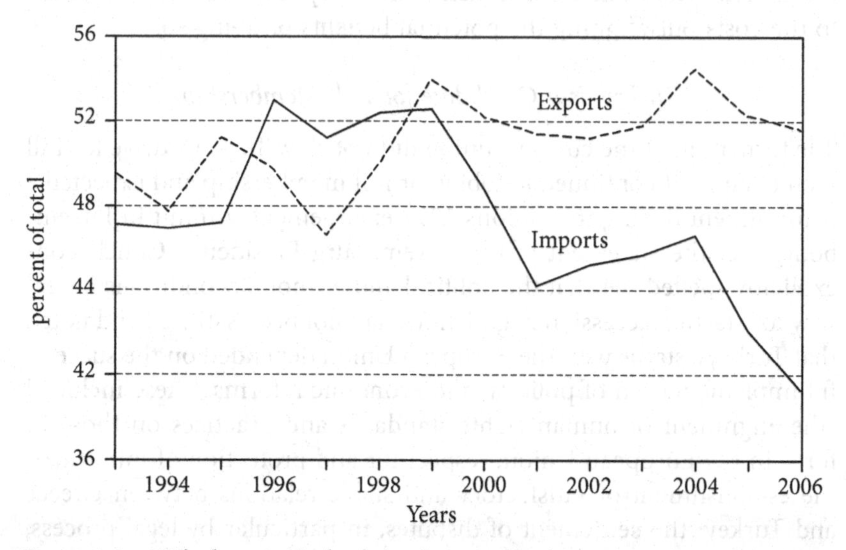

Figure 9.2 EU's share in Turkey's total exports and imports, 1993–2006. (Data from State Planning Organization, *Economic and Social Indicators 1950–2006*; Undersecretariat for Foreign Trade.)

costs in member countries. Cost-profit margins changing inversely with the volume of exports, for example, could lead to a more competitive market structure in the manufacturing sector (Mıhçı and Akkoyunlu-Wigley 2002). Such dynamic effects, which include the impact of a larger common market on productivity through economies of scale, external economies, more competitive market structure, and improved investment, are difficult to quantify. There are some qualitative assessments indicating that the union has been welfare enhancing, prompted by trade creation, and the dynamic effects have been relatively more significant than the static effects (Ülgen and Zahariadis 2004). But a complete assessment of the dynamics effect would require years of experimentation and data.

In the late 1990s, interest in the customs union issue dramatically shifted to the question of Turkey's full membership. At the time, there seemed to be a general view that even if there were expected detrimental trade effects from joining the customs union, they were worth taking given the future prospect of Turkey's full integration with the Union. Moreover, despite occasional concerns that Turkey may have to pull back from its obligations in the event that future membership does not materialize, the level of integration that had been achieved would have probably made it infeasible to end the customs union. In other words, the customs union deepened the economic integration with Europe, creating an economic environment where any reversal would have led to the costs outweighing the potential benefits of doing so.

Turkey as a Candidate for Full Membership

The formation of the customs union did not slow Turkey's drive for full membership. It continued to lobby for full membership and expected a commitment during the Union's 1997 enlargement summit in Luxembourg. Yet the statement of the Luxembourg Presidency Conclusions explicitly spelled out that the political and economic conditions necessary for starting accession negotiations had not been satisfied and noted that Turkey's status with the European Union depended on the successful implementation of political and economic reforms. These included "the alignment of human rights standards and practices on those in force in the European Union; respect for and protection of minorities; the establishment of satisfactory and stable relations between Greece and Turkey; the settlement of disputes, in particular by legal process, including the International Court of Justice; and support for negotiations under the aegis of the UN on a political settlement in Cyprus on the basis of the relevant UN Security Council Resolutions."[17] The Luxembourg Presidency Conclusions did confirm Turkey's eligibility for accession to the EU, however. It established that "[w]hile the political and economic conditions allowing accession negotiations to be envisaged are not satisfied, the European Council considers that it is nevertheless important for a strategy to be drawn up to prepare Turkey for accession by bringing it closer to the European Union in every field."[18]

Turkey's efforts to get closer to the EU thus continued, and in the 1999 Helsinki Summit the EU finally upgraded Turkey's status to candidacy for full membership. Motivated by the Helsinki decision, Turkey initiated various reforms to reinforce its bid for candidacy despite the economic and financial turmoil that had shaken its economy. Turkey's immediate goal was to obtain a firm date for opening the accession talks during the 2002 Copenhagen Summit. The Union, on the other hand, was not ready to make such a commitment. It discreetly applauded Turkey's efforts, but at the same time cautioned that introducing reforms alone was not sufficient and that the Union was much more interested in their implementation and thus needed time to assess the consequences. Clearly, the EU was unimpressed with many reforms that Turkey urgently introduced, instead emphasizing the importance of their actual implementation.

As the date of the 2002 Copenhagen meeting approached, EU officials firmly resisted Turkish requests on the grounds that Turkey was not ready and that much needed to be done before the Union would commit itself to an irreversible decision. Turkey, on the other hand, claimed readiness and did not hesitate to publicly accuse the EU of setting new standards to protract the accession talks. Boxed in between its own internal political dynamics and the EU's inflexible demands, Turkey continued to assure the Union that the implementation of reforms would follow more determinedly once the accession decision had been made. Having mostly fulfilled the Copenhagen criteria to start accession negotiations, Turkey lobbied tirelessly to make its case, yet the outcome was not all that satisfying. Turkey had hoped to start

[17] The Council of the European Union, *Presidency Conclusions*, Press Release, Nr: SN400/97, December 12, 1997, Luxembourg.

[18] The Council of the European Union, *Presidency Conclusions*, Press Release, Nr: SN400/97, December 12, 1997, Luxembourg.

accession negotiations in 2003, but instead was granted a conditional date of December 2004.

The Copenhagen decision was an improvement, because it once again reconfirmed Turkey's candidacy for full membership and also came a bit closer to setting a date for accession negotiations. In contrast to the Luxembourg summit, the sentiment of the member states in Copenhagen was also positive and more responsive to Turkish demands for full membership. In short, the Copenhagen decision was the best that the EU could offer Turkey, and Turkey had no choice but to stay the course.

In this improved environment, Turkey continued to introduce the needed reforms and pass measures for their implementation. But the EU was still unconvinced; the implementation of the newly passed reforms seemed more important than their introduction, the alleged human rights violations were still an issue, and above all, the congruity of the judicial system with the legislated reforms had not yet been achieved.

As the decision date approached, the opposition to Turkish accession, particularly in Paris and in other dissenting northern European capitals, intensified but failed to be consequential. The EU continued to raise a new concern each time Turkey met a stated requirement or introduced a reform (Tekin 2004). The issues of human rights and the death penalty were followed by problem areas of cultural and minority rights, the role of the military, and the lack of transparency in the state sector. Once all the reforms and constitutional amendments had been made, the EU's focus switched to the issue of implementation. Turkey complied once again. Then, as noted above, the issue of Cyprus was put on the table. By October 2004, the EU seemed to be running out of excuses. Thus, in December 2004, based on the October recommendation of the Commission in charge of the enlargement, the EU Council agreed to start the negotiation talks on October 3, 2005.[19]

The most important section of that historic recommendation document was paragraph 23, the framework for negotiations. Even though it was stated that the design of the framework took into account the experience of the fifth enlargement, it appeared that it was tailored to Turkey's unique position. The issues raised in the framework clearly reflected the real concerns of the member states. Given the financial and

[19] The Council of the European Union, *Presidency Conclusions*, December 16–17, 2004, Brussels.

institutional impact of Turkey's potential accession and the complexity of a negotiation process that will involve all member states, an early Turkish membership was clearly out of the question. It also seemed unlikely that the EU would conclude the negotiations before 2014, since the EU was still in the process of negotiating its budget for 2007–2013. As clearly stated in the October 2004 Commission's recommendation, "The budgetary impact of Turkish membership to the EU can only be fully assessed once the parameters for the financial negotiations with Turkey have been defined in the context of the financial perspectives from 2014 onwards" (*Recommendation of the European Commission on Turkey's Progress Toward Accession*, October 6, 2004, p. 6).

Also, in contrast to earlier enlargements, the possibility of including permanent safeguard clauses was stated in the Brussels Presidency Conclusions specifically because of a high probability of increased migration of Turkish workers. In the case of the last enlargement, there was a transition period of seven years for new member states, during which time free movement of workers was constrained. But given the demographic profile of Turkey, the framework not only allowed for the possibility of permanent safeguards but also provided for a maximum role in the decision-making process "regarding the eventual establishment of freedom of movement of persons" to individual states that might be most affected. Assuming a transition period of ten years, estimates of a likely migration potential from Turkey to the EU range from a level below 1 million to 2.9 million (Flam 2003, Hughes 2004). However, these rough estimates will likely be different from actual migration that might take place in 2014 and beyond. Both the EU's and Turkey's demographic profiles are likely to change; moreover, in view of possible variations in labor markets, what might have seemed to be a concern in 2005 could very well be an advantage for EU member states that may experience a labor shortage by 2014. We return to this issue in chapter 11.

The framework also highlighted the fact that the negotiations were open-ended, a statement that was not stressed in previous rounds of enlargements. The open-ended nature of the negotiations was specifically included in the framework to allow for possible alternatives to accession, and on the insistence of some member states, if it becomes necessary, the need to fully anchor the Candidate State (the reference is Turkey) to the European structures was added.

In spite of these highly sensitive qualifiers, however, Turkey finally achieved what it had strived for; obtaining a clear date for starting accession negotiations, an outcome that seemed almost impossible a few years earlier. Even though further conditions by the Europeans to conclude the negotiations might prove likely, it was still too early to predict what might transpire in the future. Europe, still hesitant to accept Turkey as an equal partner, hoped for a long negotiation period with the expectation of gradual changes in both political and economic environments that would ease some of the tensions within the EU that might result from early Turkish membership. As we elaborate in the next chapter, leaving behind the uncertainty surrounding its status, Turkey, on the other hand, was anxious to move forward, with heightened confidence and determination in an environment where it could continue to institutionalize its reforms and deepen its legal, political, and economic restructuring.

CHAPTER TEN

STARTING THE ACCESSION TALKS

The December 2004 European Council decision to commence accession negotiations with Turkey did not come without effort, and neither did the agreement on the common negotiation framework reached on October 3, 2005. Having been granted the status of an official candidate state, Turkey was obviously anxious to start the screening process as a prelude to accession negotiations. The European Commission had already presented a draft of the negotiation framework to the Turkish government in June 2005, stating that the conditions set by the European Council to start the talks had been fulfilled and that the next step was the adoption of the framework by the member states.[1] But some EU member states, still not ready to welcome Turkey to the EU, were yet to abandon the idea of privileged partnership status as an alternative to full admission. Hoping to change the nature of the integration process, Austria, in particular, insisted on including a provision in the accession framework that would allow for the prospect of privileged partnership, which Turkey strongly opposed. During the EU foreign ministers' meeting in Luxembourg, there was also debate over whether Turkish entry into the EU should be reassessed, not only in terms of the Copenhagen criteria but also on the basis of the EU's absorption capacity, an added condition that was not applied to previous enlargements. Austria was not the only member state that wanted these changes in the accession document. There were other states taking a similar stance, eager to anchor Turkey in the EU or at least keep the full membership prospect alive for the time being, given the adverse consequences of an outright rejection.

In the final version of the document, drafted after painstaking negotiations and deliberations on alternative scenarios, reference to privileged partnership was dropped, but the condition of absorption capacity remained. The paragraph that was the source of the controversy was

[1] As noted in chapter 8, starting the talks was contingent on the adoption of six additional items of legislation that the European Council expected Turkey to fully implement, and that condition as of June 1, 2005, was fulfilled.

ultimately worded as follows: "As agreed at the European Council in December 2004, these negotiations are based on Article 49 of the Treaty on European Union. The shared objective of the negotiations is accession. These negotiations are an open-ended process, the outcome of which cannot be guaranteed beforehand. While having full regard to all Copenhagen criteria, including the absorption capacity of the Union, if Turkey is not in a position to assume in full all the obligations of membership it must be ensured that Turkey is fully anchored in the European structures through the strongest possible bond."[2]

This final draft of the agreement was not what the Erdoğan government had hoped for, but it was acceptable. Even though added provisions appeared to be potential setbacks capable of delaying or diminishing the prospect of full membership, the wording of the document excluded those possibilities at least in the intermediate term. There was a stern reminder, however, that Turkey had to fulfill its obligations under the Additional Protocol extending the Association Agreement to all new EU member states, a step that Turkey was hesitant to take since that would have implied the recognition of the Greek Cypriot government. Turkey had signed the Protocol in July 2005, broadening the customs union to include Cyprus, but in an addendum had declared that Turkey did not recognize Greek Cypriots as the sole representative of Cyprus, firmly stating that "signature, ratification and implementation of this Protocol neither amount to any form of recognition of the Republic of Cyprus referred to in the Protocol; nor prejudice Turkey's rights and obligations emanating from the Treaty of Guarantee, the Treaty of Alliance, and the Treaty of Establishment of 1960."[3]

The EU responded with a counterstatement in September 2005, reminding Turkey of its obligations and the expectation of "full, non-discriminatory implementation of the Additional Protocol, and the removal of all obstacles to the free movement of goods, including restrictions on means of transport."[4] The EU further warned that opening negotiations on relevant chapters of the *acquis communautaire* (the entire body of EU legislation) and the overall progress in negotiations depended on whether Turkey's obligations to all EU member states were fully met.

---

[2] European Commission, *Negotiating Framework*, October 3, 2005, Luxembourg.

[3] EU-Turkey News Network, *Declaration by Turkey on Cyprus*, July 29, 2006.

[4] The Council of the European Union, *Enlargement: Turkey, Declaration by the European Community and its Member States*, 12541/05 (Presse 243), September 21, 2005, Brussels.

Cyprus has been divided since 1974, when Turkey intervened and occupied the northern part of the island after a coup by a local Greek group that supported union with Greece and was backed by Greece's military junta. Since then there have been numerous UN-sponsored peace plans to unite the divided island, but none of them have been successful. Before the Republic of Cyprus became a full member of the EU in May 2004, Turkey initiated the resurrection of UN Secretary-General Kofi Annan's peace plan that aimed at uniting the divided island.[5] That did not succeed either. The EU had already started the accession negotiation with the Greek Cypriots as the only officially recognized representatives of the Republic of Cyprus, hoping to eventually admit a united Cyprus into the EU. The Turkish Cypriots concluded the UN talks as scheduled with a settlement that seemed to be viewed as reasonable by the world community and voted in favor of the agreement in the referenda that were simultaneously held on both sides of the island. But despite pressure from the EU and the United States, the Greek Cypriots turned down this historic opportunity; the result of the referendum that was held on the Greek side was not affirmative. The Greeks had no compelling reason to agree to the terms of the settlement, since it had already been decided that full membership in the EU was imminent, irrespective of the outcome of the negotiations. The referendum that was held on both sides of the island confirmed that Turkish Cypriots desired a united island, but the proposed settlement was rejected by an overwhelming majority of the Greek voters. The island did not unify as was hoped by the EU. In the end, the Greek Cypriots were admitted into the EU as the sole representative of the Republic of Cyprus. And as a member of the EU customs union, Turkey was obligated to extend its customs union terms to include the new EU member, Cyprus. The Commission wanted Turkish ports opened to registered Cypriot vessels, but Turkey's position did not change, even after the commencement of the accession negotiations. Turkey continued to insist on not recognizing the Republic of Cyprus as long as Northern Cyprus remained isolated, and it expected the EU to honor the European Commission's 2004 decision to end the economic isolation of the Turkish Cypriots, which had remained unfulfilled.[6]

---

[5] For the full text of UN Secretary-General Kofi Annan's plan, see United Nations, *Comprehensive Settlement of the Cyprus Problem*, March 31, 2004. Also see UN Chronicle Online Edition, *Cyprus Post-Referendum*, July 30, 2004.

[6] The Commission proposed a regulation to provide financial support to the Turkish

Convinced that Turkey was determined not to act on this highly complex and sensitive issue, on November 29, 2006, the EU Commission drafted its recommendation to suspend the accession talks on eight chapters (see table 10.1). In December 2006, EU foreign ministers concurred with the Commission's recommendation and decided to keep the remaining chapters open until an agreement was reached with Turkey on this issue. Despite this complication, the formal screening process on all 35 chapters listed in the negotiation framework started, and it was finalized one year later, in October 2006. Negotiations typically begin after the completion of the screening cycle of each chapter followed by a process of opening and closing the chapter, usually with no major interruptions expected. In the case of Turkey, however, after the chapter on science and research was opened and provisionally closed in June 2006, negotiations were first stalled and started again at the end of March 2007 on the topic of enterprise and industry.

Table 10.1 Chapters of the *acquis*, October 2005–September 2006

Chapter Headings	Level of harmonization
1. Free movement of goods[b]	Uneven progress
2. Freedom of movement for workers	Limited progress
3. Right of establishment and freedom to provide services[b]	Limited progress
4. Free movement of capital	Very limited progress
5. Public procurement	Very limited progress
6. Company law	Limited progress
7. Intellectual property law	Well advanced progress
8. Competition policy	Well advanced
9. Financial services[b]	Some progress made
10. Information society and media	Progress made
11. Agriculture and rural development[b]	Limited progress
12. Food safety, veterinary and phytosanitary policy	Limited progress
13. Fisheries[b]	No progress made
14. Transport policy[b]	Some progress made
15. Energy	Some progress made

Cypriot Community for the period 2004–2006, which the Council approved in February 2006. The proposed regulation to facilitate direct trade from the Northern part of Cyprus has not yet been approved. For the Commission's proposals, see European Commission, *Commission Proposes Comprehensive Isolation of Turkish Cypriot Community*, Press Release IP/04/857, July 8, 2004, Brussels.

Table 10.1 (*cont.*)

Chapter Headings	Level of harmonization
16. Taxation	Limited progress
17. Economic and monetary union	Progress made
18. Statistics[d]	Some progress made
19. Social policy and employment	Limited progress
20. Enterprise and industrial policy[c]	Good progress made
21. Trans-European network	Limited progress
22. Regional policy and coordination of structural instruments	Progress made
23. Judiciary and fundamental rights	Some/limited progress
24. Justice, freedom and security	Some progress
25. Science and research[a]	Well prepared for accession
26. Education and culture	Alignment nearly complete
27. Environment	Low progress
28. Consumer and health protection	Progress made
29. Customs union[b]	Ready for high alignment
30. External relations[b]	Made progress
31. Foreign, security and defense policy	Overall alignment continued
32. Financial control[d]	Some progress
33. Financial and budgetary provisions	Some progress
34. Institutions	
35. Other issues	

Source: Commission of the European Communities, Staff Working Document, *Turkey 2006 Progress Report.*

[a] Opened and provisionally closed in June 2006.

[b] Negotiations were suspended in December 2006.

[c] Opened in March 2007.

[d] Opened in June 2007.

The Turkish Economy after the 2004 Brussels Summit

Still on the EU-track, Turkey continued to enjoy strong economic performance and implement far-reaching reforms despite the EU's ongoing uncertainty over how to proceed with the full-membership process. GDP grew at an annual rate of 8.9 percent in 2004 and continued its robust performance, increasing 7.4 percent in 2005 before slowing down to a 3.4 percent increase in the third quarter of 2006 and finishing the year at 6.1 percent (see table 10.2). Following a similar growth pattern, consumption was up from 8.8 percent in 2005 to 11.5 percent in the second quarter of 2006 and dropped to 2.3 percent in the next quarter. Total investment continued its growth in the first quarter of 2006, rising

Table 10.2 Selected macroeconomic indicators, 2001–2006

Year	GDP growth rate	Inflation rate	Budget deficit	Primary budget surplus	Trade balance	Current account
			% of GNP			
2001	−7.5	68.5	−16.5	6.8	−2.6	2.3
2002	7.9	29.7	−14.6	4.3	−4.0	−0.8
2003	5.8	18.4	−11.3	5.2	−5.9	−3.4
2004	8.9	9.3	−7.1	6.1	−7.9	−5.2
2005	7.4	7.7	−2.0	7.4	−9.1	−6.3
2006	6.1	9.6	−0.8	8.6	−10.1	−7.9

Sources: Central Bank of the Republic of Turkey, Electronic Data Delivery System; Turkish Treasury, *Economic Indicators*; State Planning Organization, *Economic and Social Indicators 1950–2006, Main Economic Indicators May 2007*; Ministry of Finance.

from 24 percent in 2005 to 32.1 percent, but then it decelerated to 4.4 percent in the fourth quarter of the year. The main decline was in the public-sector component of investment; a 32.8 percent increase in the first quarter of 2006 fell to negative 11.9 percent and negative 4.1 percent in the next two quarters. The change in private-sector investment, on the other hand, was relatively moderate, declining from 32.1 percent to 18.4 percent and 15 percent during the same quarters. Government spending also increased by 18.3 percent in the second quarter of 2006 but subsequently slowed down to a 14.8 percent increase in the next quarter.[7]

The deceleration of the growth rate of GDP (and its components) in the second half of 2006 was caused by tight monetary policy and high interest rates aimed at keeping inflation in check. In both 2004 and 2005, annual inflation rates were realized below the targeted levels of 12 percent and 8 percent. However, after declining from 9.3 percent in 2004 to 7.7 percent in 2005, inflation rose to 9.6 percent in 2006, a rate that was significantly above the targeted level of 5 percent. The upsurge in inflation occurred despite the formal inflation targeting that was adopted as a nominal anchor at the beginning of 2006 and was caused largely by rising crude oil prices and the depreciation of the Turkish lira during the second quarter of the year. In response, interest rates

[7] State Planning Organization, *Main Economic Indicators*, May 2007.

were raised and the money supply was tightened through open market operations to drain the excess liquidity.[8]

Fiscal policy has also been tight and on track since 2001, targeting a primary surplus of 6.5 percent of GNP, a commitment that was made by the Turkish government as part of a standby agreement with the IMF. Since then, fiscal indicators, including the primary budget surplus and the overall budget deficit, have been improving, with slight deviations from the projected levels. Fiscal performance in 2004 was particularly strong; despite the increase in crude oil prices, the primary surplus rose to 6.1 percent of GNP, and the overall budget deficit narrowed to 7.1 percent of GNP, due mainly to an increase in tax revenues and a 13 percent cut in discretionary expenditures.[9] In the next two years, efforts to increase government revenues and control expenditures continued. Consequently, the primary budget surplus increased from 7.4 percent of GNP in 2005 to 8.6 percent of GNP in 2006; the overall deficit also narrowed from 2 percent of GNP to 0.8 percent of GNP (see table 10.2).

External balance indicators were not as favorable, however. After increasing by 6.3 percent of GNP in 2005 and 7.9 percent of GNP in 2006, the current account deficit reached a new high on an annualized basis in the first quarter of 2007. The trade deficit was also growing; starting with the second quarter of 2004, both imports and exports increased at a slower pace, and that trend continued through 2005. While the slower rate of growth in exports persisted in the first quarter of 2006, the growth rate of imports accelerated, and the subsequent upward trend in export growth that started in the third quarter of 2006 was not strong enough to exceed the growth rate in total imports. Despite increases in productivity that might have increased external competitiveness through lower unit costs, the gap between exports and imports thus grew wider because of such factors as the appreciation of the Turkish lira during the second half of 2006, a higher rate of increase in import prices relative to export prices, a jump in imports from China, increasing dependency of exports on imports, and the increase in natural gas and oil prices.[10]

---

[8] IMF, *Letter of Intent*, July 7, 2006.

[9] IMF, *Letter of Intent*, April 2, 2004.

[10] The increase in imports from China was particularly striking: Its share in the total imports dramatically increased from 5.6 percent in 2005 to 6.9 percent in 2006, making that the highest increase, followed by the increase in the share of the Middle Eastern countries combined. See State Planning Organization, *Ninth Development Plan 2007–2013*, 26; Central Bank, *Balance of Payments Report 2006-III*.

With a record current account deficit, capital inflow was predictably substantial. Based on 2006 data, of the total capital inflow of $55.8 billion, net portfolio investment amounted to $7.4 billion, which was significantly below net direct investment of $19.2 billion (see table 10.3). The other category, including short-term and long-term credits obtained by the banks and the private sector, totaled $26.5 billion in 2006. The sum of all three categories exceeded the total external financing requirement, and the excess was added to the banks' foreign exchange assets and the official reserves.

Table 10.3 External financing, 2004–2006, in billion $

	2004	2005	2006
Current account	-15.6	-23.2	-31.8
Capital flows	23.6	44.5	55.8
Direct investment	2.0	8.7	19.2
Portfolio investment	8.0	13.4	7.4
Other	13.8	20.9	26.5

Source: Central Bank of the Republic of Turkey, *Balance of Payments Report 2007-I.*

As shown in table 10.4, the official reserves, which have been accumulating at an increasing rate since 2001, reached their highest level in 2006. Both domestic and external debt rose to record levels as well, but as a percentage of GDP they have been down slightly since the fourth quarter of 2004. The ratio of short-term external debt to Central Bank reserves, however, has been rising since the first quarter of 2006. This ratio, which reflects increased "external debt fragility" when it is high, had come down from 1.47 just before the 2001 crisis to 0.77 in the first quarter of 2006 and was up slightly in the second quarter of 2006 (Yeldan 2006). Overall, however, there was notable improvement in the debt structure and maturities in comparison to the period before the 2001 crisis, and even though the risk to financial stability has diminished considerably, further improvements in the debt structure will likely reduce the vulnerability of the financial system to external shocks.

From the preceding economic profile, it is clear that Turkey's vital statistics, with the exception of those related to external balances and to some degree the composition of external debt, have been improving since the 2001 crisis. Obviously, the issues of a widening current account deficit and increased domestic and external debt are a source of anxiety and will continue as such as long as domestic saving falls short

Table 10.4 International reserves, external and domestic debt, and public sector borrowing requirement, 2001–2006

Year	International reserves		External debt Total		Short term	Domestic debt	PSBR
	In billion $	% of GNP	In billion $	% of GNP	% of GNP	% of GNP	% of GNP
2001	30.2	20.7	113.6	78.0	11.2	69.2	16.4
2002	38.0	21.0	129.7	72.0	09.1	54.5	12.7
2003	45.0	18.8	144.2	60.7	09.6	54.5	9.3
2004	53.8	18.0	160.8	53.8	10.7	52.3	4.7
2005	68.7	19.0	168.8	47.0	10.3	50.3	−0.4
2006	90.8	22.7	207.4	51.9	10.5	43.7	−3.0

Sources: Central Bank of the Republic of Turkey, Electronic Data Delivery System; State Planning Organization, *Economic and Social Indicators 1950–2006*, *Main Economic Indicators May 2007*; Turkish Treasury, *Economic Indicators.*

of projected investment or the current account remains in deficit. In a dynamic economy poised for accelerated growth and development, holding back domestic investment is highly implausible. A simple national income identity suggests that to reduce dependency on foreign capital, national saving must either exceed investment or the current account must show a surplus. The latter is only possible if an economy is able to upgrade its technology, accumulate capital goods, and increase its production capacity, and that would necessitate investment, which brings us back to the issue of the inadequacy of domestic saving. For decades, a high percentage of national saving in Turkey had been used up in the financing of budget deficits. Throughout the 1990s, the budget deficit averaged 6.2 percent of GNP, and it has been only a few years since the government has been able to contribute to national saving by achieving a sustainable primary budget surplus.

Unemployment, Real Wages, and Income Distribution

Having a budget surplus for an extended period of time does not come without a cost, however. As a countercyclical contractionary fiscal measure, a budget surplus would normally result in a slower growth rate and increased unemployment, unless it is accommodated by an expansionary monetary policy. In Turkey the outcome was no different: the unemployment rate, which had come down to 6.5 percent in 2000, was up to 9.9 percent in 2006 (see table 10.5). During the same period,

Table 10.5 GNP per capita and employment data, 2000–2006

	2000	2001	2002	2003	2004	2005	2006
GNP per capita (in $)	2,965	2,123	2,598	3,383	4,172	5,008	5,477
Unemployment rate	6.5	8.4	10.3	10.5	10.3	10.3	9.9
Underemployment rate	6.9	6.0	5.4	4.8	4.1	3.3	3.6
Labor force (in 1000s)	23,078	23,491	23,818	23,640	24,289	24,565	24,776
Employed	21,581	21,524	21,354	21,147	21,791	22,046	22,330
Unemployed	1,497	1,967	2,464	2,493	2,498	2,520	2,446
Employment rate	46.7	45.6	44.4	43.2	43.7	43.4	43.2
Labor force participation rate	49.9	49.8	49.6	48.3	48.7	48.3	48.0

Sources: TÜRKSTAT, *Statistical Indicators 1923–2005*, Table 9.1; Household Labor Force Survey, *Bulletin for 2006*, 6/03/2007.

the labor force participation rate remained almost the same: it was slightly below 60 percent during the late 1980s and steadily declined to an average of 49.3 percent in the first half of the 2000s. Since 2001, the labor force participation rate and the unemployment rate have been moving in opposite directions, indicating an increase in the number of marginally unemployed or discouraged workers. Such a trend when observed in a high growth period would indeed imply "jobless growth," which is what Turkey has been experiencing, particularly during the post-2001 crisis period (Yeldan 2006).

As highlighted in the 2006 World Bank labor market study, Turkey has one of the lowest employed-to-adult-population ratios in the world; at 43.7 percent in 2006, it is much lower than the EU average, which is around 65 percent, and significantly below the EU member state employment target of 70 percent set for 2010. The labor force participation rate is also lower than the EU average, for a number of reasons, such as population growth outpacing employment growth, a high ratio of older workers in the labor force, low female participation in the labor force, and a tight job market for college graduates.[11] Also, despite strong growth

[11] See World Bank, *Turkey Labor Market Study*, World Bank Report No. 33254-TR, April 14, 2006; Eurostat, *Europe in Figures—Eurostat Yearbook 2006–07*.

since the early 1980s, job creation has been moderate, largely because of uneven sectoral shifts—the inability of the industrial sector to absorb the larger outflow of labor from the agricultural sector, creating long-term frictional unemployment. Existing labor market practices including high severance pay, early retirement age, restrictions on temporary work, a relatively long average workweek, and so on have also been a deterrent in job creation. Clearly, easing some of these practices could have a positive impact on employment and increase labor force participation.[12]

A close examination of labor data also reveals that despite a remarkable rise in labor productivity since 2000, real wages have been declining during the same period.[13] In the early stages of stabilization and structural adjustment, real wages normally increase because of wage rigidity and falling inflation, but during the recovery period, real wages first tend to decline as the economy moves to a sustainable output level and then begin to rise as economic recovery progresses on an expansionary path and the demand for labor starts to increase. After financial crises, real wages seem to fall sharply, however. As documented in the World Bank study, in Turkey real wages in manufacturing dropped significantly during periods after the crises of 1994 and 2001. After 1994, the real wage index fluctuated in an upward trend but fell again after 2001, and even though it rebounded quickly from the 2001 level, real wages were still below those of the pre-1994 crisis period.

Despite the deterioration in real wages, GNP per capita has been increasing significantly. During the 1990s, after dropping to its lowest level in 1994, it began to steadily increase during the remaining years of the 1990s, and after falling to another low in 2001 it rose more than 100 percent during the period 2003–2006. There has also been a slight improvement in income distribution. In 2002, 20 percent of the population with the lowest income received 5.3 percent of the disposable income, while 20 percent of the population with the highest income received 50.1 percent.[14] In 2003, the share of income received by all income categories (excluding the top quintile) increased slightly, while

---

[12] See IMF, *Turkey—2007 Article IV Consultation, Concluding Statement of the IMF Mission*, March 9, 2007.

[13] The index of labor productivity and real wages moved in tandem until 1980, but thereafter both indicators began to fluctuate in opposite directions, particularly after 2001 when labor productivity continued to rise as real wages moved in a downward trend (Yeldan 2006).

[14] State Planning Organization, *Ninth Development Plan 2007–2013*, 51–53; TÜRKSTAT, *2004 Household Budget Survey*, News Bulletin February 27, 2006. For the analysis and the results of income distribution for earlier dates, see Yükseler (2004).

the share of the top quintile declined. In 2004, there was no change in income distribution in favor of the lowest income group, but the share of the top quintile decreased further to 46.2 percent, and the income received by the second, third, and fourth quintiles increased. Compared to 1987 data, the changes are not very significant, but the ratio of total income received by the highest income group to that of the lowest income group decreased from 9.6 in 1987 to 7.7 in 2004, still much higher than the EU ratio, though, which was roughly 5 in 2004.

In recent years, even though there has been a modest improvement in the poverty rate, it is significantly higher than EU levels. The poverty rate defined on the basis of food and basic non-food expenditures was 27 percent in 2002, and after rising to 28 percent in 2003 it decreased slightly to 25.6 percent in 2004. Despite this modest decline, poverty in Turkey has been widespread, particularly in rural areas.[15] In 2003, the percentage of the population at risk of poverty in Turkey was almost 10 percentage points above that in the EU.[16] In an effort to eradicate poverty, Turkey has recently taken important steps, including improvements in the social insurance system, pilot implementation of family medicine, the establishment of universal health insurance, and combining the social security institutions under a single organization.[17]

More Restructuring

As the role of the state in the economy continued to decrease, measures to further strengthen the private sector, and at the same time enhance efficiency and facilitate the effective functioning of the public sector through administrative reforms, took priority. To that end, the role of the state in the economy was significantly reduced through privatization, with the public sector completely withdrawing from key industries such as iron-steel, oil refining, and telecommunications, to name a few.[18] As

---

[15] State Planning Organization, *Ninth Development Plan 2007–2013*, 52.

[16] In a hypothetical case of the absence of social transfers, the difference is less dramatic, and in some cases Turkey fares even slightly better than some member nations. In 2003, the percentage of population at risk of poverty before social transfers was 36 percent in Ireland, 32 percent in Denmark, and 31 percent in Poland, and in Turkey it was 31 percent. After social transfers, the poverty rates are much lower: 21 percent in Ireland, 12 percent in Denmark, 17 percent in Poland, and 26 percent in Turkey. For more, see Eurostat, *Europe in Figures—Eurostat Yearbook 2006–07*, 117.

[17] The 2006 social security law was annulled by the Constitutional Court, and at the time of writing the social security reform was yet to be reintroduced.

[18] As of 2006, State Economic Enterprises accounted for 5 percent of GDP and 15

the state's direct role in resource allocation decreased, the regulatory function became necessary, calling for the introduction of legislation and regulations to increase competitiveness in the economy and improve the investment environment. Government also introduced specific legislation, regulations, and guidance in the areas of information and communication technologies, energy, and transportation.

The administrative reforms involved far-reaching measures to increase the effectiveness of the public sector. These included (a) a constitutional amendment to ensure conformance with the Public Financial Management and Control Law that was amended and had gone into effect in 2006, (b) a budget accounting and reporting system to comply with international standards and strengthen fiscal transparency, (c) local administrative reforms to improve financial and managerial efficiency, and (d) the creation of an ombudsman who represents the interests of the public in the inspection and investigation of complaints against the administration.[19]

To comply with EU regulations and international standards, numerous steps were also taken in the banking and insurance sectors. An insurance bill was introduced to develop an insurance market and to introduce provisions to facilitate an effectively functioning insurance sector. With the Banks Law that went into effect in 2005, additional guidelines and standards were introduced to enhance the legal and institutional framework to increase supervision and auditing in the sector. The main objective of the law was "to regulate the principles and procedures of ensuring confidence and stability in financial markets, the efficient functioning of the credit system and the protection of the rights and interests of depositors."[20] Another priority of the law, in addition to making the sector more reliable, transparent, and stable, was to ensure its compliance with the EU banking standards and facilitate its integration with the international financial system. Thus, as a result of

percent of value added in manufacturing. See Commission of the European Communities, Commission Staff Working Document, *Turkey—2006 Progress Report*, 28, Brussels, November 2006. As of 2006, about 71 percent of 244 companies have been privatized. The gross revenue from privatization in 2006 amounted to $8 billion, bringing the total gross revenue for the period 1986–2006 to about $25.7 billion (these figures, obtained from State Planning Organization, *Pre-Accession Economic Program, 2006*, are updated based on the latest data from the Republic of Turkey Prime Ministry, Privatization Administration, http://www.oib.gov.tr/).

[19] State Planning Organization, *Pre-Accession Economic Program*, November 2006, 79–82.

[20] The Banks Association of Turkey, *Banking Law 5411*, publication no: 55, 10.

extensive restructuring during the period 2001–2003, the banking system in Turkey has become more "resilient and sound." As Pazarbaşıoğlu (2005, 172–73) concluded, most of the requirements to align Turkey's banking system to the EU were fulfilled and a significant percentage of the costs that would have been resulted from the convergence to the EU banking system has already been incurred.

By the end of 2006, Turkey appeared to have made significant progress in its reforms.[21] As noted by the European Commission, "As regards economic criteria, Turkey can be regarded as a functioning market economy, as long as it firmly maintains its recent stabilization and reform achievements. Turkey should also be able to cope with competitive pressure and market forces within the Union in the medium term, provided that it firmly maintains its stabilization policy and takes further decisive steps towards structural reforms."[22] The report from the IMF was much more upbeat on Turkey's accomplishments, however. As the IMF March 9, 2007 mission statement concluded: "Opportunities for the Turkish economy are enormous. The goal should be to build on the economic success of the last five years to firmly entrench high growth, secure low inflation, and make the economy more flexible and resilient to external shocks. Continued disciplined fiscal and monetary policies complemented by bold structural reforms are essential to lift Turkey onto a significantly higher growth trajectory. The agenda is large and some reforms could face resistance, but the rewards in terms of sustained improvements in living standards would make the effort well worthwhile."[23]

Factors Underlying Turkey's Economic Transformation

Turkey's economic transformation, despite legitimate concerns with respect to external balances and income distribution in particular, appears to be on track and irreversible. Turkey's growth, specifically during the post-2001 crisis (with an annual average growth rate of 7.2

---

[21] For a detailed impact analyses of the EU accession in agriculture, manufacturing, services, and network sectors, see Hoekman and Togan (2005).

[22] European Commission, *Enlargement Strategy and Main Challenges 2006–2007*, 54.

[23] IMF, *Turkey—2007 Article IV Consultation, Concluding Statement of the IMF Mission*, March 9, 2007.

percent), has been unmatched by any sub-period during the post-1980s. The only comparable sub-period is the 1983–86 politically stable period, when the Turkish economy grew by an annual average of 5.7 percent. The average annual rate of growth during the post-1994 crisis, including the years 1995 through 1999, was 4.0 percent. Obviously, an economy is likely to exhibit improved performance in a politically stable environment, as was the case during the post-2002 general election period. Should the credit then go to the Erdoğan government under which high growth was attained and far-reaching reforms that dramatically changed Turkey's economic structure were implemented? Or was the architect of this buoyant performance the Ecevit government, which initiated some of the most overdue reforms that set the tone for further restructuring and developed the foundation of an economic renovation that was passed down to the Erdoğan administration? As discussed in chapter 8, the Ecevit coalition government made it possible for important legislation to go through the parliamentary process before the 2002 general election. Thereafter, the restructuring efforts took a much more dynamic and definite turn. Restructuring had to continue not only to comply with the IMF conditions but also to bring Turkey closer to its EU destination. The Erdoğan government worked with a very tight timetable to undertake all the necessary measures in the areas that the EU had been insisting on as conditions for starting the membership negotiations. A process that began with the Ecevit government thus continued with added urgency and determination, creating an economic and political environment that helped lead to sustainable improvements.

How does the Washington Consensus play into this? Did "one-size-fits-all" happen to be the right size for Turkey, especially when its economic transformation is viewed from a long-run perspective? As discussed in detail in chapter 2, during the early years of the Republic, in an economic environment where investment capital and private-sector initiative were inadequate, the state found itself taking the lead in Turkey's industrialization, and that tradition continued for more than four decades. But when state-led industrialization was no longer sustainable, in the late 1970s, Turkey also lacked the resources needed to reform its state sector. At a time when policies were being redesigned for increased liberalization and privatization across the developed and emerging economies, it was no longer feasible for Turkey to continue with business as usual. Recognizing this, in the 1980s Turkey began to undo its state-dominated economic structure by implementing the emerging growth and development framework, referred to as the Washington Consensus. The "stabilize, liberalize, and privatize" agenda at first appeared to succeed as Turkey began to recover from the debt crisis of the late 1970s with improved statistics that garnered the support of international financial institutions. But with its fading economic performance during the 1990s Turkey did not fit the model country of the IMF. Öniş and Şenses (2005) wrote that "the performance of the Turkish economy deteriorated in the 1990s, notably after the decision to open up the capital account fully in 1989, in the face of rising macroeconomic instability and without the necessary regulatory and legal safeguards" (p. 270). In many other emerging economies the outcome was similar, and as Rodrik (2006) noted, "The question now is not whether the Washington Consensus is dead or alive; it is what will replace it" (p. 974).

As the search for a replacement continues, it should be noted that even though there currently seems to be agreement among theoreticians and practitioners that in most cases the Washington Consensus failed to produce its intended results, in retrospect it was one factor that changed Turkey's economic profile, but it did so at a substantial cost: frequent financial crises, chronic inflation, and deteriorating income distribution.[24] What is remarkable, however, is that the Turkish economy, after two decades of experimentation with neoliberal policies, reached a level of development that could at least withstand the rigorous EU reconditioning.

Would Turkey have experienced the latest growth cycle that began after the 2001 crisis had the EU membership prospect not been on the table, or more specifically, was the prospect of full integration with the EU the driving force of this ongoing economic transformation? In formulating a response to this question, one should acknowledge that Turkey's drive for modernization had its roots in the early years of the Republic, building Turkey's industrial base with a unique partnership between the state and the private sector upon which an industrialized outward-looking economic structure developed (see table 10.6). And it is from that foundation that today's internationally competitive, highly productive private sector emerged. Yet the accelerated pace at which recent reforms were introduced, particularly during the post-2002 gen-

[24] For more on the Washington Consensus debate, see Öniş and Şenses (2005) and Rodrik (2004, 2006).

Table 10.6 Output growth, 1924–2005

Year	GDP Growth rate	Industry		Agriculture		Service	
		Growth rate	% of total	Growth rate	% of total	Growth rate	% of total
1924–29	10.8	8.0	9.6	15.9	45.7	8.3	44.8
1930–39	6.0	11.7	13.5	6.0	43.8	5.7	42.7
1940–49	0.7	-0.3	14.9	1.7	43.0	1.0	42.1
1950–59	7.1	9.2	14.2	6.6	39.6	6.8	46.2
1960–69	5.4	9.5	18.0	1.9	33.0	6.7	49.0
1970–79	4.7	6.1	19.8	1.9	25.6	6.0	54.6
1980	-2.4	-3.6	20.5	1.3	24.2	-4.1	55.4
1981	4.9	9.9	21.5	-1.8	22.6	5.8	55.9
1982	3.6	5.1	21.9	3.3	22.7	2.3	55.4
1983	5.0	6.7	22.4	-0.8	21.6	5.3	56.0
1984	6.7	10.5	23.1	0.6	20.3	8.2	56.6
1985	4.2	6.5	23.6	-0.3	19.4	5.0	57.0
1986	7.0	13.1	25.0	3.6	18.8	5.2	56.2
1987	9.5	9.2	24.9	0.4	17.2	13.2	57.9
1988	2.1	2.1	25.1	8.0	18.3	-0.8	56.7
1989	0.3	4.9	25.9	-7.7	16.6	3.2	57.5
1990	9.3	9.3	25.9	7.0	16.3	10.1	57.9
1991	0.9	2.9	26.5	-0.6	16.1	-0.5	57.4
1992	6.0	6.2	26.5	4.3	15.8	7.1	57.8
1993	8.0	8.3	26.5	-0.8	14.5	10.5	59.0
1994	-5.5	-5.7	26.6	-0.6	15.3	-7.6	58.1
1995	7.2	12.5	27.7	1.3	14.4	7.6	57.9
1996	7.0	6.8	27.7	4.6	14.0	7.9	58.3
1997	7.5	10.2	28.1	-2.2	12.7	9.9	59.2
1998	3.1	1.8	27.6	9.6	13.4	3.6	59.0
1999	-4.7	-5.1	27.9	-5.6	13.4	-6.7	58.7
2000	7.4	6.2	27.8	3.8	13.1	7.0	59.0
2001	-7.5	-7.4	28.5	-6.0	13.6	-11.3	57.9
2002	7.9	9.1	28.8	7.5	13.6	7.5	57.6
2003	5.8	7.8	29.3	-2.4	12.5	6.9	58.2
2004	8.9	9.4	29.2	2.0	11.6	11.8	59.2
2005	7.4	6.6	28.9	5.7	11.4	8.5	59.7

Sources: TÜRKSTAT, *Statistical Indicators 1923–2005*; Central Bank of the Republic of Turkey, Electronic Data Delivery System.

eral election period, was indeed the result of an improved prospect of future EU membership, despite the barrage of discouraging statements coming from some of the EU capitals. The impact of the EU cannot be overlooked, but at the same time Turkey's more than five-decade-old drive for modernization, the unique state-private sector partnership that was behind it, and the IMF-sponsored and closely monitored adjustment and restructuring process should not be understated.

Thus far, from Turkey's perspective, the desire to join the Union, at least at the policy-making level, continues. Public support, although not as strong as it was when enthusiasm for joining the EU was heightened by the 2004 European Presidency decision to start accession talks, is still in favor of joining, but gradually waning. Recent commentaries from some member states have not been supportive of Turkey's accession, and some even appear determined to change the nature of the integration process. Member states that have traditionally been in favor of Turkish accession have become more vocal in their support as well, but the populist tendencies of some European leaders appear to have been fairly successful in keeping Europe's ongoing concerns regarding Turkey's full membership in the headlines. Will Turkey eventually join the Union? This is the question we turn to next.

CHAPTER ELEVEN

PROSPECTS FOR FULL MEMBERSHIP: A COMMENTARY

Before the December 2004 Brussels European Presidency decision, the EU's major concerns were related to a multitude of issues, including Turkey's human rights record, its internal political dynamics, the structure of its economy, and the level of its development, none of which seemed easy to remedy. It was indeed a challenge to achieve immediate results on these issues in an economic and political environment that had been weakened by continuing inflation, repeated financial crises, and a high degree of political fragmentation. Yet, in spite of such difficulties, Turkey made a genuine effort to address these and other concerns that had been raised by the EU Commission, and most of the time it seemed fairly convincing. Still, several key issues, including the size of the Turkish economy, fear of large-scale migration, institutional incompatibility, and the state of Turkish democracy, remain unsettled and may emerge as roadblocks that prolong the accession process. Moreover, even though these matters may eventually be resolved as accession talks proceed, the question of ambiguity over the future path that the EU expansion may take and the effect that will have on future Turkish membership may become major determinants, increasing the likelihood of changing the nature of Turkey's integration process.

As of this writing, the ongoing debate on the alternative paths in which European integration could ultimately proceed has not yet subsided.[1] As summed up in Casanova (2006), the central question at this time is "whether European identity, and therefore its external and internal boundaries, should be defined by the common heritage of Christianity and Western civilization or by its modern secular values of liberalism, universal human rights, political democracy and tolerant and inclusive multiculturalism" (p. 241). A decision on this issue clearly has important implications for those who aspire to join the Union. According to Keyder (2006, 80), Europe, proceeding along the first path, preoccupied with "greater unification and deepening around a core of

[1] See Casanova (2006), Grigoriadis (2006), and Keyder (2006).

shared heritage and history, with an implicit Christian consciousness," would offer no hope for those countries that are excluded. Along the second path, on the other hand, "Europe could be composed of a cool, dispassionate, carefully assessed membership, the result of deliberation and choice, based on interest and calculation. This calculation would include as a factor the moral ideal represented by a 'European' order of social democracy, where cultural values are expressed in terms of secular notions relating to legal, political and economic processes, and to the desired goals."

Will Turkey, a candidate state that has already satisfied the Copenhagen criteria, ultimately become a full member irrespective of what path the EU chooses to take? Or, more importantly, will full membership be a possibility even if the EU remains a predominantly economic union distant to the notion of common European identity that may be stretched beyond liberal democratic values and multiculturalism? As of this writing, the response is at best ambiguous. Restating Huntington's three requirements that Turkey needs to meet in order to integrate with the West, Casanova (2006) argued that Turkey has already met two conditions: Turkey's political and economic establishment have been supportive, and even though public support for joining the EU has recently been sliding, it would not be an overstatement to say that Turkey is still eager to join the EU. Yet, as far as the third requirement goes, it is not clear, as Casanova stated, if the EU is ready and willing to admit "a modern Muslim democratic Turkey into the EU" (p. 240). Clearly, from the perspective of the majority of political elites and the officials in Brussels, as a union of states the EU has already committed itself to proceed with political negotiations with Turkey. But as Le Gloannec (2006) pointed out, as a union of peoples the EU expects something more than diplomatic negotiations and "sharing treaties" that would lead to membership; instead, "a common ground must be found between the citizens of the EU and the Turks before the latter join the Union" (p. 272). Finding a common ground between Turkey and the EU has proven to be a challenge even though accession as a legal and political process is bound to continue at its own pace. But as Kastoryano (2006, 275) observed, the debates and arguments advanced thus far within the EU have clearly made Turkish accession "a class of its own," bringing to the forefront not only the question of cultural and religious differences but also the issue of geographical proximity and borders.

Making reference to the debate in France on the legitimacy of Turkish membership, for example, Göle (2006) observed, "Europe is constructed as an identity defined by shared history and common cultural values rather than as a project for the future." She continued, "In Turkey, where Europeanness is not part of a 'natural' historic legacy it is appropriated voluntarily as a political project, as a perspective, promoting a democratic frame for rethinking commonness and difference" (p. 260). From this perspective it is clear that Turkey will face the least resistance when the EU is perceived to be a project by the majority of EU citizens. In fact, the ideals of a "core Europe," restated in Benhabib and Işıksel (2006), which include the values of Judeo-Christianity, the Renaissance, and the Enlightenment, to which the EU appeals to deepen its economic and political experiment, may be the only recourse to divert Turkey from the accession path on the premise that as a predominantly Muslim nation, Turkey would have little to share with a culture that has its roots in Christianity. Benhabib and Işiksel, however, rightly remind us that the Renaissance "rediscovered the human and not just the European; the Enlightenment was obsessed with the variety of cultures, customs, and laws beyond the boundaries of Europe. One need only recall Montaigne, Montesquieu, Diderot, Herder, Rousseau, and Kant! Certainly the universality of these values need not lead to the indiscriminate openness of the institutions of the European Union to all newcomers. However, it does imply that the Copenhagen criteria, and not any newly discovered fear of "*l'étranger*" as the Muslim, must guide Europe's negotiations with Turkey" (pp. 231–32). And the debate goes on.

The preceding excerpts are only a fragment, and not necessarily a representative sample, of intriguing questions being raised in the ongoing debate on Turkish accession to the EU, a debate likely to intensify in support of either path the EU will be proceeding on and the consequent impact of that choice on Turkey's accession project. So far, the opposition to Turkish membership has not been staged on the basis of its compatibility with the European core values, at least at the official level, with the exception of perhaps some populist statements made by a number of European political figures. The opposition up until now has been expressed mainly through commentaries and occasional interviews, with very few empirical studies on the sentiments of European citizens being conducted other than a score of public opinion surveys that reveal the degree of opposition to Turkish membership.

Utilizing theoretical constructs from the opinion formation and voting behavior literature, one empirical study in particular attempts to explain the reaction to Turkey's candidacy. The study, conducted by McLaren (2007), found that the opposition to Turkish membership is not connected to economic self-interest; that is, the job status and income level of EU citizens are not statistically significant in explaining the opposition to Turkey, while they are so connected in the case of other pre-2004 candidates. There is no evidence that EU citizens are concerned about being personally disadvantaged as a result of resource reallocation that may follow Turkish entry, such as businesses relocating where labor costs are more favorable or sharing the labor market with the newcomers. The EU citizens did, however, reveal group-level concerns regarding issues such as the risk of compromising their culture and way of life. They also view Turkey's candidacy as a potential threat to "in-group resources" such as social security benefits and employment, but these were also valid concerns in explaining the opposition to other pre-2004 candidates. Looking into the level of economic development, trade volume, geographical proximity, and concentration of migrants from the candidate country in the EU as contextual factors, McLaren focused on the last factor and concluded that "[EU] citizens are most worried about the potential effects of Turkish entry on the economic and social welfare benefits of their fellow citizens and on national culture and way of life, as they were with other candidates. The difference, however, is that large-scale migration from Turkey may have created an environment in which these fears are amplified to a much greater extent than was the case with the 2004 enlargement candidates" (pp. 273–74).

While the main finding of the McLaren study may have important implications for the design of public campaigns to inform and educate the EU public by emphasizing the significant contributions of the Turkish community to the host EU member states, for example, it should be noted that the study obviously overlooked the important bridge that the Turkish community has built between Turkey and the EU in the economic, social, and political domains since the early 1960s. As both qualitative and quantitative analysis in Kaya (2004, 46) revealed, for example, the majority in the Turkish community appear to have become "politically, socially, economically and culturally integrated active agents in their countries of settlement." It should also be emphasized that further empirical investigation to identify the reasons behind the perceptions of EU citizens, which appears to be unique to Turkish candidacy, would be necessary in order to develop a complete understanding of European opposition.

The ongoing academic debate on the European identity issue and the analyses of citizen sentiment in the EU will probably weigh heavily as Turkey and the EU get closer to concluding the accession project to their mutual satisfaction. The main headlines thus far from the EU have been limited to frequent reminders from EU officials to comply with the criteria and a barrage of political commentaries on the issue of whether Turkey should be considered an equal European partner based on commonly known arguments and cited deficiencies.

One frequently cited deficiency, a likely roadblock that might prolong the accession talks, is the incompatibility of Turkey's economic institutions. In the past, Turkey perhaps overlooked many opportunities that would have brought its economy closer to EU standards in a more timely fashion. During the liberalization and stabilization period of the 1980s, for example, Turkey inadvertently overlooked the importance of realigning its political, organizational, and legal structures, key areas in which the EU has been trying to motivate Turkey to concentrate its reforms. Such restructuring was further delayed during the 1990s, when the coalition governments of the period appeared to place more emphasis on party politics and seemed preoccupied with short-term macroeconomic policy making due to recurring financial crises. Chronic high inflation and excessive public spending that characterized these decades created an economic and policy environment with an emphasis on stabilization rather than restructuring.

However, in recent years, in spite of an unfavorable macroeconomic environment and at times misguided policies that severely reduced the efficiency of financial markets and slowed down economic progress, Turkey proved to be flexible enough in adjusting to the conditions and expectations of a potential EU-member economy. The resilience that it had shown since the establishment of the Republic in the 1920s was certainly the result of the ongoing transformation involving its economic institutions and their role in the development of the Turkish economy. Even though the process was at times delayed because of destabilizing internal and external factors, after the turbulent decades of the 1980s and 1990s, Turkey was finally on track and much more focused on redirecting its economic transformation toward its ultimate destination, the European Union accession. Turkey's economic improvement has been acknowledged in various EU documents, and even though there are several concerns that will likely be dealt with during the accession negotiation process, overall the state of its economy has become less of an issue in comparison to the time when Turkey had not yet been recognized as a candidate state.[2]

Despite this remarkable economic transformation, strong opposition to Turkish membership in the EU remains and does not seem to abate. There are also signs that the opposition will continue, even during the long process of accession negotiations. Those who oppose Turkish membership point out the size of the Turkish economy and its likely burden on EU institutions and markets. Assuming that Turkey becomes a full member in 2015, they argue that by then it will probably be one of the most populated states in the EU. But, as Lammers (2006) reported, assuming that the economic growth differential between the EU and Turkey remains unchanged, and given the size and comparatively higher growth rate of its population, Turkey's contribution to EU total output by 2015 is likely to be about 3.2 percent.[3] The cost to the EU measured in terms of what Turkey will receive under Common Agricultural Policy and the Structural Funds is not expected to be in excess of any amount in the range of 0.15 to 0.2 percent of the EU's GDP, according to estimates by Derviş et al. (2004).

Furthermore, the fear of migration may pose a roadblock during the accession talks, even though it is likely that by the time Turkey is admitted as a full member, Turkey's economic profile will be more conducive to the functioning of a much more efficient labor market that may actually deter migration. In the short run, however, as Turkey begins to implement the new labor law introduced in 2003 and to align its labor market with the EU in accordance with the *acquis*, there could be a significant decline in employment with likely negative spillover effects on European labor markets. For example, as the simulation exercise by Taymaz and Özler (2005, 253–56) showed, employment in manufacturing could decrease significantly as employment policies and the wage structure are applied uniformly within the entire manufacturing sector in accordance with the *acquis*. With the adoption and enforcement of such employment policies and wage structure, small informal sector

[2] But still, Turkey, with its lowest per capita income and largest agricultural sector, will become the largest recipient of financial support from the EU budget, which is estimated to be around 4 percent of its GDP (Lammers 2006).

[3] Hughes (2004) also noted that, given the size of its population, Turkey is likely to have limited influence on economic policy matters, but its weight on the Union's foreign policy issues will be considerable, although it will not be the only player determining the future of EU's foreign policy.

firms will be required to pay taxes and social security benefits and consequently they will lose their cost advantage and thus their market share. As Togan (2005, 326–27) noted, the decline in total employment could be much higher when the impact of the EU regulations on the small informal firms of agriculture and service sectors is also taken into account. Taymaz and Özler pointed out, though, that with simulated faster GDP growth rates such "short-term transitory-costs" stemming from the elimination of the informal sector could be reduced.

With increased productivity and economic growth, therefore, it can be argued that in the long run there would likely be little spillover effects on the European labor markets. Flam (2003) forecasted that under the assumption of no restrictions and a GDP per capita growth rate of 5.5 percent in Turkey, the Turkish immigrant population could increase from 2.2 million in 2000 to 3.5 million in 2030. The simulation results of Erzan, Kuzubaş, and Yıldız (2004) indicated a net migration of 1–2.1 million, significantly lower than the likely migration of 2.7 million if Turkey does not become a full member. Relying on reported figures in various studies, Lammers (2006) provided a range of 2–3 million and does not consider this to be a significantly high figure given that it will constitute less than one percent of the population of EU-15. Even if, in the worst case scenario as perceived by the EU, increased migration from Turkey becomes a possibility, there will most likely be some set of mutually agreed upon safeguards that would control the direction and the magnitude of migration.

Another area of concern is the state of Turkish democracy. Even though democracy in Turkey has continued to flourish since the 1950s (when the multiparty system was adopted) the process at times was interrupted and produced outcomes that gave little cause to celebrate, particularly throughout the post-1980 period. Despite the universal acceptance and practice of democracy in the nation, it was rare for the opposition and ruling parties to come to an agreement on issues related to public and national interest, for example. Polarization was common, and disagreements were always voiced openly and strongly, from time to time leading to political crises and increased speculation of military intervention. Having witnessed numerous interventions in the past, the Turkish public is indeed aware of the plusses and minuses of military rule, and it has finally reached a level of maturity that values a political environment with a functioning democracy free of disruption. In recent years, military intervention in Turkey has been a thing of the past, even though internal political dynamics still make it necessary for the military to continue to express its views publicly. It is not a common practice in any of the EU states for the military to make public statements on economic and political matters, so the military's influence in Turkey is obviously a concern for the EU.

Another issue that is publicly debated with respect to Turkey's full membership prospects is whether Turkey is a European country and if it should be categorized with or compared to any state inside or outside Europe that might be inspired by Turkey's quest for full membership.[4] The issue certainly has strategic significance for the Union's future enlargements, especially when countries such as Russia and Ukraine, for instance, apply for full membership. Obviously, each applicant will likely be evaluated and treated on a case-by-case basis, if and when that happens. But the view that if Turkey is admitted to the Union, so too should these nations be admitted, arguably has little relevance, considering that none of the nations usually mentioned has participated in European institutions or contributed to the well-being of Europe to the extent that Turkey has since the late 1940s. As confirmed in the Commission's October 6, 2004, recommendations: "For major periods of European history, Turkey has been an important factor of European politics. Turkey is a member of all important other European organizations and has since the Second World War played an important role in contributing to the shaping of European policies" (p. 2). One organization in particular is the Council of Europe, which was founded in 1949 with the aim of achieving the unity of its members, among which were five of the original six members of today's EU and other members, including Turkey, who joined the Council the same year it was founded.[5]

[4] This is a question that was openly raised by the former French president and past chairman of the European Union's Constitutional Council, Valéry Giscard d'Estaing. In a public statement that has been less frequently quoted than the widely publicized *Le Monde* interview, d'Estaing voiced his opposition, stating that "first, except for Istanbul, Turkey is not located on the European Continent, but mainly in Asia. Second, if we start admitting countries not located in Europe, by which criteria do we reject membership by any state? If we want to have a real, deep integration, it must be with people of comparable conditions, politically, economically, and culturally, all located on the European soil." And he added, "It is simply not historically consistent for it to belong to Europe." See "Europe, Austria and Turkey," *New Perspectives Quarterly*, Spring 2000, 18–20. Also see *Le Monde*, November 8, 2002, and *Guardian*, November 11, 2002, 17.

[5] Interestingly, some of the current EU members were not among the nations that established the Council; it took more than six years before even Austria, for example, became a member.

Turkey's claim to membership has its roots in the Treaty of Rome, as is the case for any European state. As was clearly stated in the Preamble of the 1963 Ankara Treaty, even at the time, the Community recognized that "the efforts of the Turkish people to improve their standard of living will facilitate the accession of Turkey to the Community at a later date." In the Preamble, the Community resolved "to preserve and strengthen peace and liberty by joint pursuit of the ideals underlying the Treaty establishing the European Economic Community."[6] From these statements, it is clear that not only was Turkey treated no differently than any other European nation committed to the ideals of the Treaty of Rome, but its eligibility for full membership was also unequivocal. Today, the EU clearly recognizes Turkey as a "European state" in the same context the term had been used in the Treaty.[7]

Yet the issue of whether Turkey is European does not seem to go away. It was once again addressed by the newly elected French President Sarkozy, who during his election campaign did not refrain from disqualifying Turkey on the basis of his unique characterization of the "Europeanness" of Turkey. In his campaign messages, he consistently pointed out that a culture that belongs to Asia cannot and should not integrate in the EU, and judging from the statements he has made since becoming president, his position has not changed, and he continues to support the idea of proceeding with accession negotiations leading to a special status for Turkey rather than the full membership. Other EU leaders appear to be less vocal on this issue. But Redmond (2007, 316) observed, "It sometimes seems that the concept of 'Europeanness' is not really a working criterion for EU membership but rather an emergency escape route to which the current EU is keen to retain access." It usually takes one influential voice to lead the way.

Another concern that has been repeatedly voiced by those who oppose Turkish membership is the risk that Europe would take by extending its borders to the Middle East and the Caucasus. This argument is based on the premise that under the geopolitical entanglements of our times, bordering the EU with nations of the Middle East and the Caucasus will be destabilizing and likely to present security problems for Europe. In the event that such complications were to occur, the implication is

[6] *Agreement Establishing an Association between the European Economic Community and Turkey*, Ankara, September 12, 1963.

[7] See Böttcher (2004, 5).

that the EU will be better off with a nonmember Turkey acting as a buffer against negative spillover effects. Obviously, in this argument, the well-being of an ally that has been devoting its strategic assets to the defense of Europe for decades does not seem to be a relevant issue. Moreover, if Turkey becomes a full member, and thus the EU's borders are extended, it appears that some skeptics seem to even overlook the likely positive spillover effects of the spread of democracy and human rights in the region.[8]

The EU has proven itself capable of raising new issues and hinting about new roadblocks that may further delay accession, or as it has done in the past, overlooking even legitimate shortcomings of a candidate and moving on with accession.[9] Will the Union's resistance to Turkish full membership finally discourage Turkey's policy makers from taking further steps to reform their society along the lines of the EU standards? The response at this time would probably be "not yet," given the long list of the EU's past demands and Turkey's prompt response in complying with them. Turkey thus far has proven itself capable of overcoming most of the deficiencies that were clearly stated by the official bodies of the Union and seems committed to further its economic restructuring to close the gap with the current member states. As the negotiation continues uninterrupted, it is expected that many of the concerns stemming from Turkey's size and the development level of its economy will diminish. Economic growth and development are likely to gain a fresh dynamism that would lead to considerable improvement in major economic indicators, as has been the case for most of the recent entrants into the Union. The size of the economy is likely to become an asset for the Union rather than a liability. The young, dynamic population

[8] And there are more issues and concerns likely to capture the headlines as the accession process proceeds at times in a "wait and see" mode. Many unresolved complications relating to Turkey's internal and external policy challenges, including the Cyprus question, Kurdish separatism, the Armenian issue, and even ongoing disputes with Greece, persist as potential setbacks that could very likely derail the accession process. Each of these issues has a complicated history that warrants careful analysis. For the EU, the main challenge is how to maintain its credibility as an even-handed broker since concerned parties in some of these disputes are insiders, while Turkey is making its case from the outside. For more on these disputes and Turkey's internal and external policy challenges, see Aybet (2006).

[9] See, for example, Redmond (2007), who cited various enlargement cases in which the EU took risks with new members and argued that "Turkish accession 'can be done'—it just needs the same vision and political will that has been displayed at key moments in the Union's past" (pp. 316–17).

of Turkey, rather than being a threat for the mature European labor markets, is likely to be more involved in its growing dynamic markets. Moreover, as a future EU member with a flourishing private sector and stable economy, it seems that Turkey will be a magnet for direct foreign investment and thus close the gap with member nations, maybe much sooner than expected.[10] Two bright spots are definitely the human capital that has been accumulating despite Turkey's inadequate investment in that area and the development of an entrepreneurial class that has been gradually preempting the state.

It should be noted that the decision-making bodies of the Union are clearly aware of Turkey's potential contribution to the EU and the region as a whole. But it is the European public that is not yet convinced. Very few in Europe have the opportunity to enjoy the rich cultural diversity and traditions of Turkey, and many are unaware of the impressive developments that have been taking place since the establishment of the Republic. The prospects for membership will be strengthened if Europe begins to take a good look at an inevitable member, impartially and with the demeanor of accepting rather than rejecting. It is perhaps then that cultural and social differences might begin to seem less irreconcilable than most Europeans might now believe. After all, the Turkish people have been enjoying European cultures as well as their own for centuries, and that has definitely had an immense impact on the growth and maturity of their society. Today, an overwhelming majority in Turkey accepts and is willing to face challenges similar to their European contemporaries, and they rightly do so because they do not feel alien to European civilization.

In closing, it should be stressed that Turkey has made a phenomenal transition from an emerging economy to a maturing economy, and it will not be far from being considered a matured economy once the negotiation process reaches its logical conclusion. It is a shared perception that Europe's contribution in this process is uncontestable. The goal of EU membership not only motivated many of the recent reforms that the economy badly needed but also helped the nation to question its deficiencies and at least attempt to leave behind some of its outdated social and political institutions. EU membership is expected to speed up this transition with likely external benefits to Europe and

[10] See Dutz, Us, and Yılmaz (2005).

beyond. Democracy in Turkey has been establishing its roots since Atatürk's revolution. It is a way of life that many Turks cherish, have paid dearly to maintain, and seem determined to nurture, in spite of all likely adversities, including potential roadblocks that may prolong their journey to their destination.

BIBLIOGRAPHY

Aizenman, J. 2004. Financial opening and development: Evidence and policy controversies. *American Economic Review Proceedings* 94(2): 65–70.

Akat, A. S. 2000. The political economy of Turkish inflation. *Journal of International Affairs* 54(1): 265–82.

Akçay, O. C., C. E. Alper, and S. Özmucur. 1996. Budget deficit, money supply and inflation: Evidence from low and high frequency data for Turkey. Working Paper, Department of Economics, Boğaziçi University, İstanbul.

——. 2002. Budget deficit, inflation and debt sustainability: Evidence from Turkey, 1970–2000. In Kibritçioğlu, Rittenberg, and Selçuk 2002, 77–96.

Aktan, O. 1972. Effects of joining the EEC on the Turkish economy. PhD diss., University of Oxford.

——. 1996. Liberalization, export incentives and exchange rate policy: Turkey's experience in the 1980s. In Togan and Balasubramanyam 1996, 177–97.

Aktan, O., and T. Baysan. 1985. Türk ekonomisinin dünya ekonomisine entegrasyonu: Liberasyon, karşılaştırmalı üstünlük ve optimum politikalar [Integration of the Turkish economy into the world economy: Trade liberalization, comparative advantage and optimum policies]. *METU Studies in Development* 12(1–2): 49–106.

Akyürek, C. 1999. An empirical analysis of post-liberalization inflation in Turkey. *Yapı Kredi Economic Review* 10(2): 31–53.

Akyüz, Y. 1990. Financial system and policies in Turkey in the 1980s. In Arıcanlı and Rodrik 1990, 98–131.

Akyüz, Y., and K. Boratav. 2002. The making of the Turkish financial crisis. Discussion Paper 158, United Nations Conference on Trade and Development, April.

Alper, E. 2001. The Turkish liquidity crisis of 2000. *Russian and East European Finance and Trade* 37(6): 58–80.

Alper, E., and M. Üçer. 1998. Some observations on Turkish inflation: A "random walk" down the past decade. Paper presented at the Conference for Stabilization in an Emerging Market: The Case of Turkey, January 23, Boğaziçi University, İstanbul.

Alper, E., H. Berüment, and K. Malatyalı. 2001. The effect of the disinflation program on the structure of the Turkish banking sector. *Russian and East European Finance and Trade* 37(6): 81–95.

Altınkemer, M., and N. K. Ekinci. 1992. Capital account liberalization: The case of Turkey. Research Department Discussion, Paper 9210, The Central Bank of the Republic of Turkey, Ankara.

Altuğ, S., and A. Filiztekin, eds. 2006. *The Turkish economy: The real economy, corporate governance and reform*. New York: Routledge.

——. 2006. Productivity and growth, 1923–2003. In Altuğ and Filiztekin 2006, 15–62.

Anand, R., A. Chhibber, and S. van Wijnbergen. 1990. External balance and growth in Turkey: Can they be reconciled? In Aricanli and Rodrik 1990, 157–82.

Arcayürek, C. 2001. *Baba'sının kızı* [Daddy's girl]. Ankara: Bilgi Yayınevi.

Arıcanlı, T., and D. Rodrik, eds. 1990. *The political economy of Turkey*. New York: St. Martin Press.

Aşıkoğlu, Y. 1992. Strategic issues in exchange rate liberalization: A critical evaluation of the Turkish experience. In Nas and Odekon 1992, 101–23.

Atiyas, I. 1990. The private sector's response to financial liberalization in Turkey: 1980–82. In Arıcanlı and Rodrik 1990, 132–56.

Aybet, G. 2006. Turkey and the EU after the first year of negotiations: Reconciling internal and external policy challenges. *Security Dialogue* 37(4): 529–49.

Balassa, B. 1978. Exports and economic growth: Further evidence. *Journal of Development Economics* 5(2): 181–89.
——. 1986. Policy responses to exogenous shocks in developing countries. *American Economic Review Papers and Proceedings* 76(2): 75–78.
Barlow, R., and F. Şenses. 1995. The Turkish export boom: Just reward or just lucky? *Journal of Development Economics* 48(1): 111–33.
Başlevent, C., H. Kirmanoğlu, and B. Şenatalar. 2005. Empirical investigation of party preferences and economic voting in Turkey. *European Journal of Political Research* 44:547–62.
Baysan, T. 1974. Economic implications of Turkey's entry into the Common Market. PhD diss., University of Minnesota.
Baysan, T., and C. Blitzer. 1990. Turkey's trade liberalization in the 1980s and prospects for its sustainability. In Arıcanlı and Rodrik 1990, 9–36.
Bell, M., B. Ross-Larson, and L. E. Westphal. 1984. Assessing the performance of infant industries. *Journal of Development Economics* 16(1–2): 101–28.
Benhabib, S., and T. Işıksel. 2006. Ancient battles, new prejudices, and future perspectives: Turkey and the EU. *Constellations* 13(2): 218–33.
Boratav, K. 1990. Inter-class relations of distribution under 'structural adjustment': Turkey during the 1980s. In Arıcanlı and Rodrik 1990, 199–229.
Boratav, K., C. Keyder, and Ş. Pamuk. 1984. *Krizin gelişimi ve Türkiye'nin alternatif sorunu*. İstanbul: Kaynak Yayınları.
Boratav, K., O. Türel, and E. Yeldan. 1995. The Turkish economy in 1981–92: A balance sheet, problems and prospects. *METU Studies in Development* 22(1): 1–36.
——. 1996. The macroeconomic adjustment in Turkey, 1981–1992: A decomposition exercise. *Yapı Kredi Economic Review* 7(1): 3–19.
Böttcher, B. 2004. Turkish accession to the EU—the way is the goal. *EU Monitor Deutsche Bank Research* (September 1): 4–11.
Bruno, M., S. Fischer, E. Helpman, N. Liviatan, and L. Meridor, eds. 1991. *Lessons of economic stabilization and its aftermath*. Cambridge, Massachusetts: The MIT Press.
Bruno, M., and J. Sachs. 1985. *Economics of worldwide stagflation*. Cambridge, Massachusetts: Harvard University Press.
Calvo, G. A., and E. G. Mendoza. 1996. Petty crime and cruel punishment: Lessons from the Mexican debacle. *American Economic Review Proceedings* 86(2): 170–75.
Cardoso, E. 1991. From inertia to megainflation: Brazil in the 1980s. In Bruno, Fischer, Helpman, Liviatan, and Meridor 1991, 143–86.
Casanova, J. 2006. The long, difficult, and tortuous journey of Turkey into Europe and the dilemmas of European civilization. *Constellations* 13(2): 234–47.
Celasun, M. 1986. Income distribution and domestic terms of trade in Turkey 1978–1983. *METU Studies in Development* 13(1–2): 193–216.
——. 1989. Income distribution and employment aspects of Turkey's post-1980 adjustment. *METU Studies in Development* 16(3–4): 1–31.
——. 1990. Fiscal aspects of adjustment in the 1980s. In Arıcanlı and Rodrik 1990, 37–59.
Celasun, M., and D. Rodrik. 1989. Turkish experience with debt: Macroeconomic policy and performance. In *Developing country debt and the world economy*, ed. J. D. Sachs, 193–211. Chicago: The University of Chicago Press.
Celasun, O. 1998. The 1994 currency crisis in Turkey. Policy Research Working Paper 1913, The World Bank.
Chenery, H. 1975. Foreword. In *Economy-wide models and development planning*, ed. C. R. Blitzer, P. B. Clark, and L. Taylor. London: Oxford University Press.
Collins, S. 1990. Lessons from Korean economic growth. *American Economic Review Papers and Proceedings* 80(2): 104–107.
Conway, P. 1988. The impact of recent trade liberalization policies in Turkey. In Nas and Odekon 1988, 47–67.

——. 1990. The record on private investment in Turkey. In Arıcanlı and Rodrik 1990, 78–97.
Corbo, V., J. de Melo, and J. Tybout. 1986. What went wrong with the recent reforms in the Southern Cone. *Economic Development and Cultural Change* 34(3): 607–40.
Demirgüç-Kunt, A., and E. Detragiache. 1998. Financial liberalization and financial fragility. Development Research Group, The World Bank.
Derviş, K. 2003. Turkey: Return from the brink, attempt at systematic change and structural reform. Practitioners of Development Seminar Series, July 2, The World Bank.
Derviş, K., D. Gros, F. Öztrak, Y. Işık, and F. Bayar. 2004. Turkey and the EU budget prospects and issues. In Emerson and Aydin 2004, 76–81.
Dibooğlu, S., and A. Kibritçioğlu. 2004. Inflation, output growth and stabilization in Turkey, 1980-2002. *Journal of Economics and Business* 56(1): 43–61.
Dornbusch R. and S. Fischer. 1991. Moderate inflation. Policy Research Dissemination Center, The World Bank.
Dutz, M., M. Us, and K. Yılmaz. 2005. Turkey's foreign direct investment challenges: Competition, the rule of law, and EU accession. In Hoekman and Togan 2005, 261–93.
Edwards, S. 1993. Openness, trade liberalization, and growth in developing countries. *Journal of Economic Literature* 31(3): 1358–93.
Edwards, S., and S. Teitel. 1986. Introduction to growth, reform, and adjustment: Latin America's trade and macroeconomic policies in the 1970s and 1980s. *Economic Development and Cultural Change* 34(3): 423–31.
Ekinci, N. K., and K. A. Ertürk. 2007. Turkish currency crises of 2000-2001, revisited. *International Review of Applied Economics* 21(1): 29–41.
Emerson, M., and S. Aydin, eds. 2004. *Turkey in Europe Monitor.* Center for European Policy Studies, Brussels.
Erdilek, A. 1988. The role of foreign investment in the liberalization of the Turkish economy. In Nas and Odekon 1988, 141–59.
Erlat, H. 2002. Long memory in Turkish inflation rates. In Kibritcioğlu, Rittenberg, and Selçuk 2002, 97–122.
Ersel, H., and E. Kumcu. 1995. İstikrar programı ve kamu dengesi [Stabilization program and public sector equilibrium]. In *Türkiye için yeni bir orta vadeli istikrar programına doğru* [Toward new intermediate term stabilization program for Turkey], 171–92. İstanbul: TUSIAD.
Ertuğrul, A., and F. Selçuk. 2001. A brief account of the Turkish economy, 1980–2000. *Russian and East European Finance and Trade* 37(6): 6–30.
Ertuğrul, A., and E. Yeldan. 2003. On the structural weaknesses of the post-1999 Turkish dis-inflation program. *Turkish Studies Quarterly* 4(2): 53–66.
Ertuna, O. 1986. The macroeconomic stability: The Turkish case 1950–1979. *Yapı Kredi Economic Review* 1(1): 93–108.
Erzan, R., U. Kuzubaş, and N. Yıldız. 2004. Growth and immigration scenarios for Turkey and the EU. In Emerson and Aydin 2004, 114–25.
Feder, G. 1982. On exports and economic growth. *Journal of Development Economics* 12(1-2): 59–73.
Feldstein, M. 1986. Supply-side economics: Old truths and new claims? *American Economic Review Papers and Proceedings* 76(2): 26–30.
Fischer, S. 2001. Distinguished lecture on economics in government: Exchange rate regimes: Is bipolar view correct? *Journal of Economic Perspectives* 15(2): 3–24.
Flam, H. 2003. Turkey and the EU: Politics and economics of accession. Seminar Paper 718, Institute for International Economic Studies, Stockholm University.
Fry, M. J. 1986. Turkey's great inflation. *METU Studies in Development* 13(1-2): 95–116.

Gazioğlu, Ş. 1986. Government deficits, consumption and inflation in Turkey. *METU Studies in Development* 13(1–2): 117–34.
Göle, N. 2006. Europe's encounter with Islam. *Constellations* 13(2): 248–62.
Grabbe, H. 2004. From drift to strategy: Why the EU should start accession talks with Turkey. Reform Essays, Center for European Reform, London.
Grigoriadis, I. N. 2006. Turkey's accession to the European Union: Debating the most difficult enlargement ever. *SAIS Review* 26(1): 147–60.
Gülalp, H. 1995. Islamist party poised for national power in Turkey. *Middle East Report* (May–August): 54–56.
——. 2001. Globalization and political Islam: The social bases of Turkey's Welfare Party. *International Journal of Middle East Studies* 33(3): 433–48.
——. 2002. Using Islam as a political ideology: Turkey in historical perspective. *Cultural Dynamics* 14(1): 21–39.
Hale, W. 1980. Ideology and economic development in Turkey, 1930–1945. *Bulletin* (British Society for Middle Eastern Studies) 7(2): 100–17.
——. 1981. *The political and economic development of modern Turkey*. London: Croom Helm.
Harrison, G. W., T. F. Rutherford, and D. G. Tarr. 1997. Economic implications for Turkey of a customs union with the European Union. *European Economic Review* 41:861–70.
Healey, D. T. 1972. Development policy: New thinking about an interpretation. *Journal of Economic Literature* 10(3): 757–97.
Heymann, D. 1991. From sharp disinflation to hyperinflation, twice: The Argentine experience, 1985–1989. In Bruno, Fischer, Helpman, N. Liviatan, and L. Meridor 1991, 103–41.
Hoekman, B. M., and S. Togan, eds. 2005. *Turkey: Economic reform and accession to the European Union*. Washington, DC: The World Bank and Center for Economic Policy Research.
Hughes, K. 2004. Turkey and the European Union: Just another enlargement? Exploring the implications of Turkish accession. A Friends of Europe Working Paper, Brussels.
Humphrey, D. D., and C. E. Ferguson. 1960. The domestic and world benefits of customs union. *Economia Internationale* 13:197–213.
İnselbağ, I., and B. Gültekin. 1988. Financial markets in Turkey. In Nas and Odekon 1988, 129–40.
Jung, W. S. and P. Marshall. 1985. Exports, growth and causality in developing countries. *Journal of Development Economics* 18(1): 1–12.
Kaya, A. 2004. A bridge, or a breach, between Turkey and the European Union, Working Paper 5. In Emerson and Aydin 2004, 37–46.
Kastoryano, R. 2006. Turkey/Europe: Space-border-identity. *Constellations* 13(2): 275–87.
Kazgan, G. 1985. *Ekonomide dışa açık büyüme* [Outward-looking growth]. İstanbul: Altın Kitaplar Yayınevi.
Keyder, Ç. 1981. *The definition of peripheral economy: Turkey 1923–1929*. London: Cambridge University Press.
——. 1984. İthal ikameci sanayileşme ve çelişkileri [Import substituting industrialization and its inconsistencies]. In Boratav, Keyder, and Pamuk 1984, 13–35.
——. 2006. Moving in from the margins? Turkey in Europe. *Diogenes* 53(2): 72–81.
Keyman, F., and Z. Öniş. 2004. Helsinki, Copenhagen and beyond: Challenges to the new Europe and the Turkish state. In *Turkey and European integration: Accession prospects and issues*, ed. M. Uğur and N. Canefe. London: Routledge.
Khan, M. S. 1986. Developing country exchange rate policy responses to exogenous shocks. *American Economic Review Papers and Proceedings* 76(2): 84–87.

Kibritçioğlu, A. 2004. A short review of the long history of high inflation in Turkey. In *Inflation: Concepts and Experiences*, ed. S. M. Rao, 84–109. Hyderabad: The ICFAI University Press.
Kibritçioğlu, L., L. Rittenberg, and F. Selçuk, eds. 2002. *Inflation and disinflation in Turkey*. Alderhost: Ashgate.
Kiguel, M. and N. Liviatan. 1991. The inflation-stabilization cycles in Argentina and Brazil. In Bruno, Fischer, Helpman, Liviatan, and Meridor 1991, 191–239.
Kongar, E. 1998. 21. *Yüzyılda Türkiye* [Turkey in the 21th Century]. İstanbul: Remzi Kitabevi.
Kopits, G. 1987. Structural reform, stabilization, and growth in Turkey. IMF Occasional paper 52, Washington, DC.
Kramer, H. 1996. Turkey and the European Union: A multi-dimensional relationship with hazy perspectives. In Mastny and Nation 1996, 203–32.
——. 2004. Whither Turkey's EU accession? Perspectives and problems after December 2004. *AICGS Advisor*, September 30. American Institute for Contemporary Studies, Johns Hopkins University, Washington, DC.
Krueger, A. O. 1992. *Economic policy reform in developing countries*. Cambridge, Massachusetts: Blackwell Publishers.
Kuyucuklu, N. 1983. *Türkiye iktisadı* [Turkish Economy]. İstanbul: Okan Dağıtımcılık Yayıncılık.
Lammers, K. 2006. The EU and Turkey—Economic effects of Turkey's full membership. *Intereconomics* (September–October): 282–88.
Layard, R., and S. Nickell. 1989. The Thatcher miracle? *American Economic Review Papers and Proceedings* 79(2): 215–19.
Le Gloannec, A.-M. 2006. Is Turkey Euro-compatible? French and German debates about the non-criteria. *Constellations* 13(2): 263–74.
Levy-Yeyati, E., and F. Sturzenegger. 2003. To float or to fix: Evidence on the impact of exchange rate regimes on growth. *American Economic Review Papers and Proceedings* 93(4): 1173–93.
Lipsey, G. 1960. The theory of customs unions: A general survey. *Economic Journal* 70:496–513.
Little, I., T. Scitovsky, and M. Scott. 1970. *Industry and trade in some developing countries: A comparative study*. London: Oxford University Press.
Mastny, V., and R. C. Nation, eds. 1996. *Turkey between east and west: New challenges for a rising regional power*. Boulder, Colorado: Westview Press.
Martin, P., and H. Rey. 2006. Globalization and emerging markets: With or without crash. *American Economic Review* 96(5): 1631–51.
Metin, K. 1998. The relationship between inflation and the budget deficit in Turkey. *Journal of Business, Economics and Statistics* 16(4): 412–22.
Metin-Özcan, K., H. Berüment, and B. Neyaptı. 2004. Dynamics of inflation and inflation inertia in Turkey. *Journal of Economic Cooperation* 25(3): 63–86.
Mead, J. E. 1955. *The theory of customs union*. Amsterdam: North-Holland.
McLaren, M. L. 2007. Explaining opposition to Turkish membership of the EU. *European Union Politics* 8(2): 251–78.
Mıhçı, S., and A. Akkoyunlu-Wigley. 2002. The effect of trade liberalization on the concentration and profitability of the Turkish manufacturing industries. Economics Department, Hacettepe University, Ankara.
Nas, T. 1977. Effects of Turkish-EEC customs union on Turkish manufactured exports. PhD diss., Florida State University, Tallahassee.
Nas, T., and M. Odekon, eds. 1988. *Liberalization and the Turkish economy*. New York: Greenwood Press.
——, eds. 1992. *Economics and politics of Turkish liberalization*. Bethlehem: Lehigh University Press.

Nas, T., and M. Perry. 2000. Inflation, inflation uncertainty, and monetary policy in Turkey. *Contemporary Economic Policy* 18(2): 170–80.
——. 2001. Turkish inflation and real output growth, 1963-2000. *Russian and East European Finance and Trade* 37(6): 31–46.
Nas, T., A. Price, and C. Weber. 1986. *A policy oriented theory of corruption.* American Political Science Review 80(1): 107–19.
Nelsen, B. F., and A. C.-G. Stubb. 1998. *The European Union: Readings on the theory and practice of European integration.* 2nd ed. London: Lynee Rienner Publishers, Inc.
Neyaptı, B., and N. Kaya. 2001. Inflation and inflation uncertainty in Turkey: evidence from past two decades. *Yapı Kredi Economic Review* 12(2): 21–25.
Neyaptı, B., F. Taşkın, and M. Üngör. 2003. Has European customs union agreement really affected Turkey's trade? Department of Economics, Bilkent University, Ankara.
Nishimizu, M., and S. Robinson. 1984. Trade policies and productivity change in semi-industrialized countries. *Journal of Development Economics* 16(1–2): 177–206.
Odekon, M. 1992. Turkish liberalization: From the perspectives of manufacturing firms. In Nas and Odekon 1992, 29–46.
Okyar, O. 1965. The concept of étatism. *The Economic Journal* 75(297): 98–111.
Ortiz, G. 1991. Mexico beyond the debt crisis: Toward sustainable growth with price stability. In Bruno, Fischer, Helpman, Liviatan and Meridor 1991, 283–322.
Öniş, Z. 1986. Stabilization and growth in a semi-industrial economy: An evaluation of the recent Turkish experiment, 1977–1984. *METU Studies in Development* 13(1–2): 7–28.
——. 1996. The state and economic development in contemporary Turkey: Etatism to neoliberalism and beyond. In Mastny and Nation 1996, 155–78.
——. 2006. Globalization and party transformation: Turkey's Justice and Developmant Party in perspective. In *Globalising democracy: Party politics in emerging democracies,* ed. P. Burnell. London: Routledge.
Öniş, Z., and S. Özmucur. 1990. Exchange rates, inflation and money supply in Turkey: Testing the vicious circle hypothesis. *Journal of Development Economics* 32(1): 133–54.
Öniş, Z., and F. Şenses. 2005. Rethinking the emerging post-Washington Consensus. *Development and Change* 36(2): 263–90.
Özatay, F. 1996. The lessons from the 1994 crisis in Turkey: Public debt (mis)management and confidence crisis. *Yapı Kredi Economic Review* 7(1): 21–37.
Özatay, F., and G. Sak. 2002. Banking sector fragility and Turkey's 2000–01 financial crisis. In *Brookings Trade Forum: 2002,* ed. S. M. Collins and D. Rodrik, 121–72. Washington, DC: Brookings Institution Press.
Pamuk, Ş. 1984. İthal ikamesi, döviz darboğazları ve Turkiye, 1947–1979 [Import substitution, foreign exchange bottlenecks, and Turkey]. In Boratav, Keyder, and Pamuk 1984, 36–68.
Pazarbaşıoğlu, C. 2005. Accession to the European Union: Potential impacts on the Turkish banking sector. In Hoekman and Togan 2005, 187–208.
Redmond, J. 2007. Turkey and the European Union: Troubled European or European trouble? *International Affairs* 83(2): 305–17.
Redmond, J., and G. G. Rosenthal, eds. 1998. *The expanding European Union: Past, present, future.* London: Lynee Rienner Publishers, Inc.
Rodrik, D. 1988. External debt and economic performance in Turkey. In Nas and Odekon 1988, 161–83.
——. 1991. Premature liberalization, incomplete stabilization: the Özal decade in Turkey. In Bruno, Fischer, Helpman, Liviatan, and Meridor 1991, 323–53.
——. 2004. Rethinking growth policies in the developing world. Luca d'Agliano Lecture in Development Economics for 2004. Kennedy School of Government, Harvard University, Cambridge, MA.

——. 2006. Goodbye Washington consensus, hello Washington confusion? A review of the World Bank's economic growth in the 1990s: Learning from a decade of reform. *Journal of Economic Literature* 44(4): 973–87.

Rodrik, D., and A. Velasco. 2000. Short-term capital flows. In *Annual World Bank Conference on Development Economics 1999*, ed. B. Pleskovic and J. E. Stiglitz, 59–90. Washington, DC: The World Bank.

Sachs, J. D. 1996. Economic transition and the exchange-rate regime. *American Economic Review Proceedings* 86(2): 147–52.

Sayarı, S. 1992. Politics and economic policy-making in Turkey, 1980–1988. In Nas and Odekon 1992, 26–43. Bethlehem: Lehigh University Press.

Selçuk, F. 2001. Seigniorage, currency substitution, and inflation in Turkey. *Russian and East European Finance and Trade* 37(6): 47–57.

Soydan, A. 2003. Financial liberalization, currency substitution and seigniorage: evidence from Turkey. Middlesex University Business School, The Burroughs, Hendon, London.

Sönmez, M. 1982. *Türkiye ekonomisinde bunalım* [Crisis in the Turkish economy]. İstanbul: Belge Yayınları.

Summers, L., and L. H. Pritchett, 1993. The Structural-adjustment debate. *American Economic Review Papers and Proceedings* 83(2): 383–89.

Şenses, F. 1983. An assessment of Turkey's liberalization attempts since 1980 against the background of her stabilization program. *METU Studies in Development* 10(3): 271–321.

——. 1988. An overview of recent Turkish experience with economic stabilization and liberalization. In Nas and Odekon 1988, 9–28. New York: Greenwood Press.

——. 1990. An Assessment of the pattern of Turkish manufactured export growth in the 1980s and its prospects. In Aricanli and Rodrik 1990, 60–77.

Tanzi, V. 1986. Fiscal policy responses to exogenous shocks in developing countries. *American Economic Review Papers and Proceedings* 76(2): 88–91.

Taymaz, E., and Ş. Özler. 2005. Labor market policies and EU accession: Problems and prospects for Turkey. In Hoekman and Togan 2005, 223–60.

Tekin, A. 2004. Future of Turkey-EU relations: A civilisational discourse. *Futures* 1–16.

Tekin-Koru, A., and E. Özmen. 2003. Budget deficits, money growth and inflation: the Turkish evidence. *Applied Economics* 35(5): 591–96.

Tezel, Y. S. 1982. *Cumhuriyet döneminin iktisadi tarihi* [The economic history of the Republic]. Ankara: Yurt Yayınevi.

——. 2005. *Transformation of state and society in Turkey: From the Ottoman Empire to the Turkish Republic.* Ankara: Roma Yayınları.

Togan, S. 1996. Trade liberalization and competitive structure in Turkey during the 1980s. In Togan and Balasubramanyam 1996, 5–51.

——. 2005. Economic implications of EU accession for Turkey. In Hoekman and Togan 2005, 311–30.

Togan, S. and V. N. Balasubramanyam, eds. 1996. *The Economy of Turkey since liberalization.* Houndsmills: Macmillan.

Tükel, A., M. Üçer, and C. Van Rijckeghem. 2006. The Turkish banking sector: A rough ride from crisis to maturation. In Altuğ and Filiztekin 2006, 276–303.

Türkeş, M. 1998. Critique of studies of the Kadro (Cadre) movement. *METU Studies in Development* 25(4): 663–78.

——. 2001. A patriotic leftist development-strategy proposal in Turkey in the 1930s: The case of the Kadro (Cadre) movement. *International Journal of Middle East Studies* 33(1): 91–114.

Tyler, W. G. 1981. Growth and export expansion in developing countries: Some empirical evidence. *Journal of Development Economics* 9:121–30.

Üçer, M., C. Van Rijckeghem, and R. Yolalan. 1998. Leading indicators of currency crises: A brief literature survey and an application to Turkey. *Yapı Kredi Economic Review* 9(2): 3–23.

Ülgen, S., and Y. Zahariadis. 2004. The future of Turkish-EU trade relations. EU-Turkey Working Paper 5, Center for European Policies, Brussels.

Ülken, Y. 1981. *Atatürk ve iktisat* (Atatürk and Economics). Ankara: Türkiye İş Bankası Kültür Yayınları.

Utkulu, U., and D. Seymen. 2004. Trade and competitiveness between Turkey and the EU: Time series evidence. Turkish Economic Association Discussion Paper 2004/8, Ankara.

Uygur, E. 1993. Liberalization and economic performance in Turkey. United Nations Conference on Trade and Development Discussion Paper No. 65. August, Geneva, Switzerland.

Vanek, J. 1962. *International trade: Theory and economic policy*. Homewood: Irwin.

Viner, J. 1950. *The customs union issue*. New York: Carnegie Endowment for International Peace.

Waterbury, J. 1992. Export-led growth and the center-right coalition in Turkey. In Nas and Odekon 1992, 44–72.

Yavuz, M. H. 1997. Political Islam and the Welfare (Refah) Party in Turkey. *Comparative Politics* 30(1): 63–82.

Yeldan, E. 2006. Turkey 2001–2006: Macroeconomics of post-crisis adjustments. Global Policy Network.http://www.gpn.org.

Yükseler, Z. 2004. 1994, 2002 ve 2003 yılları hanehalkı gelir ve tüketim harcamaları anketleri [1994, 2002 and 2003 household income and expenditure surveys]. Discussion paper 2004/23. Turkish Economic Association. Ankara.

INDEX

Printed in the United States
by Baker & Taylor Publisher Services

Printed in the United States
by Baker & Taylor Publisher Services